This book offers a revisionary account of key epistemological concepts and doctrines of St. Thomas Aquinas, particularly his concept of *scientia* (science), and proposes a new interpretation of the purpose and composition of Aquinas's most mature and influential work, the *Summa theologiae*, which presents the *scientia* of sacred doctrine, i.e. Christian theology. Contrary to the standard interpretation of the *Summa* as a work for neophytes in theology, Jenkins argues that it is in fact a pedagogical work intended as the culmination of the philosophical and theological studies of very gifted students.

Jenkins then considers our knowledge of the principles of a science. He argues that rational assent to the principles of sacred doctrine, the articles of faith, is due to the influence of grace on one's cognitive powers, because of which one is able immediately to apprehend these propositions as divinely revealed. His study will be of interest to readers in philosophy, theology and medieval studies.

KNOWLEDGE AND FAITH IN THOMAS AQUINAS

KNOWLEDGE AND FAITH IN THOMAS AQUINAS

JOHN I. JENKINS, CSC

University of Notre Dame

CAMBRIDGE
UNIVERSITY PRESS

PUBLISHED BY THE PRESS SYNDICATE OF THE UNIVERSITY OF CAMBRIDGE
The Pitt Building, Trumpington Street, Cambridge CB2 IRP, United Kingdom

CAMBRIDGE UNIVERSITY PRESS
The Edinburgh Building, Cambridge CB2 2RU, United Kingdom
40 West 20th Street, New York, NY 10011–4211, USA
10 Stamford Road, Oakleigh, Melbourne 3166, Australia

© Cambridge University Press 1997

First published 1997

Printed in the United Kingdom at the University Press, Cambridge

Typeset in Baskerville 11/12½ pt

A catalogue record for this book is available from the British Library

Library of Congress cataloguing in publication data
Jenkins, John I.
Knowledge and Faith in Thomas Aquinas / John I. Jenkins.
p.   cm.
Includes bibliographical references and index.
ISBN 0 521 58126 5 (hardback)
1. Thomas, Aquinas, Saint, 1225?–1274.
2. Knowledge, Theory of – History.
3. Theology, Doctrinal – History – Middle Ages, 600–1500.
I. Title.
B765.T54J46   1997   95–43918   CIP

ISBN 0 521 58126 5 hardback

To my Mother and Father

Inter homines autem maxime aliquis est parentibus debitor.

Thomas Aquinas, *Summa contra gentiles* III, cap. 128

Contents

Acknowledgments

I have been working on this book on and off for ten years, and have been thinking about the issues it treats for an even longer time. The people who have helped me during this long gestation are too numerous to list, but I will try to mention some of the most prominent. Of course, I alone am responsible for the views presented in this work.

Many of the ideas for this work were first developed in a D.Phil. dissertation at Oxford University, where I was extremely fortunate to have studied. I wish to thank Brian Davies, OP, Anthony Kenny and Richard Swinburne, all of whom supervised the writing of my dissertation at some stage in its composition. Each of them was generous with his time and helpful in his criticisms. My thanks also go to those at my college, Campion Hall, who supported me. And last but not least, thanks to the friends at Oxford who sustained me in many ways.

I am fortunate to teach at the institution at which I was an undergraduate, so many of those who taught me as a student now teach me as a colleague. Parts of this work were read at departmental colloquia, and I benefited from comments and criticisms. David Burrell, CSC, Scott MacDonald, Alfred Freddoso, Ernan McMullin, David Solomon, Phil Quinn, Paul Weithman, Joseph Wawrykow and Martha Merritt have all read and commented on parts of this work at some stage in its composition. Peter Adamson helped me prepare the final version. Ralph McInerny deserves special thanks, for he not only read, commented upon and discussed parts of this work with me, but has consistently supported me in my work.

Michael J. Buckley, SJ, gave me my first Latin copy of Aquinas's *Summa theologiae* when I was a student in theology, and he made room in a very busy schedule to read and discuss its contents with me. (We only made it through the first question of the *Prima pars* of the *Summa* during that term, and this book is in many ways the fruit of my continuing efforts to understand that question.) Mike has continued to be a friend and mentor, and I am very grateful to him for his help and friendship through the years.

Alasdair MacIntyre has profoundly influenced this work and its author in several ways. First, his writings have inspired and illumined my study of Aquinas. Secondly, he has been generous in reading and commenting on various parts of various drafts of this work. And thirdly, by his integrity, his dedication to inquiry and his search for what is true and good, he has embodied for me much of what it means to live a philosophical life. I am extremely grateful for his help, support and example.

Three anonymous readers to whom Cambridge University Press sent my manuscript provided very helpful comments, and I have incorporated many of their suggestions. I am also indebted to some excellent editorial staff at Cambridge University Press, particularly Hilary Gaskin and Rosemary Morris. My friend Dianne Phillips suggested the image for the cover of this book.

As I try to teach my students, I continue to be surprised by how much I learn in the effort. My thanks go to the students at Notre Dame, whom I have had the very great privilege to teach and to learn from in so many ways. I hope they have learned as much as I have. Thanks also to the communities at Dillon Hall, Old College and Moreau Seminary where I have been living while at Notre Dame. They have supported me and patiently awaited the publication of this book.

I am grateful to the Lynde and Harry Bradley Foundation and the University of Notre Dame, which supported me during a sabbatical year during which I worked on this project.

Finally, two groups deserve my special gratitude. The first is the Congregation of Holy Cross, of which I am a member. It has been generous in providing me the financial resources and time needed for me to pursue my studies and research. More importantly, my superiors and friends in the community have been unwavering in their encouragement and fraternal understanding. I am profoundly blessed to have such brothers.

The second group is my family. My parents must have thought it odd to have a son with such a passionate interest in philosophy, but their support and encouragement to follow my interests has always been unhesitating and unqualified, even when they may not have understood just what those interests were. And I could have asked for no better friends and companions in life than my sisters and brothers. In writing this work, as in all the significant endeavors of my life, my family has been a constant and indispensable source of strength, encouragement and illumination. Through their example I have learned about the Love which made us, and which draws us back to Himself. And to my parents I dedicate this book.

Note on the text

TRANSLATIONS AND CITATIONS OF THE WORKS OF AQUINAS

All translations of passages from Aquinas's works quoted in this book are mine. I have tried to render Aquinas's words as literally and accurately as I could, sometimes perhaps at the expense of elegant English.

There is no single edition of Aquinas's works which is wholly adequate. For the most part I have used the Leonine edition of Thomas Aquinas, *Opera omnia* (1882–). This edition, however, is not yet complete, and another edition has of course been used when no Leonine text is available. Also, some of the early works in the Leonine edition have been improved by later editions based on the earlier Leonine edition. Most notably, Robert Busa's *S. Thomae Aquinatis opera omnia* is based on the Leonine texts which were available by 1971, and in some cases he included corrections of these texts. For some works, then, I have used Busa's texts.

When citing the *Summa theologiae*, I follow the convention of giving the part, question, article and part of the article. Thus "*ST* II–II.1.6. ad 2" refers to the second part of the second part of the *Summa theologiae*, question one, article 6, response to objection two. If there is no reference to a part of the article, the reference is to the corpus of that article. Citations of the *Quaestiones disputatae* are similar, though of course there is no reference to a part of the work.

When referring to one of Aquinas's commentaries on Aristotle, I give the book (if there is more than one) in large roman numerals, the *lectio* in small roman numerals. I also give the paragraph numbers which were introduced in the Marietti editions of Aquinas's works. Although these are not medieval divisions of the texts and although my translation is generally not based on the Marietti edition, these paragraph numbers are often included in English editions and can be helpful in locating a passage.

Abbreviations

The following short titles of Aquinas's works are used throughout the book. The Latin editions on which my translations are based can be found in the bibliography. Also listed there are English translations of Aquinas's works which I have consulted, and by which I have often been helped in my translations.

ST	*Summa theologiae*
SCG	*Summa contra gentiles*
SSS	*In quattuor libros Sententiarum*
De potentia	*Quaestiones disputatae de potentia*
De ver.	*Quaestiones disputatae de veritate*
In De anima	*Sententia libri De anima*
In Ethica	*Sententia libri Ethicorum*
In Meta.	*Expositio in libros Metaphysicorum*
In Periherm.	*Expositio in libros Perihermenias*
In Physica	*Expositio in libros Physicorum*
In Post. anal.	*Expositio libri posteriorum*
In De Trin.	*Super Boethium de Trinitate*

Introduction

The questions of Thomas Aquinas about knowledge and faith are not ours. Twentieth-century philosophers have tried to find in Aquinas answers to our questions, but with predictable results: his detractors have found him either confused or simple-minded, while many of his supporters have tended to assimilate his thought to one or another modern philosophers. Both, I contend, have misunderstood his thought. We cannot find our questions in Aquinas's writings because the interrelated cluster of epistemic concepts denoted by the terms he uses – such as *cognitio, intelligere, notitia, credere, opinio, fides* and especially *scientia* – differ in varying degrees from our concepts of cognition, understanding, knowledge, belief, opinion, faith and science. Thus when Aquinas raises broadly epistemic questions, he does so in a different conceptual framework, and in this framework a different set of propositions is considered unproblematic, and another set is open to question. There are undoubtedly affinities between Aquinas's questions and our own, and many of his concerns are quite similar to ours. Still, I want to argue, in an important sense which has not been fully appreciated in the literature, Aquinas asks different questions and pursues different ends in his inquiries. My particular concern in this work will be with the central notion of *scientia* in Aquinas, and how this concept plays a role in the *scientia* of sacred doctrine, the *scientia* of Christian theology which is based upon faith and presented in Aquinas's *magnum opus*, the *Summa theologiae*.

Our misunderstandings and misinterpretations of Thomas Aquinas are due at least in part to the peculiar way in which his works have been received during most of the twentieth century. Philosophers are especially interested in the question of cognition and knowledge, and until approximately the end of the Second Vatican Council in 1965 there was a rather sharp dichotomy in philosophical attitudes toward Aquinas.[1] As Anthony Kenny put it, looking back in 1969, as a philosopher Aquinas had been at the same time undervalued and overvalued.[2] In most circles of at least Anglo-American philosophy, with a few exceptions, Aquinas's works were either entirely ignored or treated in a cursory fashion and readily dismissed.[3] But among Neo-Scholastic philosophers who described themselves as Thomists, Aquinas was often regarded as a unique source of definitive answers to the philosophical problems of the day. Although these Thomists disagreed sharply among themselves about what Aquinas's views actually were and how they resolved the central questions of modern philosophy, they argued that, once understood, Aquinas's writings did provide the answers. Thus, to the extent Aquinas's thought was not simply neglected, it was portrayed as constituting one of the competing answers to contemporary philosophical questions.

Consider, for example, the various treatments in twentieth-century Thomism of Aquinas's epistemological views. For Joseph Maréchal the "fundamental problem" in the theory of knowledge was: "Do we meet in consciousness . . . an [absolute, objective] affirmation, surrounded by all the guarantees demanded by the most exacting critique?"[4] Maréchal believed that Kant's transcendental critique, which was for him the apogee of modern philosophy's attempt to respond to this fundamental problem, could be supplemented by Aquinas's account of cognition to render, on grounds Kant would accept, a realist, Thomistic metaphysics. Maréchal's Kantian turn in the reading of Aquinas, which became known as Transcendental Thomism, was taken up and developed by Bernard Lonergan under the influence of C. S. Pierce,[5] and by Karl Rahner under the influence of Martin Heidegger.[6] Alongside this Maréchalian reading a broadly Cartesian reading of Aquinas could be found.[7] In contrast, two very influential Thomists, Jacques Maritain and Etienne Gilson, rejected the critical program of Descartes and Kant as a philosophical dead-end and a distortion of Aquinas. As Gilson put it, "you must either begin as a realist with being, in which case you will have knowledge of being, or begin as a critical idealist, in which case you will never have contact with being."[8] Aquinas, Gilson held, had the correct view of the matter, and according to it we are immediately aware of the existence of the objects of sense perception and intellectual understanding. On Maritain's version of Thomism, we are implicitly aware of being in our apprehension of any idea, and we become fully aware when we abstract the idea of being.[9] Gilson and Maritain, then, held that a true Thomism must reject the 'critical problem' of modern philosophy, but they nevertheless presented their respective versions of Thomism as the true account of knowledge for which contemporary philosophers were seeking.

Regardless of how we judge the philosophical adequacy of these various Thomisms, it is clear that they approach the texts with contemporary philosophical problems in mind, they employ the vocabulary of the modern philosophers and they seek in Aquinas answers to these contemporary questions. This is most apparent in the Maréchalian and Cartesian versions of Thomism. But it is true even for Gilson and Maritain, though perhaps to a lesser extent. The 'critical problem', they believe, cannot be found in Aquinas nor should it be taken seriously as a philosophical problem. But once this point is recognized, they contend, we find in Aquinas the correct account of *knowledge*, just as their philosophical contemporaries offered different accounts of this concept.

Much of the work of these Thomists is useful, and some of it brilliant, and I do not want to disparage their efforts. The pervading spirit of their work, however, is to read Aquinas's works as providing an alternative answer, and indeed the most satisfactory answer, to contemporary philosophical questions. But this effort to present Aquinas as a participant in the discussions of modern philosophy has naturally led to an assimilation of Aquinas's thought to our own, and to a practice of expressing his thought within our conceptual framework. I want to suggest that this treatment of Aquinas's thought by his advocates – as well as by his detractors – has distorted it. The contemporary philosophical idiom in which these scholars have tried to express Aquinas's thought has in many respects been a procrustean bed, one on which commentators have tended to slice away whatever in Aquinas's inquiries seemed to express different concerns, to ask different questions, and to have different aims from those of participants in the contemporary debate.

In the present work, then, I will carefully examine the notion of *scientia* in Aquinas, and will be particularly interested in the differences between Aquinas's concept and our epistemic concepts. My contention will be that Aquinas's distinctive notion of *scientia* shaped his thought and writing in ways which have not been fully appreciated in the literature. Since Aquinas was a theological Master or teacher, a *Magister Sacrae Paginae*, the *scientia* of sacred doctrine, or

Christian theology, was the heart of his work and interests throughout his life. And the *Summa theologiae*, whose subject was sacred doctrine, was not only his last and greatest composition, but in many ways summed up the intellectual work of his life. Thus as we examine Aquinas's concept of *scientia* our special concern will be with the *scientia* of sacred doctrine in the *Summa theologiae*.

In the first chapter of this book I examine Aquinas's understanding of Aristotle's notion of ἐπιστήμη (in Aristotle's text) or *scientia* (in the Latin translation Aquinas used), as this is presented in Aquinas's commentary on the *Posterior Analytics*. The Aristotelian view as presented in this work and in Aquinas's commentary is complex and not easily summarized. A noteworthy feature of this account, however, is that a condition for perfect *scientia* of some predication is that not only must one know the cause of this predication being true (in the Aristotelian sense of formal, material, efficient or final cause), but one must also know the cause better than its effect. The reason for this rather stringent requirement is that, for perfect *scientia*, one's awareness of the cause must eventually become the cause of one's awareness of the effect.

This condition for *scientia*, which seems strange to modern ears, has important implications for the process of acquisition of *scientia* within a certain field. To acquire such *scientia* two stages are necessary. In a first stage one becomes familiar with the fundamental concepts within the field and discovers the causes, and thus becomes able to say which causes bring about which effects. In addition to this, however, a second stage is also required which will make the causes sufficiently well known that they become the foundation of one's thinking in that field, and one's knowledge of the causes becomes the cause of one's knowledge of the effects. To use an anachronistic example, consider a car mechanic who knows very well that when octane is combined with oxygen and a spark is applied, combustion occurs. He may even be able to recite the cause of this; he may have learned, through reading it or being told, that octane reacts with oxygen because it has the chemical structure of an alkane hydrocarbon. However, though he in some sense knows the cause of octane's combustibility, he does not have *scientia* of this fact until he becomes so familiar with the respective structures of hydrogen, carbon and alkane hydrocarbons such as octane that his knowledge of octane's combustibility flows from, is caused by, his knowledge of these chemical forms. The second stage in the acquisition of a *scientia* is meant to bring about the required familiarity with the cause in a field. Its purpose is to induce habits of thought, intellectual habits, in virtue of which a person's knowledge of the cause becomes the cause of, the epistemic grounds for, his knowledge of the effect. Its purpose, that is, is to make one's thinking in a particular field mirror the order of causality.

In chapter two I argue that in the *Summa theologiae* Aquinas adopts the Aristotelian notion of *scientia*, or at least something quite close to it. The structure of the *scientia* of the *Summa theologiae*, sacred doctrine or Christian theology, differs from other forms of *scientia* which humans can have, for in it humans participate in God's own *scientia*. The principles of this *scientia* are the articles of faith which have been revealed by God and accepted in faith. Although these principles cannot be fully understood and must remain mysteries in this life, and although this *scientia* transcends many of the limitations to which other *scientiae* are subject, sacred doctrine is properly a *scientia* subject to the fundamental conditions of an Aristotelian *scientia*.

In chapter three I draw the consequences of the preceding analysis for our understanding of the *Summa theologiae* and sacred doctrine. There I argue that the *Summa* was not written for neophytes in the study of theology, as has been widely thought, but was a pedagogical work for very advanced students who had come to the second stage in the acquisition of this *scientia*. That is, it was intended as a work for students who were already familiar with Christian theology, its concepts and principles, and the philosophy it presupposes, but who stood in need of the intellectual habituation by which the principles in the field, the articles of faith, become the foundation and cause of their thinking about matters in this field. Thus the *Summa theologiae* offers a synoptic view of the field which, as much as possible, moves from causes to effects so that the proper habits of thought are instilled.

My interpretation of Aquinas on *scientia* and sacred doctrine raises a question about his view of how we apprehend the principles of the various *scientiae*. If one's knowledge of principles is to be the cause of one's knowledge of conclusions, and if *scientia* is to be a practical ideal for inquiry and pedagogy, it must be a practical possibility for us to know the principles of the *scientia* and to know them better than its conclusions. In chapters four to six I take up this question. In chapter four I give a general sketch of Aquinas's account of our apprehension of the principles of *scientiae* which are not based upon divine revelation, but on natural human cognitive powers. Aquinas, I contend, held views according to which the required apprehension of principles in these *scientiae* is at least possible.

In chapter six I consider assent to the principles of sacred doctrine, the articles of faith. Against the standard interpretations, I argue that Aquinas did not think that this assent is inferred from any conclusions of natural theology, nor that it is due to a command of the will which overrides a lack of evidence. Rather one is able immediately to apprehend these propositions as divinely revealed. To prepare for this, I consider in chapter five the nature of grace, which elevates our natural powers, and the theological virtues and Gifts which are due to divine grace.

In the final chapter, I take up two final objections to my reading of the *Summa theologiae* as a whole and the sort of intellectual virtue which it was trying to instill. This will provide an opportunity to review the way we can acquire the *scientia* of sacred doctrine. The perfection of this *scientia*, which is the highest wisdom, is only attained after one's life on this earth when he enjoys the vision of the divine essence and knows other things through God's essence. In this life, however, we can attain an inchoate realization of it which will help us attain the perfect state. I summarize just how the *Summa theologiae* is meant to instill the imperfect state.

"Philosophy in the ancient world began in wonder," Henry Frankfurt recently observed. "In the modern world, of course, it began in doubt."[10] One might add that the philosophy which began in wonder sought wisdom, while that which began in doubt sought indubitable, or certain, or reliable information about the world. If we take philosophy in its classical sense, as the love of and search for wisdom, the whole of Aquinas's thought, even his Christian theology, can be called philosophical. And, in this wider sense of philosophy, the whole of Aquinas's thought stood within the ancient philosophical tradition. Aquinas was, of course, distinguished from earlier pagan thinkers in that he believed the wisdom philosophy sought could not be fully attained by strictly natural human powers, or in this world. He learned much from his reading of Aristotle and Aristotelians, but his fundamental concern was to understand and articulate a Christian wisdom. This wisdom could not be had through natural, human reasoning, but was possible only through Christian faith and through living a life informed by love of God and neighbor, a love which is realizable only if God elevates us beyond our nature. According to Aquinas's Christian vision, we attain perfect wisdom in heaven, when we will see God as He is (Mt 5:8), and know all other things in and through our grasp of divine essence. Then we will know perfectly, even as we are known (1 Cor. 13:12). Indeed, then we will be like God, for we will see God as He is (I Jn 3:2).

My contention, then, is that we distort Aquinas's thought if we remove it from this ancient philosophical tradition and try to find and make central the issues of modern philosophy. A further consequence of my study will be that we miss the impetus and tenor of his thought if we consider elements of it apart from the specifically Christian wisdom which is its end, its *telos*. Aquinas's writings have, I believe, been subject to both sorts of distortion.[11]

My concern in what follows, then, will be with understanding certain pivotal aspects of Aquinas's thought, particularly his concept of *scientia* and the nature of his project in the *Summa theologiae*. I will not try to argue whether Aquinas is right or wrong, whether ultimately his views can be defended or whether they must be rejected. As was said, scholarship on Aquinas has often been hampered because scholars were too quick to try to defend his views as viable in the contemporary philosophical debate, and failed to understand them fully. We shall find that simply to understand Aquinas on several key points on which he has been misunderstood will be quite enough to occupy us in the following pages. A sustained and systematic critique or defense of Aquinas's views must be the subject of subsequent work.

Nevertheless, although my concern will be limited to the historical or interpretive question of what Aquinas thought, I hope it will be of some use to those interested in the viability of contemporary Thomism. Since the end of the Second Vatican Council the influence of the central figures of twentieth century Neo-Scholasticism – such as Maréchal, Maritain and Gilson – has waned. But in their place has arisen some excellent work on both understanding and developing Aquinas's views.[12] My hope is that my efforts will aid this strand of contemporary Thomism.

Among Neo-Scholastic Thomists we find a tendency to define Thomism by some set or core of unalterable doctrines. Difficulties arose, however, when someone argued that one or more of these doctrines was not in fact in Aquinas's writings, or was in fact false. Alasdair MacIntyre has argued that a better way to think of

Thomism is as a tradition. A tradition is defined with respect to a certain language, shared beliefs, institutions and practices. In the course of time debates, conflicts and inquiries lead those working within a tradition to modify and revise not only the doctrines under consideration, but also aspects of the shared language, background beliefs, institutions and practices. Nevertheless the continuity of debate and inquiry makes for the continuity of an identifiable tradition.[13] If we understand Thomism as a tradition, we can see how we can critique or modify certain doctrines of Aquinas, and yet still remain faithful to the tradition.

Certainly there is much in Aquinas's thought which contemporary thinkers, even contemporary Thomists, will find untenable in light of subsequent scientific, philosophical and theological developments. It would truly be miraculous (in Aquinas's sense of this term) if, given the work of the past seven hundred years, that were not the case. However, I believe that any careful study of Aquinas's views will reveal much that is philosophically and theologically suggestive, true and profound. The most viable contemporary Thomism is one which takes its start from Aquinas's texts, but subjects Aquinas's claims to critical examination, and develops and revises them in light of this subsequent criticism and inquiry. It is this sort of work which constitutes a Thomistic tradition. It is hoped that my effort to reach a better understanding of this medieval Master will also illumine possibilities for the Thomistic tradition.

PART ONE

Scientia

CHAPTER ONE

'Scientia' in the 'Posterior Analytics'

"We think that we have *scientia simpliciter*, and not in a sophistical way, accidentally," writes Aristotle at the beginning of chapter two of the first book of the *Posterior Analytics*.[1] Aristotle's work is devoted to an analysis of the concept of ἐπιστήμη, which is rendered as *scientia* in the medieval Latin translations, and Aquinas's concept of *scientia* has its roots in the *Posterior Analytics*. Our attempt to understand Aquinas's concept of *scientia*, then, must begin with a careful examination of Aristotle's work and Aquinas's commentary on it. This will enable us to see in following chapters how this concept shapes Aquinas's understanding of sacred doctrine and his project in the *Summa theologiae*.

The prospect of analyzing and explaining the theory of *scientia* found in the *Posterior Analytics* is daunting. Aristotle's *Posterior Analytics* and Aquinas's commentary on this work are complex, philosophically difficult, often obscure and fraught with questions and problems for any interpreter. Moreover, an interpreter is confronted with an enormous amount of scholarly literature on these works, both contemporary and historical. And in both contemporary and historical scholarship, one finds little consensus even on fundamental questions. If our treatment of Aristotle's work and Aquinas's commentary in this chapter is to be manageable, we must set some limits on our discussion.

We will first of all restrict our treatment by focusing on Aquinas's understanding of Aristotle's work, and avoiding alternative interpretations which have been generated by centuries of scholarly controversy. Thus my primary interest in this chapter will not be so much in Aristotle's *Posterior Analytics* itself as in Aquinas's understanding of that work, whether or not his understanding is correct. Though I believe Aquinas's reading of Aristotle is astute and for the most part defensible, I will not try to defend it here against all the challenges which could be raised. My intention is simply to set forth some central components of the doctrines of the *Posterior Analytics* as Aquinas understood them, and thus gain insight into Aquinas's thought. For ease of reference I will henceforth use the initials *PA* to refer to the *Posterior Analytics* as Aquinas understood this work.

Secondly, my discussion of the *PA* will be limited in scope. My intention in this chapter is simply to argue, on the basis of a careful reading of the texts of Aristotle and Aquinas, that there are certain general features of the *PA* notion of *scientia* whose existence and importance have not been widely recognized, and, as I will go on to argue in subsequent chapters, these features are critical for grasping Aquinas's understanding of the *scientia* of sacred doctrine and his project in the *Summa theologiae*. Thus there are many important passages in the *Posterior Analytics* and in Aquinas's commentary, and many important claims made in these passages, which I will not discuss. Moreover, I will not discuss many of the interesting philosophical questions and problems to which the issues I will discuss give rise. And, finally, I will not discuss at length much of the secondary literature on the *Posterior Analytics* and on Aquinas's commentary.[2]

No doubt questions and problems will remain at the end of my work. Indeed, I will be disappointed if my efforts do not generate further questions and problems. I will have accomplished my goal if I can make a case, on the basis of a careful reading of relevant texts, for a revisionary understanding of some key epistemological tenets of Aquinas, of his understanding of Christian theology and of his project in the *Summa theologiae*.

I.I PRELIMINARY REMARKS

Before embarking on a detailed examination of the texts, it will perhaps be helpful to begin with a preliminary discussion of the issues which will be addressed in the coming chapter. Thus I begin in this section with an overview of the theory of demonstration Aquinas found in Aristotle's *Posterior Analytics*, and then make some remarks about the translation of some key terms in Aristotle's and Aquinas's texts.

The account of scientific demonstration in the *PA* turns on a distinction between certain derivative facts and other essential facts. The essential facts are in some way expressed in the definition of a subject, and from these other derivative facts are demonstrated. Very roughly and briefly, the theory is as follows. Consider one of Aristotle's favorite examples, the demonstration of the inherence of the attribute *having interior angles equal to two right angles* (i.e. interior angles equal to 180°) in a subject. Such a demonstration must be constructed within a particular science, and a science is identified and individuated by the subject genus or kind that it treats. This subject genus is some natural kind in the world that we can investigate.[3] In the case of our example, the science is of course geometry, whose subject genus is spatial magnitude.

If the inherence of *having interior angles equal to two right angles* can be demonstrated within the science of geometry, the necessary inherence of this attribute will be established in a demonstrative syllogism which proceeds from principles which concern an essence or nature within the subject genus. Moreover, this demonstration must proceed from the most fundamental, the most inclusive genus in which this attribute inheres necessarily. For instance, it is possible to construct a syllogism proving that *having interior angles equal to two right angles* necessarily inheres in something *qua* isosceles triangle; but this would not be a scientific demonstration, for it is possible to establish that it inheres in virtue of a more fundamental, more inclusive nature – viz. triangle.

In this way one demonstrates the inherence of all derivative, necessary attributes of the essences within the genus which a particular science studies. Aquinas calls these derivative, demonstrable attributes *per se* accidents (which is the Latin phrase which translates Aristotle's καθ᾽ αὑτό). Of course, there are other accidents which do not belong *per se* to their subject. For instance, *being blue* or *being bronze* do not belong to a triangle *qua* triangle, and so they are not demonstrable in a science. They are mere accidents.[4]

As the *PA* presents it, then, a demonstrative syllogism begins from principles which assert the existence of, and essential facts about, the science's proper subject, and from these proceeds to demonstrate the *per se* accidents of its subject.[5] Much of the scholarship on the *PA* has concentrated on what is required for a demonstrative syllogism, and how it can be constructed. But the theory of demonstration is set forth in the *PA* in order to elucidate the concept of *scientia simpliciter* (ἐπιστήμη ἁπλῶς in Aristotle's Greek text), complete or unqualified scientific knowledge, and for this it is not enough simply to construct a demonstrative syllogism. As M. F. Burnyeat has pointed out with regard to Aristotle's *Posterior Analytics*, the aspirant to unqualified scientific knowledge must attain such a grasp of the principles, of the essences or natures within the subject genus, that this apprehension of the principles becomes the cause of, the epistemic ground for, his assent to the conclusion.[6] That is, for scientific knowledge, it is not enough to construct a demonstrative syllogism whose conclusion asserts that a particular attribute inheres in a particular subject. The syllogism must also express the *grounds* for one's belief that the conclusion is true.

Let us attempt to illustrate Burnyeat's point by introducing another example from the *PA*, the demonstration making clear the cause of the fact that vines shed their leaves annually.[7] It is one of the more elaborate examples in the *Posterior Analytics* or in Aquinas's commentary, and we will return to it several times in the course of our discussion in this chapter. The example, however, is unclear in several respects. We will here tentatively present what seems to be the relevant demonstration, but it will be necessary to add further refinements and qualifications before we arrive at a syllogism which meets the strict standards of scientific demonstration. The gradual ascertainment of the demonstration in this case will be helpful, for the initial tentative presentation will provide an intuition about what is involved in demonstrations, while the addition of further refinements in subsequent discussion will be instructive about the full requirements of a scientific demonstration.

A person can come to construct a demonstrative syllogism in the following way. Through ordinary observation one can come to know that vines shed their leaves annually, and one may seek the cause of this fact. One also easily observes that not only vines, but also fig trees and other plants, shed their leaves. One can then discover that all deciduous plants belong to the genus of broad-leaved plants. One discovers, then, that *being broad-leaved*, having this generic form, is the cause of the deciduousness of vines.[8] Moreover, since this is the genus of vine, *being broad-leaved* is in the definition of vine. Consequently one has arrived at that part of the essence of vine which is the cause of its deciduousness.

This case contains a slight complexity, for there is a more proximate cause of the deciduousness of vines than being broad-leaved. This is the fact that all broad-leaved plants have their sap congeal at the leaf stalk.[9] Thus we can (tentatively) conclude that in order to demonstrate that vines are deciduous we need the following sorties:

(1) All vines are broad-leaved.
(2) All broad-leaved plants are sap-congealers at the leaf stalk.
(3) All sap-congealers at the leaf stalk are deciduous.

(4) All vines are deciduous.

Burnyeat's point is that although one may discover the causes of
the deciduousness of vines, and be able to construct the above
sorties, this is not sufficient for scientific knowledge that vines are
deciduous. It is also necessary that one come to believe (4) because
of, on the grounds of, (1)–(3).[10] For scientific knowledge one must, of
course, identify the appropriate causes and be able to construct
demonstrative syllogisms. But, Burnyeat argues, it is further required
that one's apprehension of these causes become sufficiently complete
and sure that this apprehension becomes the cause of, the ground
for, one's assent to the conclusion. And for this one must undergo a
process of "intellectual habituation," a certain cognitive re-structuring so that one's belief that something is the cause of the inherence
of an attribute becomes the epistemic ground for one's belief that the
attribute inheres. As Aquinas's Aristotle puts it, what is better known
by nature – i.e. the cause – must become better known *to the inquirer* –
i.e. as epistemic ground for another belief. Only then does one attain
scientia simpliciter.

In this chapter I will argue that the interpretation of Aristotle's
Posterior Analytics sketched in the previous paragraphs is in fact
Aquinas's interpretation of Aristotle; and moreover, it is the core of
Aquinas's own account of scientific knowledge. Most importantly, I
will argue that a key condition of *scientia* for Aquinas is that the
principles of a demonstration be better known than the conclusion,
and that this has important consequences which have been overlooked
by commentators. For I will argue in subsequent chapters that this is
the understanding of scientific knowledge which Aquinas brings to his
treatment of Christian theology (which he calls "sacred doctrine"),
and that it determines the purpose and structure of his *Summa theologiae*
in ways which have not been appreciated. Our task in this chapter,
then, will be to examine carefully Aristotle's *Posterior Analytics* and
Aquinas's commentary on this work so that we can elaborate the
account of scientific knowledge described above and establish that it
is in fact Aquinas's understanding of Aristotle's account.

There are, however, problems with the translation of key terms in

Table 1.1. *Translations of Aristotle's Greek terms*

Aristotle	Aquinas's Latin	My English translation
ἐπίστασθαι	scire	———
εἰδέναι	scire	———
ἐπιστήμη	scientia	———
γιγνώσκειν	cognoscere	to apprehend
γνῶσις	cognitio	apprehension/cognition
γιγνώσκειν	noscere	to know
γνῶσις	notitia	knowledge
———	innotescere	to become known

Aristotle's text and in Aquinas's commentary. Indeed, a central tenet of my work will be that certain key terms in Aquinas's discussions of cognitive and epistemic matters simply do not translate straightforwardly into twentieth-century English.[11] Although I will render some of them into English, the reader should be aware that translations are tentative and imperfect. A list of key terms for our interests may be found in table 1.1. Since in Aquinas's Latin translation of the *Posterior Analytics* Aristotle's Greek terms γιγνώσκειν and γνῶσις were translated in two different ways depending on context, I list both translations.

Several comments on these translations are necessary. First, there is no single English expression which will serve as a wholly satisfactory translation of *cognitio* or *cognoscere*. In Aquinas's writing these words seem to be generic terms for intentional, mental activity. In most cases, the terms refer to the apprehension, whether sensible or intellectual, of a thing or proposition. Thus, in what follows I will, for the most part, translate *cognitio* by *apprehension* and *cognoscere* by *to apprehend*. Although this strategy will generally render Aquinas's texts, the reader should beware of two disadvantages. First, though Aquinas's Latin flows smoothly, some translations will seem forced and stilted. Secondly, *apprehension* and *to apprehend* tend to imply that the mind has been successful in grasping its object, whereas *cognitio* and *cognoscere* can be used of false and illusory mental states. Although these are serious difficulties with this strategy for translation, I know of no alternative which does not bring with it equally or more serious problems.

In a few contexts Aquinas uses *cognitio* to refer not to the apprehension in which the mental activity of some being issues, but to the whole collection of mental processes which lead to apprehension. In these cases I will translate *cognitio* by *cognition*.

In Aquinas's commentary on the *Posterior Analytics*, *noscere* and *notitia* are near synonyms of *cognoscere* and *cognitio*, but the former pair of terms seem to be used in a more restricted sense. They seem to signify only intellectual *cognitio*, and *cognitio* which successfully apprehends its object. That is, *notitia* seems to be true belief with positive epistemic status, and *noscere* seems to be to have such a belief. Thus I will translate these terms by *knowledge* and *to know*. Aquinas uses *innotescere* as the passive form of *noscere*, and so I will translate it with *to become known*.

Scientia is the subject of my study, and, as I hope will become clear in the course of the discussion, any translation into contemporary English would be misleading. Thus I will continue to use the Latin *scientia* (singular) and *scientiae* (plural), as I have already. For the verb *scire*, I will use *to have scientia*. Since the adjective *scientialis* presents problems of gender and number agreement and case inflections, I will render it as *scientific*; though the reader should be aware that this English word is used for the Latin term. For other related terms, I will translate the word as is appropriate for the context.

I.2 *SCIENTIA* AND THE DEMONSTRATIVE SYLLOGISM

We turn now to a more detailed analysis of the *Posterior Analytics* and Aquinas's commentary on this work. The opening chapters of the *PA* contain an argument that a demonstrative syllogism is necessary for *scientia*, and they begin to identify the conditions such a syllogism must meet. Since *scientia* is the result of a demonstrative syllogism, this initial characterization of such a syllogism is critical to the *PA*'s account of *scientia*. And, as we will see, critical to his analysis of a demonstrative syllogism are the conditions its premises must meet. In this section we will identify these conditions as they are understood and discussed in Aquinas's commentary, and in subsequent sections we will examine them more fully.

In the proemium to his commentary on the *Posterior Analytics* Aquinas discusses the subject and purpose of Aristotle's work. The *Prior* and *Posterior Analytics*, writes Aquinas, fall within what is called judicative logic, "because [its] judgment is with the certitude of *scientia*."[12] The *Prior Analytics* concerns only syllogistic form, but Aquinas writes that there is also a study "from the matter, because the propositions employed are *per se* and necessary, and this is the purpose of the book of the *Posterior Analytics*, which concerns the demonstrative syllogism."[13] The end or goal of the demonstrative syllogism is *scientia*, and it is in virtue of this end that demonstration is constituted as it is.[14] Thus, while the *Prior Analytics* considers only the validity or invalidity of various syllogistic forms, the *Posterior Analytics* considers the further conditions on the propositions of a syllogism which make it productive of *scientia*, which make it a scientific demonstration. Most importantly, it is concerned with what sort of premises are required for it to be a syllogism which issues in *scientia*.

The first chapter of the *Posterior Analytics* begins with the argument that a demonstrative syllogism is necessary for *scientia*. Aristotle opens the work with the sweeping claim: "All teaching and all intellectual learning comes about from already existing knowledge."[15] As Aquinas explains, Aristotle's strategy is to move from this most general claim to what is required for the particular cognitive state which is *scientia*. As Aquinas writes, "to show the necessity of the demonstrative syllogism, Aristotle begins by asserting that apprehension among us [humans] is acquired from some pre-existing apprehension."[16] Aristotle attempts to establish the general claim inductively in the first chapter, Aquinas says, by considering various *scientiae* and arts. Aquinas's Aristotle then goes on to argue that *scientia*, as a particular form of apprehension, also proceeds from pre-existing apprehension.

The *PA* then gives us an initial sketch of what must be pre-known for *scientia* of some conclusion. "*Scientia* through demonstration seeks a certain conclusion in which a proper accident is predicated of a certain subject, and the conclusion is inferred from certain principles."[17] For such a demonstration, regarding the subject the demonstrator must have previous knowledge of 'what it is' (*quid est*) – i.e. of the essence of the subject. He must also already know 'that it exists' (*quia est*) – i.e. he must know that individuals with this essence exist. Moreover, of the attribute whose inherence is to be demonstrated, he must know only what the terms signify (for the existence of the attribute – its inherence in a subject – is established in the demonstration). And finally, he must have prior knowledge of the truth of the principles from which the conclusion is inferred.

Aristotle's text and Aquinas's commentary are dense, abstract and sparing of illuminating examples. It may be helpful here to depart from the texts and return to the example of the deciduousness of vines. As before:

(1) All vines are broad-leaved.
(2) All broad-leaved plants are sap-congealers at the leaf stalk.
(3) All sap-congealers at the leaf stalk are deciduous.

---

(4) All vines are deciduous.

In the first chapter of the *PA* Aristotle is saying that in order to have *scientia* of (4) one must have prior knowledge of the *quid est*, the essence, of vine. Since the genus of vine is broad-leaved plant, a prior knowledge of the essence, which is expressed in the genus-difference definition, would yield knowledge of (1). Secondly, it is a requirement of a *PA scientia* that one know that the subject exists. The reason for this requirement is not discussed extensively, but it seems that given an Aristotelian account of universals as existing *in res*, if one knows of no individuals then there are no objects of one's *scientia*; there is nothing for one's *scientia* to be *about*. Thirdly, of the attribute, *being deciduous*, one must know only what the term means or signifies, for its existence is established in the demonstration. The *PA* adds that one must know the truth of the principles – in this case propositions (1), (2) and (3) above.[18]

Having argued in chapter one for the need for the demonstrative syllogism and the prior knowledge it requires, in chapter two the *PA* "begins to delimit (*determinare*) the demonstrative syllogism."[19] The *PA* here invokes common understanding.[20] According to this common understanding, "to have *scientia* of something is to apprehend that thing perfectly, and this is to grasp the truth of it: for the principles of the being of the thing and the truth of the thing are the same."[21] *Scientia*, then, as perfect apprehension, requires a grasp of the truth, and hence of the principles of a thing. Aquinas adds in his commentary, "therefore, it must be that the one having *scientia*, if his apprehension is perfect, apprehends the cause of the thing of which he has *scientia*."[22] That is, if one is to have *scientia*, perfect apprehension of the inherence of an attribute A in a subject S, then one must know the cause of S being A, and one must know it *as* the cause.[23] Moreover, if the apprehension is to be perfect, it must be *cognitio certa*, which, Aquinas explains, could not be if the thing could be otherwise. Thus, "it is further required that something of which one has *scientia* cannot be otherwise."[24] Hence, one must know that A belongs to S necessarily.[25]

The point here seems to be simply to elaborate and provide further support for what we have seen sketched in chapter one of the *PA*. If one is to have *scientia* that vines are deciduous, one must apprehend the cause of this attribute, the fact that vines are broad-leaved, which in turn is part of the essence of vine. Moreover, if one can have *scientia* of this fact, it must be the case that this is a necessary attribute of vines, which is due to their essence.

In characteristically Aristotelian fashion, the *PA* moves from this initial, general delineation of *scientia* to a more detailed analysis of the demonstrative syllogism through which the *scientia* so delineated can be realized. The *PA* describes the demonstrative syllogism in terms of both its end or goal and its 'matter,' its constituents. In terms of its end, as we have seen, "demonstration is a scientific syllogism, that is one producing *scientia*."[26] Later, Aquinas writes, Aristotle "asserts the consequence by which the material definition of demonstration is concluded from premises when he says that if 'to have *scientia*' signifies what we said – viz. to apprehend the cause of a thing, etc. – it is necessary that demonstrative *scientia* (i.e. *scientia* which is acquired through demonstration) proceeds from propositions [which are] true, primitive and immediate . . . and moreover from [propositions] better known, prior to and causes of the conclusions."[27] These six conditions on the premises of a demonstrative syllogism are critical, and we will discuss each of them below.

The first two chapters of the *PA*, then, arrive at definitions of the demonstrative syllogism in terms of both its end or goal, and its matter or constituents. This is, however, only an initial sketch, and the reader should keep in mind that we find important qualifications on it in subsequent chapters. One often finds in Aristotle's works that these initial formulations are based on a loose inductive argument and on common opinions, and some key terms are left ambiguous and unclear. Only in subsequent analysis and argument are these formulations clarified and further supported. Thus we must turn to subsequent analysis and argument to understand the respective senses of terms such as *necessity, cause* and *primitive*.

A second point to note is that the notion of *scientia* sketched in these opening chapters is of *scientia simpliciter, scientia* in an unqualified sense, which is perfect apprehension.[28] As will become clear in the course of the *PA*, Aristotle and Aquinas will accept as *scientia* certain types of apprehension which do not fulfill all the conditions for *scientia* in a perfect or unqualified way. Aristotle's strategy in the *PA* is to describe the perfect or paradigmatic instance of *scientia*, but then to consider as *scientia* other forms of apprehension which fulfill the conditions for perfect *scientia* in only a partial or qualified way. Thus, as we shall see, although perfect *scientia* is only of absolutely necessary truths, we can also have *scientia* of what occurs "for the most part."

We turn now to the subsequent chapters of the *PA*, in which this initial analysis of *scientia* is elaborated. As was mentioned above, we will not attempt to discuss exhaustively the various lines of argument in the later chapters of the *PA*, but will seek only a general portrayal of the view of *scientia* it presents. It will be most useful to organize our discussion around the various conditions on the premises of a demonstrative syllogism stated in the material definition above. The first of the conditions – that the premises are (1) true – is self-explanatory. The rest, however, require further elucidation. Four conditions are closely related, and I will call them, for reasons to be explained, the *priority cluster of conditions*. These are that the premises of a demonstration are (2) primitive, (3) prior, (4) immediate, and (5) state the cause of the conclusion. The central condition, I shall argue, is the primitiveness condition, and we will begin with and concentrate on it. After considering this priority cluster, I will turn to the (6) 'better-known' condition.

1.3 THE PRIMITIVENESS CONDITION

Chapter four of the *PA* states that there are three ways in which an attribute may be universally predicated of a subject: it may be (1) "said of all", (2) said *per se* or (3) said primitively of the subject. Although the primary concern in this chapter is with the primitiveness condition, the *PA* first considers the other two sorts of universal predication. This is because, of these three, each successive kind of predication entails but is not entailed by the previous. Thus each successive sort of universal predication can be understood as adding further conditions to the previous. As Aquinas explains:

These three [kinds of universal predication – viz., 'Said of all,' 'said *per se*' and 'said primitively'] are related by adding to each [successive one] in turn. For every *per se* predication is also universal [i.e. 'said of all'], but not conversely. Similarly every primitive predication is a *per se* predication, but not conversely. Thus the rationale for [Aristotle's] order of treatment in these [kinds of predication] becomes evident.[29]

We will follow the *PA* in approaching our discussion of the primitiveness condition by considering in order each of these three kinds of universal predication.

The first sort of universal predication is one in which one term is 'said of all' (*dici de omni*) of another. As Aquinas writes, "something is 'said of all' . . . when there is nothing to be found under the subject of which the other term is not predicated."[30] That is, a predicate is 'said of all' if the predication is what we would normally call a *universal predication* (which is more narrow than the *PA* sense of 'universal predication'). Thus A is said of all of B if all Bs are As.[31] At least in the paradigm case, the premises of a demonstrative syllogism are universal in this sense.

The second sort of universal predication is one in which the predicate is said of a subject *per se* (καθ' αὐτό in Greek), which is, literally, "through itself." The preposition *per*, writes Aquinas, "denotes a relationship to a cause."[32] Thus an attribute is said *per se* of a subject if it has, in some sense, the subject itself as the cause of its inherence. The *PA* goes on to distinguish four modes of perseity according to the various ways in which the subject itself can be the cause of the inherence of an attribute.

The first mode of perseity is that in which the intrinsic causality is due to the form: "when that which is attributed to something pertains to its form."[33] Because the definition signifies the form and essence of the thing, the first mode occurs

when of a given thing is predicated either [its] definition or something posited in [its] definition (and this is what [Aristotle] means [when he says] that *per se* are whatever are in *that*, namely, the *quod quid est* – that is, in the definition indicating the *quid est*), whether these are put in the nominative or in one of the oblique cases.[34]

That is, what is predicated *per se* in the first mode is, first of all, the definition. But, secondly, it includes whatever is contained in that definition. What is contained consists not only of what is predicated in the nominative case in the definition, as *figure* is in the definition of triangle, 'a figure bounded by three lines.' It also includes what is posited, though not predicated, in an oblique case. The phrase *by . . . lines*, though not predicated of triangle in the nominative case, nevertheless posits something in an oblique case in the definition (viz. lines). Hence, Aquinas writes, "line is in a triangle *per se*."[35] The point seems to be that a proposition such as *A triangle has three lines* would be *per se* in the first mode. Thus a thing's definition, or any component of the definition – whether predicated of the thing or posited as belonging to it – is predicated *per se* in the first mode.

Something is said *per se* of a subject in the second mode with respect to what is called the material cause. Here the *PA* speaks of an attribute whose proper subject is placed in its definition:

The second mode of making a *per se* statement occurs when this preposition *per* denotes the relationship to a material cause, as when that to which something is attributed is the proper matter and proper subject of that thing. And the proper subject must be placed in the definition of an accident.[36]

The example Aquinas gives here is snubness (*simus*), which is defined as 'curvature of the nose.' Nose is the sole or proper subject of this attribute, and so it is in its definition. Hence snubness belongs to nose, its proper subject, in the second mode of perseity.

Both the first and second mode of perseity are based in definitions, then, but in different ways. In the first mode an attribute, A, belongs to a subject, S, just if A is in the definition of S. Thus *being a figure* belongs to triangle in this mode of perseity. But in the second mode an attribute, A, belongs to a subject, S, just if S is in the definition of A as its proper subject. Other examples of the second mode of perseity which the *PA* offers are straight and curved, which belong to line; odd and even, which belong to number; and equilateral and scalene, which belong to triangle. These and all such attributes belong *per se* to their proper subjects in the second mode.

Aristotle includes a third mode of being *per se*, which does not have the sense of being related to an intrinsic cause, but has the sense of 'being alone' (i.e. existing apart or independently). This mode is not relevant to demonstration.

Aristotle finally "presents the fourth mode, according to which this preposition *per* denotes a relationship to an efficient cause, even to some other thing."[37] In some cases the efficient cause of the attribute is extrinsic to the subject, as, for example, if there is lightning while someone is walking. Lightning of course is not caused by anything in virtue of it being a walking thing, and so the cause here is not *per se*, but extrinsic. Such a predication is *per accidens*, a mere accident, whose inherence cannot be demonstrated scientifically. However, in the case of *The one who has been slain dies*, the predication is *per se*. The *PA*'s point here seems to be that for the subject as described in this predication – i.e. for the thing with the form indicated – the effect follows as an (in some sense) necessary effect.[38] In the example, for a living thing which has received a blow of a certain sort, death follows as the necessary effect. In this case the cause is intrinsic, and the predication is not *per accidens*. Other examples of *per se* predications of this sort would be *Triangles have interior angles equal to two right angles* and *Vines are deciduous*. Predications of this sort are *per se* in the fourth mode.[39]

The premises of a demonstrative syllogism, then, must be universal in the sense that they are *per se* predications. As the *PA* envisions demonstrations, they seem generally (though not always) to move from predications which are *per se* in the first or second mode to conclusions which are *per se* in the fourth mode. As we said above, they move from certain essential facts, which are in some way expressed in the definition of the subject, to other derivative facts. Thus *having angles equal to two right angles* is true of triangles because of what is intrinsic to triangles: their essential form, which is expressed in the definition. And *being deciduous* is true of broad-leaved plants because of their generic form, which is part of their essence and definition. Scientific demonstration, then, moves from principles stating certain intrinsic, essential facts about a subject to conclusions about *per se* accidents, which inhere because of these intrinsic facts.

Thirdly, the premises of a demonstration must be universal in the sense that they are primitive (*primo*). The primitiveness condition entails that the premises are 'said of all' and *per se* in the appropriate senses, but it places a further requirement on demonstration. Aquinas writes:

Something is said to be predicated primitively of another in relationship to those things which are prior to the subject and contain it. For to have three angles, etc., is not predicated primitively of isosceles, for it is priorly predicated of something prior, namely of triangle.[40]

Primitiveness here is defined in terms of priority and containment of a subject. The point of the example seems to be that the attribute *having three angles* is 'said of all,' and is *per se* with respect to the subject isosceles, for it is a necessary attribute of isosceles which is due to its essential form. Yet, Aquinas says, it does not inhere primitively in isosceles, for there is a subject, triangle, in which the attribute inheres *per se* and is 'said of all' and that subject is a more general kind which includes isosceles. As Aquinas explains: "That having three [angles] does not inhere primitively in isosceles is not because it is not universally predicated of it, but because it is [predicated] more widely; that is, in more than isosceles, since it inheres commonly in all triangles."[41]

What seems to be presupposed here is a hierarchical structure of genera and species which we might represent as follows:

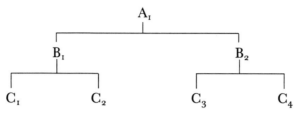

The kind on each level of this structure contains as species those below it which are connected by lines. An attribute P may belong to C_4, for example, as 'said of all' and *per se*, but still may not belong primitively, for P may belong *per se* to all of B_2, or even all of A_1. One has only found a primitive predication for a given attribute when one has found the genus in the hierarchy to which the attribute belongs as 'said of all' and *per se*, but which does not belong *per se* to any member outside that genus. Thus a primitive predication is convertible: not only is it the case that all Ss are Ps, but all Ps are Ss. A primitive predication, then, is one in which something is 'said of all' and is *per se*, but the predicate is also convertible with the subject. The *PA*, then, requires that demonstration proceed ultimately from principles which are primitive predications.

Let us return to our 'deciduous' example to gain a better understanding of the primitiveness condition and the constraints it places on demonstration. Let us label the syllogism formulated above *I*:

I. (1) All vines are broad-leaved.
    (2) All broad-leaved plants are sap-congealers at the leaf stalk.
    (3) All sap-congealers at the leaf stalk are deciduous.

    _____

    (4) All vines are deciduous.

This demonstration served as a useful example above, for it began from premise (1), which predicates a part of the essence of vine, a part of its definition, and it establishes' the inherence of a *per se* accident of that subject. However, in light of our discussion of primitiveness we will have to revise our understanding of this case of scientific demonstration, for the premises of syllogism (1) do not meet the primitiveness condition. Primitive propositions are convertible, and though it is true that all vines are broad-leaved, it is not true that all broad leaved plants are vines.

The difficulty with syllogism (1) is that it does not demonstrate the attribute, *being deciduous*, of its primitive subject, broad-leaved plants. The syllogism which does do this is the following:

II.   (1) All broad-leaved plants are sap-congealers at the leaf stalk.
      (2) All sap-congealers at the leaf stalk are deciduous.

---

      (3) All broad-leaved plants are deciduous.

As the *PA* understands deciduousness, premises (1) and (2) are 'said of all'; premise (2) seems to be a *per se* predication in the first mode;[42] and both (1) and (2) are convertible propositions, and hence could be primitive predications.

A problem with this example and with the *PA*'s theory of demonstration generally, however, is that it is difficult to understand the perseity of propositions like premise (1). The *PA* often seems to imply that demonstrations proceed from definitions which make clear the essence of the subject, and thus, it seems, the principles of demonstrations should be definitions; they should be *per se* propositions in the first or second mode. In the *PA*, however, definitions are taken to include only the genus and difference proper to the species. For example, the definition of triangle is *figure* (genus) *bounded by three lines* (specific difference). A conundrum for any interpreter of the *PA* is that it is not clear how all *per se* accidents in a field can be demonstrated from such definitions. The texts seem unclear on this point. On balance, though, I think it is best to say that in premise (1) and others like it the predicate is not taken from the definition of the subject, but is an immediate, indemonstrable *per se* attribute. Propositions in which such an attribute is predicated of a subject can serve as premises of a demonstration. On this interpretation, then, *being a sap-congealer at the leaf stalk* is an immediate, indemonstrable attribute of broad-leaved plants, and premise (1) is a *per se* predication in the fourth mode. Hence, this premise, like premise (2) is 'said of all,' *per se* and (since it is convertible) primitive.[43]

But how then are we to understand the demonstration that *vines* are deciduous? This is best understood as a syllogism of a different sort from those which, like syllogism II, meet the strict primitiveness condition. It is one which takes the results of a demonstration establishing that an attribute inheres in all members of a genus and applies this to a particular species of that genus. The syllogism in question is:

III. (1) All broad-leaved plants are deciduous.
   (2) All vines are broad-leaved plants.

---

   (3) All vines are deciduous.

Application syllogisms such as III have premises which are 'said of all' and are *per se*, but not primitive.

It seems to be these sorts of application syllogisms about which Aquinas writes in the following passage:

> If we would like to know why certain things such as *being asleep* and *being awake* are found in man and horse – Let *animal* be that in which A, the middle, is found; and let B, i.e. the major extreme, stand for items that inhere in every animal, e.g. *being asleep* and *being awake*. Let certain species of animals, such as *man, horse, cow*, be taken as minor extremes, namely C, D, E. In this way it is manifest that the reason why B, i.e. *being asleep* or *being awake*, is found in D, i.e. in *man*, is that it is because of A, i.e. because man is an *animal*. Then the same should be done in regard to the others, and the same structure of proof must be observed in all.[44]

Application syllogisms are extremely important in a *scientia*, for they establish important truths about the species within a genus. They do not meet the primitiveness condition in an unqualified way. They can, however, be said in a qualified way to proceed from primitive principles, for they apply the results of demonstrations like II above, which have primitive premises. And they do yield *scientia* about a species.[45]

1.4 FURTHER CONDITIONS FOLLOWING ON PRIMITIVENESS

The primitiveness condition entails or is closely connected with other conditions on the premises of demonstrations that are discussed in the *PA*. In this section we will consider the further conditions (A) that the principles of a demonstration are of the same genus as the conclusion, (B) that they are necessary and (C) that they are eternal.

As Aquinas explains in his commentary on chapter seven of Book 1: "After the Philosopher shows that demonstrations are from what is *per se*, he here concludes that demonstration is from proper principles, not from extraneous or common principles."[46] Proper principles are those whose terms are from the same genus as the conclusion, whereas extraneous principles have one or more terms from a different genus, and common principles have terms common to more than one genus. Aquinas is here saying that the terms of the principles of a demonstration must all be from the same genus, and he implies the 'same genus' requirement is a consequence of the *per se* requirement, which, as we have seen, is entailed by the primitiveness condition.

It is easy to see how the 'same genus' requirement follows from the perseity requirement. A genus in the *PA* consists of the common generic nature, the various specific natures which are in that genus and the attributes which belong to something by virtue of its having that generic or one of the specific natures. Each *scientia* treats a particular subject genus, and it demonstrates the attributes which belong to things *per se* by virtue of being a member of that genus; that is, it demonstrates what belongs to things by virtue of having the generic or one of the specific natures. Arithmetic, for example, is concerned with the genus of number, and demonstrates the *per se* or proper accidents of number. It will also demonstrate proper accidents which belong to some species of number, such as the odd, even or prime. It is clear, then, that the terms of a demonstration must be from the same genus – i.e. they must denote the generic nature, a specific nature of that genus or an attribute which belongs *per se* to that genus or species – for if a term denotes an attribute which is not in the subject genus, the predication cannot be *per se*. As Aristotle writes, "it is necessary that the extreme and middle [terms of a demonstrative syllogism] be of the same genus. For if they are not *per se*, they will be accidents."[47]

There are two exceptions to the 'same genus' requirement for principles of *scientiae* which deal with a particular genus. The first is the common principles or *dignitates*. These are principles which apply commonly to genera and their *scientiae*, such as:

(1) It is not possible both for the affirmation and denial of a
    proposition to be true at the same time.
(2) Either a proposition or its negation is true.
(3) If equals are taken from equals, equals remain.

(1) and (2) are called "first among common principles."[48] The *PA* argues, however, that (1) cannot be used as a premise in demonstrations.[49] (2) does play a role in the special *scientiae* as a principle in *reductio ad absurdum* arguments.[50] Principles such as (3) are employed in demonstrations, but only insofar as they are applied to the genus

of that *scientia*. Thus geometry uses (3) as speaking of equal magnitudes, arithmetic uses it as speaking of equal number, and so on.[51]

A second exception to the 'same genus' requirement concerns the concept of a subaltern *scientia*, which will be extremely important for Aquinas's understanding of sacred doctrine as a *scientia*. In some cases a higher *scientia* demonstrates propositions which serve as the principles of another *scientia* which is subordinate or subaltern to the higher *scientia*. For example, the *scientia* of optics is subaltern to geometry: "hence it is clear that when what are lines *simpliciter* are taken as visual lines, there is in a certain way a descent to another genus."[52] Euclid, for instance, held that rectilinear rays emerge from the viewer's eye in a cone whose vertex is in the eye and whose base is in the visual object. He postulated that the apparent size of an object depends upon the angle under which the object is perceived. It is easy to see that one could employ geometrical principles to show that objects further away would be seen under a lesser angle than one closer, and hence appear smaller. In this sort of demonstration, the *PA* holds, although the terms are not of the same genus *simpliciter*, they are of the same *secundum quid*.[53] In these cases, the one who possesses the subaltern *scientia* knows its principles *quia* (that) but not *propter quid* (because of which). That is, he knows only the fact that they are true, but not the demonstration of why they are true. One who has the higher *scientia*, on the other hand, knows them both *propter quid* and *quia*.[54]

There are also two *scientiae* which are exceptional in that they do not treat a particular genus, and have special relationships to the common principles. First philosophy or metaphysics "is about what is common, because its examination is of common things, namely of being and the parts or attributes of being."[55] Since it considers all being, it is not restricted to a particular genus of being, but considers all things insofar as they are. It uses the common principles as its proper principles and moves from these to establish the proper principles of the particular *scientiae*.[56] The second exception is dialectic, which argues from common logical notions to establish what belongs to one or another particular *scientia*.[57]

Such, then, is the 'same genus' requirement and the qualifications the *PA* makes regarding it. Another condition which is closely connected with the primitiveness condition is that the demonstrative *scientia* must be necessary. Although in the *PA* the primitiveness condition flows from the necessity condition discussed above, it is in

the discussion of primitiveness and perseity that the *PA*'s understanding of necessity is clarified. Aristotle opens the *Posterior Analytics*
I.6 as follows:

If demonstrative *scientia* proceeds from necessary principles (for that of
which one has *scientia* cannot be otherwise), and the things which are *per se*
belong necessarily to their objects (for in the one case they are in the *quid est*;
in the other case they are in the *quid est* of things predicated of their objects,
and the predicates are opposties one of which belongs necessarily) it is
evident that demonstrative syllogisms are from things of this sort: for
everything belongs either in this way or accidentally, and what is accidental
is not necessary.[58]

This passage, along with the rest of this chapter and Aquinas's
commentary, makes clear that in the *PA* necessity and perseity are
equivalent, as are their opposites, non-necessity and accidentality.
The necessity requirement, which was one of the two fundamental
conditions which emerged from the initial examination of common
understanding of *scientia*, is met by the fact that the premises and
conclusion of a demonstration are *per se* predications, in one of the
modes of perseity.

Chapter eight of the *PA* discusses another feature of scientific
demonstration:

It is evident too that if the propositions on which a syllogism depends are
universal, it is necessary for the conclusion of such a demonstration – [i.e.]
of demonstration *simpliciter*, as it can be called – to be eternal too. There is
therefore no demonstration or *scientia simpliciter* of corruptible things, except
in a certain way, viz. accidentally.[59]

As Aquinas explains in his commentary, the premises of a demonstrative syllogism are universal in the sense of 'said of all,' which, as
we have seen, is entailed by the primitiveness condition. Furthermore, in demonstrative syllogisms (as opposed to dialectic) the
premises, and hence the conclusion, of a demonstrative syllogism are
'said of all' not for a particular time or place, but absolutely.
Therefore the premises, and hence the conclusion, of a demonstration must be of what is eternal, and cannot be of what is corruptible.

At first blush, the requirements of necessity and eternity seem
extremely, even impossibly, stringent. But, as was mentioned above,
these stringent conditions define the paradigm instance of *scientia*,
and forms of apprehension which fulfill these conditions in only a
qualified or imperfect manner may nevertheless be (non-paradigmatic) *scientia*. Thus, the *PA* recognizes that certain truths can be

necessary and eternal in a qualified way. An attribute A may belong to a subject S necessarily in the manner required for demonstration, even though there are exceptions to it so belonging. For example, Aquinas holds that the potencies of the soul are proper accidents of a human being,[60] and among these is the power of sight.[61] Some people are blind, however, and are not actually able to see. Although such a person has an aptitude for sight rooted in his nature, a defect in the matter of his body prevents him from actually seeing.[62] Hence, although *being able to see* belongs necessarily to *human*, there are exceptions to the proposition *Humans are able to see.*[63]

Thus, although in early chapters of the *PA* the necessity and eternity requirements are asserted without qualification, subsequent discussion and resolution of puzzles lead to important qualifications of the conditions for *scientia*. Regarding the necessity requirement, for example, in *Posterior Analytics* 1.6 and in Aquinas's *lectiones* on this chapter, the propositions of a demonstrative syllogism are all said to be necessary. But in 1.30 and *lectio* xlii we find a distinction between propositions which are strictly necessary and those which are 'for the most part' (ὡς ἐπὶ τὸ πολύ / *ut frequenter*). In certain *scientiae*, such as arithmetic and geometry, the conclusions of demonstrative syllogisms are always true. In the natural *scientiae*, they are "true as 'for the most part' [*frequenter*] and are defective in a small part."[64] The latter are acceptable in demonstrations "insofar as there is something of necessity in them."[65] The point here seems to be that the attribute is *per se* and hence necessary (in the *PA*'s sense of the term) in that it is due to the subject's essence. However, the actual presence of the attribute may be obstructed by some defect in the matter of the individual.

Differences among the *scientiae* in their realization of the necessity requirement are further explained in *Posterior Analytics* 1.27 and *lectio* xli, where we find a hierarchical ordering of *scientiae* according to priority and certitude (*certitudo*).[66] What we have here, it seems, is a ranking of *scientiae*, from the paradigm cases to less perfect instances, with respect to the conditions of necessity and certitude. The mathematical *scientiae* which abstract wholly from sensible matter, such as arithmetic and geometry, are more certain (*certior*) than those which do not, such as music and harmonics, "because uncertainty is caused because of the changeability of sensible matter; hence the nearer one is to it, the less is *scientia* certain."[67]

Similarly, the *PA* admits important qualifications regarding the eternity of conclusions of demonstrative syllogisms. The *PA* recognizes that although demonstration *simpliciter* treats universal and eternal form, it is *secundum accidens* about particulars which exemplify such forms, and thus it is *secundum accidens* about what is not eternal. In his commentary Aquinas distinguishes two kinds of cause in which demonstration and *scientia* may be *secundum accidens* about what is not eternal:

For some things are not eternal with respect to time, but are eternal in relation to the cause: because it never fails that if the cause is in place, the effect follows. For example, a failure (*defectus*) of the [light of the] moon: for it never fails that there is always an eclipse of the moon whenever the earth is diametrically interposed between the sun and the moon. But some things are not eternal even in relation to the cause: because clearly the cause can be impeded. For a human being with two hands is not always produced from human seed, but there is sometimes a defect (*defectus*) due to an impediment either of the agent or of the material cause.[68]

Thus, although being eternal is a requirement of demonstrations, the *PA* recognizes cases in which demonstrations are not of the eternal. In some of these, the effect always occurs when the cause is present; in others, even when the cause is present the effect may fail because of an intervening agent or a defect in the matter. Demonstration and *scientia* are *simpliciter* of universal and eternal forms, but because these forms are instantiated in matter, and certain things are true of the individual as material, they are *secundum accidens* about what is not eternal.

Critics have often pointed to the seeming narrowness of the *PA* account of *scientia*, claiming that only an axiomatic system such as mathematics could satisfy its strict conditions. But, as Scott MacDonald has recently written, the account "is more subtle and resilient than many critics have allowed."[69] An important source of this subtlety and resilience, as MacDonald notes and as we have seen, is that while it places strict conditions on paradigmatic cases of *scientia*, it nevertheless recognizes that these conditions can be met in a qualified way when limitations in the knower, or in the object of knowledge, prevent complete fulfillment of the strict conditions. In these cases one can attain *scientia*, albeit of a non-paradigmatic sort. Thus the *PA* notion of *scientia* has a wider application than may initially seem. And, as we shall see, this resilience and flexibility of the *PA* notion will be extremely important in Aquinas's understanding of sacred doctrine as a *scientia*.

I.5 PRIORITY, CAUSALITY AND IMMEDIACY

The conditions we will next consider are that the premises of a demonstration must (A) be prior, (B) state the cause of the conclusion and (C) be immediate. As we will see, these conditions do not add many substantive constraints on a demonstration beyond those which flow from the primitiveness condition. However, they do serve to clarify and reiterate the constraints we have already discussed.

The third condition stipulates that the premises of a demonstrative syllogism must be prior to the conclusion. This condition is not extensively discussed in the *Posterior Analytics* or in Aquinas's commentary, so we must look to other works to shed some light on its import. In *Categories* 12 and *Metaphysics* v.11 we find Aristotle's most lengthy discussions of priority and posteriority, and Aquinas commented only on the latter. In the *Metaphysics* commentary Aquinas explains: "For the principle in any genus is that which is first (*primus*) in the genus. And that is said to be prior which is nearer to some determinate principle."[70] But since *principle* can be taken in many ways, so can *prior*. Aquinas distinguishes several senses of *prior* in this *lectio*: there is priority according to (1) place, (2) time, (3) motion, (4) discrete things, (5) cognition and (6) being. It seems that, with respect to the requirements for demonstration in the *PA*, we can immediately rule out taking *prior* with respect to place, time, motion and discrete things.[71] As for sense (5), priority in cognition, the term is used in this way in Aquinas's commentary,[72] but Aquinas explicitly rules it out as not being relevant to scientific demonstrations, for they proceed not from what is better known to us but from what is better known *simpliciter*.[73] Thus the priority required for scientific demonstrations must be (6), priority in being.

With regard to priority in being, the *Metaphysics* distinguishes three different modes. The first mode is non-reciprocity in being: "according to which those are said to be *prior* which can be without other things but the other things cannot be without them."[74] Aquinas in his commentary on this passage in the *Metaphysics* cites the *Categories*, where Aristotle explains further:

Secondly, [that is called *prior* which] . . . does not reciprocate as to implication of existence. For example, one is prior to two because if there are two it follows at once that there is one, whereas if there is one there are not necessarily two; so the implication of the other's existence does not hold reciprocally from one. And that from which the implication of existence does not hold reciprocally is thought to be prior.[75]

In the first mode of priority of being, then, a certain thing A is prior to another thing B just if B cannot exist without A, but A can exist without B. In this sense of priority, triangle is prior to isosceles, for something can exist as a triangle without being isosceles, but nothing can exist as isosceles without being a triangle. Thus, in this sense of *prior*, the priority condition stipulates that for all attributes which belong both to triangle and isosceles, the inherence of an attribute in isosceles must be demonstrated from its inherence in triangle. Consequently the proposition *All isosceles triangles have three angles* must be demonstrated from *All triangles have three angles*. *Prior* in this sense seems to be the comparative for the superlative *primus* or *primitive*, which we have considered above; for, in this sense, one form is prior to another if the former is closer to that form which is primitive, in the sense set forth above. Aquinas does use 'prior' in this way.[76] However, in this sense of *prior* the condition of priority is redundant, for it adds nothing to the condition of being primitive.

The second mode of priority of being "is considered according to the order of substance to accident."[77] Aquinas explains:

Because being is said in many ways and not univocally, it must be that all senses of being are referred back to one primary sense, according to which something is said to be being which is the *per se* existing subject of other beings. And because of this the first subject is said to be prior: hence substance is prior to accident.[78]

Priority taken in this sense seems to reinforce an important condition, which is implied by the primitiveness condition. Consider, for example, the terms *human, rational animal* and *risible*. Both *rational animal* and *risible* are 'said of all,' *per se* and primitively of humans. Hence it may not be clear, with only the conditions so far discussed, whether and why *Humans are risible* is to be demonstrated from *Humans are rational animals* or the other way round. But priority of being in this second sense requires that we demonstrate the inherence of proper accidents, such as *being risible* in humans, from substantial form, such as *being a rational animal*.[79]

Of course, there are many *scientiae* whose subjects are not metaphysical substances, but are from one of the other categories of being. Arithmetic, for instance, takes its subjects from the category of quantity, and geometry treats spatial magnitude. In these cases, the priority condition in this sense does not of course require that demonstration proceed from a metaphysical substance. Rather, it is from that which is the subject of other attributes in the genus – "the *per se* existing subject of other beings" (as Aristotle says in the passage quoted above).

The third mode of priority of being is closely connected with the priority of a cause to its effect. Before discussing that sense of priority, then, let us turn to the fifth condition on the premises of a demonstration, that they state the cause of the conclusion. As was clear from our discussion of perseity above, however, the cause cannot be an extrinsic efficient cause, for then it would not be *per se*, and would thus violate the primitiveness condition. The cause must be intrinsic to the subject as described in the predication. Hence, it must be either the essential form, which is stated in the definition, or the matter, in the sense of a subject of an attribute, which is in the *ratio*, and hence in the definition of the attribute. An attribute which is *per se* in the fourth mode will be an effect of the subject's form or proper matter, but it can also be the cause of other *per se* attributes. Thus, from premises which state these sorts of causes a demonstration establishes a thing's proper accidents.

The condition of causality, as restricted by the primitiveness condition, does not so much add substantive conditions to that of priority as specify its sense. As Aquinas explains, the condition of priority follows from that of causality:

Aristotle proves that the premises (*propositiones*) of a demonstration are the causes of the conclusion, because we have *scientia* when we apprehend the causes. And from this he furthermore concludes that they are prior and better known, because every cause is naturally prior and better known than its effect.[80]

As Aristotle states in the *Categories*, this is a sense in which something is prior which differs from non-reciprocity of existence (i.e. being *primitive*): "for of things which reciprocate as to implication of existence, that which is in some way the cause of the other's existence might reasonably be called prior by nature."[81] It can perhaps be said that the causality requirement specifies the sense of the priority requirement of demonstrations.

We can return to the third and final mode of the priority of being mentioned in the *Metaphysics* commentary, which is "considered according to the division of being into act and potency."[82] Certainly, the premises of a demonstration cannot be prior in potency. However, insofar as they signify the cause of the conclusion, they are prior in act, for a cause always has more actuality than its effect. The third mode of priority, then, seems to reiterate the causality condition with respect to the relationship between actuality and potentiality.

The fifth condition on the premises of a demonstration in the *PA* states that the principles of demonstration are immediate, and this is defined in terms of priority. As Aquinas explains:

Aristotle defines an immediate proposition, and says that an immediate proposition is one to which there is not another prior . . . For it was said above that demonstration is from what is prior. Therefore whenever some proposition is mediate (i.e. having a middle term through which the predicate is demonstrated of the subject) it must be that those propositions from which something is demonstrated are prior: for the inherence of the predicate term of a conclusion in the middle term is prior to its inherence in the subject; and the inherence of the middle term in the subject is prior to the inherence of the predicate in the subject.[83]

The middle term in a syllogism is, of course, the 'B' term in a syllogism, such as one of the form:

$$A \text{ is } B.$$
$$\underline{B \text{ is } C.}$$
$$A \text{ is } C.$$

A predication *A is B* is immediate – i.e. without a middle term – just if there is no other term, B*,which can be predicated *per se* of A and which is prior to B (in the senses discussed above), and thus from which *A is B* can be demonstrated. For example, in syllogism (II) above we said that premise (I), *All broad-leaved plants are sap-congealers at the leaf stalk*, is immediate because there is no prior *per se* predicate of broad-leaved plants from which *being a sap-congealer at the leaf stalk* could be demonstrated. Hence, the condition of immediacy stipulates, in terms of the form of a syllogism, that demonstrations proceed from predications for which there is no prior term.

1.6 THE PRIORITY CLUSTER OF CONDITIONS

The primitiveness, priority, causality and immediacy conditions delineate the sort of objective priority which the premises of a demonstrative syllogism must have with respect to its conclusion. Thus I call them the *priority cluster of conditions*, or just the *priority conditions*. Before turning to the sixth and final condition, the 'better known' condition, I will summarize and make several comments about the concept of demonstrative *scientia* which the conditions so far considered delimit.

On the *PA* view, each *scientia* is of a discrete genus, which is a certain natural kind. A *scientia* deals with things only by virtue of their being members of that genus or of a species of that genus. Its demonstrations establish what is true of things because they have the form or matter proper to that genus or its species. And only predications of this sort can be the object of demonstrations within that *scientia*.

In the *PA* account, primitiveness is the pivotal condition for the premises of a demonstrative syllogism, a syllogism producing *scientia*. The priority, causality and immediacy conditions for the most part clarify and reiterate what was stated or implied by the primitiveness condition.

The primitiveness condition requires first that premises be universal predications (in our sense of *universal*), in which the predicate is said universally of the subject. Secondly, they must be *per se* in one of three ways or modes. An attribute A belongs to a subject S *per se* in the first mode just if A is in some way in the definition of S (e.g. *being a figure* belongs to triangle). In the second mode A belongs to S just if S is in the definition of A as its proper subject (e.g. straight belongs to line). In the fourth mode of perseity (the third mode is not relevant to our concerns), A belongs to S by virtue of what S is, by virtue of its form or proper matter (e.g. *being deciduous* belongs to vine). Demonstrations begin from certain premises which are *per se* predications, and conclude that an attribute belongs to the subject as a *per se* or proper accident. Thirdly and finally, primitiveness requires that demonstrations of the inherence of A in S proceed from the primitive cause of A, the cause in the genus in which A universally and exclusively inheres *per se*.

A demonstrative syllogism whose premises meet the priority cluster of conditions is a *propter quid* syllogism. (This is the Latin translation of Aristotle's ὁ τοῦ διότι συλλογισμός, and it literally means a 'because of which' syllogism.) Only such demonstrations can produce *scientia simpliciter*. The *PA* recognizes, however, that there are valid, sound and informative syllogisms which do not meet the priority cluster of conditions, for they proceed from effects to establish a cause. One may establish syllogistically, for example, that

the planets are near because they do not twinkle.[84] Such a syllogism
is a demonstration *quia*, a demonstration 'of the fact.' Such a
syllogism may be an important stage in the acquisition of *scientia* (as
we will see below), and the *PA* speaks of them as producing *scientia* in
a qualified sense, but they do not produce *scientia simpliciter*.

Let us try to gain an intuitive sense of the *PA* account of scientific
demonstration by returning to the anachronistic example mentioned
in the Introduction. A car mechanic knows that when gasoline is
combined with oxygen and a spark is applied combustion occurs. He
knows the fact but does not know the 'why,' as Aristotle puts it.
When he learns a little chemistry, he discovers that octane is the
combustible agent in the gasoline with which he is familiar, and he
can then construct a syllogism from premises which are universal and
per se. Octane would be defined by its chemical structure, and this
would provide the syllogism's major premise, which would be *per se*
in the first mode. Combustibility would be an immediate *per se*
attribute of this chemical structure, and this would provide the minor
premise. And from these premises one could draw the conclusion
that octane is combustible.

However, our mechanic would not yet have a scientific demonstration or *scientia* of the combustibility of octane, for he has not yet found
the primitive cause. Octane is combustible because it has the simple
hydrocarbonic structure of an alkane, which it shares with methane,
ethane, propane, butane and other compounds. The combustibility
of octane, then, must be demonstrated from the combustibility of
alkane hydrocarbons generally. Only when one has identified the
form by virtue of which an attribute is universally and exclusively *per
se* present can one have a scientific demonstration and *scientia* of the
inherence of that attribute in a subject.[85] And such a demonstration
would proceed from premises which are prior to the conclusion,
which state the cause of the conclusion and which are immediate.

The above discussion of the *PA*'s complex theory of demonstration
has been somewhat brief and general, but it is perhaps sufficient to
give some idea of the constraints the priority conditions place on
scientific demonstration. Before we turn in the next section to the
final condition, it will be helpful for subsequent discussion to make
three comments about the *PA* theory as so far presented.

My first comment is that, on the basis of the priority conditions
above, the *PA*'s concept of *scientia* clearly differs from our concept of
knowledge and even of scientific knowledge in at least two ways.

First, the class of propositions which can be the object of *scientia* is much more restricted than those which can be known, or even scientifically known, in our sense of these terms. A scientific demonstration moves from premises which are primitive and *per se* in the first and second mode to a conclusion which is *per se* in the fourth mode. Hence, only universal, *per se* propositions can be the object of *scientia*. We cannot, therefore, have *scientia*, that Aristotle was born in Stagira, that the average American spends x number of hours watching TV, or that y per cent of infants are born with genetic defects. Moreover, of those propositions of which we can have both *scientia* and scientific knowledge (in our sense of this term), the conditions for having each state are different. On many accounts of scientific knowledge, establishing regularities, such as establishing that the stars are distant by a *quia* demonstration, could be possible objects of fully acceptable scientific knowledge, but they could not be the object of *scientia simpliciter*.

The second comment I want to make is that before the demonstrator is in a position to construct a demonstrative syllogism, he must already have discovered a great deal in a particular scientific field. As we have seen, the first chapter of the *PA* discusses how demonstrative *scientia* proceeds from prior knowledge. In his commentary on this chapter Aquinas writes:

That of which *scientia* through demonstration is sought is a conclusion in which a proper accident is predicated of some subject: and this conclusion is inferred from certain principles. And because apprehension of simples precedes apprehension of composites, it is necessary that before apprehension of a conclusion is had, the subject and attribute are apprehended in some way. And similarly there must be previous apprehension of the principle from which the conclusion is inferred, since from the apprehension of a principle one comes to know the conclusion.[86]

Of the subject of the *scientia*, then, the demonstrator must have previous knowledge of both 'what it is' (*quid est*), the essence, and 'that it exists' (*quia est*), that individuals with that essence exist. Of the attribute, the demonstrator must have previous knowledge only of what the term signifies, for that it exists is established in the demonstration. The demonstrator must also have prior knowledge of the truth of the principles from which the conclusion is inferred.[87] Thus, before one can begin to construct demonstrations within a field, a great deal must already be known about its fundamental forms and terms.

It seems, therefore, that before one can construct a demonstrative syllogism, for many *scientiae* a somewhat extended period of inquiry and discovery is required. Although the *PA* does not discuss at any length the methods and procedures which belong to this initial period, its statements about what must be previously known for demonstration seem clearly to imply that there is a prior stage in which these discoveries are made.

One method which is discussed in the *PA* is the demonstration *quia*. Because such demonstrations move from effect to cause, they immediately produce only a qualified, non-paradigmatic *scientia*, not *scientia simpliciter*. But there is an important difference between the non-paradigmatic character of *scientia* based on demonstration *quia* and that of, for instance, *scientia* of an eclipse, which, as we have seen above, is non-paradigmatic because the moon is not eternally eclipsed. In the latter case the defect is in the *object* of *scientia*, and this cannot be altered. Eclipses of the moon, unlike geometrical or arithmetic truths, are not eternal and unchanging truths, and thus cannot be apprehended as such. However, in the case of demonstrations *quia*, although we may initially apprehend the cause through the effect, we may nevertheless eventually come to understand the cause better so that we can apprehend the effect through the cause. Thus *scientia* based on demonstration *quia*, unlike *scientia* of an eclipse, can be an imperfect *scientia* which is useful in one's progress toward more perfect *scientia*. As we will see below, this is how the *PA* views many demonstrations *quia*.

The third and final comment I want to make about the *PA* concerns its clearly foundationalist picture of the justification for *scientia* and its relationship to skepticism. Foundationalism is a certain view about the ways one's beliefs are justified or have some positive epistemic status, such as being known, or (in the case of the *PA*) being *scientia*. According to a foundationalist account, some beliefs – the foundations – are justified of themselves and not because of their relationship to other beliefs; whereas other, non-foundational beliefs are justified by their relationship with other beliefs and ultimately owe their justification to foundational beliefs. The *PA* account of *scientia* is clearly foundational, for demonstrations productive of *scientia* proceed from principles which are not themselves known through demonstration, and we have *scientia* of other truths by way of demonstrations which employ these indemonstrable principles as premises.

Some versions of foundationalism in the history of philosophy had appeal because they were thought to furnish a response to skeptical objections. A skeptic is one who claims that we do not know much or most of what we think we know. The strategy of a skepticism-driven foundationalism is to find foundational beliefs which are indubitable, or incorrigible or in some way immune to skeptical objections. (Generally, these are beliefs about the contents of and relationships among one's own ideas, or about what is evident to the senses.) From these foundations one can deduce other beliefs which would be equally secure. Well-known versions of this sort of foundationalism are found in René Descartes's *Meditations* and in John Locke's account of knowledge (though not of probability and judgment) in *An Essay Concerning Human Understanding.*

The third point I want to make is that although some have attempted to understand the foundationalism of the *PA* account of *scientia* along the lines of a skepticism-driven foundationalism, this is mistaken.[88] For, according to that sort of foundationalism, foundational beliefs are immune to skeptical doubt, or at least to refutation; and one's *scientia* of the conclusions one deduces would be equally sure. But this is not the *PA* view. It is true that demonstrations proceed from indemonstrable principles and, if the demonstrator is to have *scientia*, he must have good reasons to believe that the premises meet the priority conditions. As discussed above, the object of *scientia* must be necessary, not simply in the sense that S apprehends p and p is necessary, but in the sense that S apprehends that necessarily p. And this will not meet the stronger necessity condition unless the demonstrator has good reason to believe that his premises meet the priority conditions, and thus apprehends that his conclusion is *per se*. However, the *PA* makes clear that these reasons need not be indubitable, for according to it the claim to have *scientia* is defeasible. That is, there is no requirement in the *PA* that one's claim to have *scientia* be impervious to skeptical challenges. For Aristotle admits, "it is difficult to apprehend whether one has *scientia* or not";[89] and Aquinas comments, "many opine that they have *scientia* if they have a syllogism proceeding from premises which are true and primitive, but this is not true."[90] And elsewhere Aquinas says that one may falsely believe that he has *scientia* if he takes a non-necessary middle as necessary.[91] Thus, although the *PA* requires that one who claims to have *scientia* has good reason to think his principles meet the priority conditions, this claim need not be such that it is beyond skeptical doubt or challenge. The *PA* does not seem to be particularly concerned with skepticism in its formulation of the conditions for *scientia*.[92]

1.7 THE 'BETTER KNOWN' CONDITION

We turn now to the sixth and final condition, that the premises of a demonstrative syllogism are 'better known' than the conclusion. A central thesis of mine in this work will be that this condition has not been widely understood and its significance for reading Aquinas has not been appreciated. In this section I will attempt to clarify just what its import is, and in coming chapters I will argue for its significance for understanding Aquinas's concept of *scientia* and his work on that *scientia* which was his primary concern, sacred doctrine.

In his *lectio* on chapter two of the *Posterior Analytics* Aquinas explains that because the premises of a demonstration identify the cause of what is asserted in the conclusion, they are better known, "because every cause is naturally both prior to and better known than its effect."[93] Moreover, Aquinas adds, the cause is better known not only with regard to 'what it is,' but also 'that it is'; it is better known not only with regard to its quiddity or nature, but also with regard to the fact that it exists. This inference from *A causes B* to *A is better known than B*, which initially seems quite odd to us, is explained by the *PA*'s distinction between what is better known *simpliciter* and *quoad nos*, or to us. Aquinas explains:

> And because *prior* and *better known* are said in two senses, namely 'to us' and 'by nature,' Aristotle thereupon says that those propositions from which a demonstration proceeds are prior and better known *simpliciter* and by nature, but not to us. And to elucidate this Aristotle says that what are prior and better known *simpliciter* are those things which are removed from sense perception, while the things better known to us are closer to sense perception – viz. particulars.[94]

The point here seems to be that what has causal or perhaps logical priority can be said to be 'better known' in some absolute sense, apart from the limitations of a particular knower or class of knowers. Since the premises of a demonstrative syllogism are the universal, *per se* propositions which state the cause of the conclusion, they are 'better known' in this absolute sense; they are better known *simpliciter*. However, given the epistemic limitations of a particular class of knowers, such as humans, effects may be previously and better known than their causes. Apprehension of the premises of a demonstration requires a full grasp of the universal natures involved. Human cognition is such, though, that it begins from sense perception of particulars,[95] and only gradually, and perhaps falteringly, moves toward a grasp of universal natures.[96] Thus we can observe immediately that the sun is eclipsed, but it is only gradually that we move to apprehend the nature of the eclipse, which is the middle term and cause. Thus, although the premises of a demonstrative syllogism are better known *simpliciter*, they are often initially less well known *to us*.

If the 'better known' condition requires only that the premises be better known *simpliciter*, it adds no substantive constraint on demonstrative syllogisms. Any premise which meets the priority cluster of conditions would also be better known *simpliciter*. Does the 'better known' condition add any further, substantive constraint?

The *PA* makes clear that it does. The *Posterior Analytics* begins with the universal claim, "all teaching and intellectual learning comes from already existing knowledge."[97] Aquinas understands the first chapter of the work to argue from this general claim to the particular claim that *scientia* arises from a demonstrative syllogism,[98] in which the conclusion is inferred from premises or principles. As Aquinas explains, "it must be that the principle from which the conclusion is inferred is previously apprehended (*precognoscatur*), since from apprehension of the principle the conclusion becomes known."[99] In such a syllogism, Aquinas tells us, our apprehension of the premise or principle is the cause of our apprehension of the effect. As he writes, "principles are related to conclusions in demonstrations as efficient causes in natural things to their effect (hence in the second book of the *Physics* propositions of a syllogism are classified in the genus of efficient cause)."[100] And because the demonstrator's grasp of the principle is the cause of his grasp of the conclusion, the principle must be better known *to him*:

Because we believe something which has been concluded and we have *scientia* of it through the fact that we have a demonstrative syllogism, and this insofar as we have *scientia* of a demonstrative syllogism, it is necessary not only to apprehend previously the first principles of the conclusion, but also to apprehend them better than the conclusion.[101]

Although initially the premises of a demonstrative syllogism may be better known *simpliciter* but not to us, the 'better known' condition for perfect *scientia* requires that they become better known to us and the cause of – in the sense of being the epistemic ground of or reason for – our assent to the conclusion. The 'better known' condition, then, places constraints not just on the construction of a syllogism, but on our apprehension of the propositions of the syllogism; it concerns not just objective relations among Aristotelian causes and effects, but the demonstrator's doxastic structure. I will call this part of the 'better known' condition – viz. that the principles of a demonstration be better known to us and the cause or epistemic ground of our assent to the conclusion – the *doxastic causality* condition.

Our interpretation of the long quotation at the end of the last paragraph but one is complicated by the fact that Aristotle states in his text that "either some or all" principles must be better known to us, and Aquinas gives three possible readings of this phrase. Aquinas believes each of the three readings is compatible with the *PA* doctrine, and each preserves the doxastic causality condition, albeit with some qualifications. It will be useful to consider briefly these three readings, for each brings out a different aspect of the *PA* doctrine.

According to the first reading, Aristotle is saying that, for some principles, once proposed they are better known than the conclusion; in the case of others, they need to be proven and so initially are not better known, for they are not known at all. Aquinas offers an example: "The fact that [1] an exterior angle of a triangle is equal to its opposite interior angles is, until proven, as unknown as the fact that [2] a triangle has three angles equal to two right angles."[102] The reference here seems to be to Euclid's *Elements* 1.32, where (1) is first proved, and then this proposition is used as a premise to prove (2). (1) is not known until it is proved in a demonstrative syllogism, and so it is not initially better known than the conclusion. However, once it is deployed as a principle in a demonstrative syllogism to prove (2), it is better known to the demonstrator, and is the cause of his grasp of (2). This qualification meets the doxastic causality condition, but it points out that this condition is compatible with principles of one syllogism being first proven by higher principles in another syllogism.

According to another reading, Aristotle is saying "that some principles are apprehended priorly in time with respect to the conclusion, but others come to be known simultaneously with the conclusion."[103] Perhaps an example of this is one discussed in Book II of the *PA*, the awareness of an eclipse for a person viewing it from outer space: "If we were to situate ourselves in a place above the moon, we would see how the moon became eclipsed by entering the earth's shadow. Then we would no longer ask *if* it is or *why* it is, but both would at once be obvious to us."[104] In such a case the conclusion (*that* it is) and the principle (*why* it is) are grasped simultaneously and equally well; and thus the latter is not previously and better known. Such cases, however, would seem to be rare and relatively uninteresting in a *scientia*, for with respect to them there would be no point to inquiry or discursive thought.

The third reading addresses a problem which arises from something mentioned above. In the natural *scientiae*, as we have seen, effects are often initially better known to us, and we sometimes must discover causes by a demonstration *quia* which moves from effects to causes. However, Aquinas also says that for a demonstrative syllogism "the principle from which the conclusion is inferred must be previously apprehended (*precognoscatur*),"[105] for the conclusion must be derived from it. But in the natural *scientiae* in which the effect is often known prior to and better than the cause, how can we ever construct a demonstrative syllogism in which the principle is known prior to and better than the conclusion?

Aquinas seems to address this issue in his third reading, when he writes:

There are some conclusions which are best known inasmuch as they are received from the senses, as, e.g., *The sun is eclipsed.* Hence the principle through which it is proved – viz. *The moon is interposed between the sun and earth* – is not better known *simpliciter,* though it is better known in the way proceeding from cause to effect.[106]

In those cases in which the effect is initially better known, Aquinas seems to recognize two stages in the approach to *scientia.* In the first, effects are apparent to sense, and by a demonstration *quia* one may discover the cause. However, in the second, "in the way proceeding from cause to effect," one must construct a demonstrative syllogism whose premises meet the priority cluster of conditions, and which hence is better known *simpliciter.* And what is more, if the doxastic causality condition is to be met, one must attain a familiarity with, a clear apprehension of, the truth of the principles, so that they become better known than the effect (expressed in the conclusion of the demonstration), and so eventually he comes to believe the effect exists or occurs because he believes the cause exists or occurs.

We can now discern important features of the *PA* doctrine on the nature of *scientia* and on the way in which we attain this state. As mentioned above, our discussion of the priority cluster of conditions has shown that they place stringent constraints on demonstrative syllogisms beyond validity and soundness, and that the demonstrator must have good reason to believe that these further conditions are met by his premises. Consequently, if a demonstrator is to have a properly demonstrative syllogism and have good reason to believe it is such, he must have discovered a great deal before he constructs his syllogism. He must, as we have seen, have discovered the quiddity and existence of the subject, and the quiddity of the attribute. Hence, within a *scientia*, he must have a full understanding of the natures or basic concepts of the *scientia*, and must have grasped the existence of the subject.

The *PA*, then, implies that there must be an *initial* or *first stage* of inquiry devoted to these preparatory discoveries. In some *scientiae*, such as arithmetic or geometry, this first stage may not be problematic or involved, for the principles and concepts of these *scientiae* may be relatively readily grasped. In the natural *scientiae*, however, the natures and powers of things are often hidden, and can only be discovered through more accessible effects.[107] In such cases, the inquirer may need to employ demonstrations *quia* in order to discover causes,[108] as when one attempts to demonstrate that the planets are near because they do not twinkle.[109]

A subsequent *second stage* involves the construction of *propter quid* demonstrations, which proceed from principles which are true and meet the priority cluster of conditions. But, as we have seen, it is also required that the demonstrator and his demonstration meet the doxastic causality condition, and thus undergo a sort of cognitive re-structuring, so that his belief that something is a cause itself becomes the cause of (in the sense of epistemic ground of or reason for) his belief that something else is the effect. In certain *scientiae*, such as mathematics, our belief in the effect flows naturally from our belief in the cause. But in other *scientiae*, such as all the natural *scientiae*, we naturally know the effects prior to the cause. In such *scientiae*, then, the second stage will involve not only the construction of syllogisms, but a kind of re-arrangement in our doxastic structure, so that the causes, which were formerly less familiar, become more familiar and better known; and the effects, formerly better known, come to be believed on the grounds of our belief in the cause.

What is required at this second stage is what Burnyeat has called "intellectual habituation."[110] We must undergo a process of familiarization with the principles so that they become the foundation of our thinking and reasoning within a certain area. Not only must we construct a *propter quid* syllogism within a particular field, but such syllogisms must come to express the way we think about facts described. And this requires that what is better known by nature comes to be better known to us. It requires that, in some sense, our doxastic structure comes to mirror the causal structure of the world.

This is what Aristotle (or at least Aristotle as Aquinas understands him) is speaking of in the *Metaphysics* when he describes the end or goal of inquiry:

All men begin, as we said, by wondering whether [things] are as the [apparent] automatism of marvelous occurrences [is] to those who do not yet see the cause; or changes in the course of the sun [which turns toward the south in the summer solstice, and toward the north in the winter solstice], or the incommensurability of the diagonal [of a square with its side]. For it seems marvelous to all if something were not measured by numbers. But we must advance to the contrary and more worthy position, as the proverb says, and as also happens in these matters when people have learned: for nothing would surprise a geometer more than if the diagonal turned out to be commensurable.[111]

The goal of inquiry, then, is to acquire such a familiarity with the causes in the field under study that the effects come to be not surprising but expected on the basis of our apprehension of the causes. It is not enough simply to reason to the cause, for immediately upon discovery of it the cause may still be less well known than its effects, and even inferred from these effects. There must be a clear apprehension of the cause, such that from it flows an awareness of its effects. What is required is the induction of a habit of thinking about a field. As Aristotle writes elsewhere:

Let us not fail to notice, however, that there is a difference between arguments from and those to the first principles. For Plato, too, was right in raising this question and asking, as he used to do, "are we on the way from or to the first principles?" There is a difference, as there is in a race-course between the course from the judges to the turning point and the way back.[112]

As the runners in a race must not only run to the turning point in the course but must also run back again, so in inquiry we must not only reason correctly to the actual causes in a field, we must also engage in a process of reasoning from causes to their effects. This second process of reasoning belongs to what we are calling the second stage of inquiry, and its purpose is to establish an intellectual disposition of thinking of effects in relation to their cause, to make second nature the reasoning from cause to effects within a field.

If the above understanding of the 'better known' condition as the doxastic causality condition is correct, it gives us a different picture of the *PA* than has commonly been presented. Moreover, it gives us a different perspective on how *scientia* is acquired and passed on. And, if Aquinas's concept of *scientia* was shaped by the *PA* account, it should have an effect on the way he presented and instructed others in a *scientia*. In coming chapters I will argue that it did have such an effect.

In an influential article, Jonathan Barnes claimed that in Aristotle's *Posterior Analytics*

> The theory of demonstrative science was never meant to guide or formalize scientific research: it is concerned exclusively with facts already won; it does not describe how scientists do, or ought to, *acquire* knowledge: it offers a formal model of how teachers should *present and impart* knowledge.[113]

This view of the *Posterior Analytics* as a pedagogical theory, when it is applied to what we are calling the *PA*, the *Posterior Analytics* as Aquinas understood it, holds an important grain of truth. The *PA* is not exclusively or even primarily concerned with the acquisition of new knowledge, and the construction of a demonstrative syllogism requires that most of the discoveries have already been made. Although the *PA* does discuss the sort of discovery which belongs to the first stage, it focuses primarily on the second stage, which involves the construction of a demonstrative syllogism and cognitive re-structuring, as we are calling it. The *PA*, then, is very much about pedagogy, but it is pedagogy of a sort which seems unusual to us.

Barnes's view is, however, misguided in other ways. First, it fails to recognize that the *PA* does have something to say about the first stage of inquiry, which is concerned with the discovery of new knowledge. Secondly, it views the *PA* as concerned simply with the most effective heuristic method for a teacher who knows the science to communicate its contents to neophytes. It fails to see that what is essential to the acquisition of *scientia* is cognitive re-structuring, a grasping of effects in light of causes, and that this must be undergone not only by students but even by the one who first makes many discoveries within a scientific field. Thirdly and most importantly, Barnes fails to acknowledge that the heuristic which is the concern of the *PA* is the odd (to us) one of intellectual habituation to achieve cognitive re-structuring, so that effects are believed by virtue of beliefs about their causes. Once we eliminate these misunderstandings, we can better see the very interesting sort of pedagogy with which the *PA* is concerned.

1.8 CONCLUSION

Much of the work of post-Cartesian, modern philosophers in epistemology was driven by worries about skeptical objections that we do not know much, or most, or even all of what we think we know. As I said in section 1.6 above, some of these philosophers formulated a foundationalist theory of justification which could, they hoped, overcome skeptical worries by admitting as foundational only beliefs which were indubitable, or at least sufficiently obvious and secure, so they could withstand skeptical objections, and other beliefs could be justified on the basis of these. A characteristic of these sorts of views was the stipulation that the foundational beliefs be evident to the autonomous investigation of the rational subject, for any reliance on authority or other mediating presuppositions, they believed, would be open to skeptical challenge, and assent to them would not be fully rational.

As we have said, some have interpreted the *PA* and Aquinas's foundationalism along the lines of this modern tradition. But although Aquinas recognizes that certain truths may be *per se nota* ("known of themselves," i.e. self-evident) to us, the goal of inquiry is that we may come to grasp what is *per se notum* in itself, and reason to conclusions from these truths. We can only do this, however, by undertaking a period of training and discipline under the guidance of those more accomplished with the field, so that we may acquire the intellectual habits to apprehend what is *per se notum* as such. The concern here is not with skeptical worries and the focus is not on autonomous, individualistic investigation; it is rather with the sort of intellectual formation required so that what is most intelligible in itself becomes most intelligible to us.

Central to our interpretation of Aquinas is the notion of apprenticeship, which Alasdair MacIntyre has discussed in an illuminating way.[114] In order to become a skilled furniture-maker, for example, a person who already possesses an innate potentiality for that craft must submit himself to a teacher, and accept on the teacher's authority instruction about and guidance in the acquisition of habits necessary to become adept in the craft. Similarly, if we are to acquire the intellectual virtue of *scientia*, we must submit ourselves to the training and guidance of masters within a field so that we may acquire the needed habits and realize fully our cognitive potentiality. Only then can we make competent judgments about what is truly intelligible. Only then can we attain the cognitive perfection of *scientia*.

This understanding of Aquinas's views on *scientia*, I will argue in the coming chapters, brings about a shift in our understanding of his *magnum opus*, the *Summa theologiae*. Before this case can be made, however, we must consider in the next chapter how the *PA* analysis is relevant to the *scientia* of the *Summa theologiae*, sacred doctrine.

CHAPTER TWO

'Scientia' and sacred doctrine

Sacred doctrine, the *scientia* based upon Christian revelation, is the subject of the *Summa theologiae*, and in chapter three I will argue that the study we have made of the *PA*'s concept of *scientia* will enable us better to understand Aquinas's project in that work. However, as we shall see, sacred doctrine is in many ways a peculiar *scientia*, and some have argued that it is only a *soi-disant* Aristotelian *scientia*, not one in the strict sense of the term. If this is so, then the conditions for a *PA scientia* may not be relevant to sacred doctrine and the *Summa theologiae*. The most important work on this question is perhaps Marie-Dominique Chenu's *La théologie comme science* which, though published over fifty years ago now, has exerted and continues to exert great influence on scholarly thought in this area.[1] Chenu claims that although sacred doctrine can be called a *scientia*, it is such only in an attenuated or deficient sense.

In this chapter I will argue that, while sacred doctrine has features which distinguish it from other human *scientiae*, it is nevertheless fully a *PA scientia* and it shares with other human *scientiae* central features which our analysis in chapter one identified. My argument will proceed dialectically, beginning with a consideration of a *prima facie* case for, and Chenu's arguments against, taking sacred doctrine as straightforwardly a *PA scientia*. We will then consider sacred doctrine against the background of other sorts of *scientiae* discussed in the *Summa theologiae*, and argue that this perspective enables us to resolve some puzzles which arose from our dialectical treatment, to respond to Chenu's arguments and to understand the nature of sacred doctrine as a *scientia* in the *Summa theologiae*.

2.1 CHENU: SACRED DOCTRINE AS A QUASI *SCIENTIA*

Let us call the *identity thesis* the thesis that the concept of *scientia* in the *Summa theologiae*, and more particularly the concept of *scientia* as it applies to sacred doctrine, can be straightforwardly identified with the *PA* notion or notions. As we have seen, the *PA* describes a paradigmatic notion of *scientia*, *scientia simpliciter*, which fully and perfectly fulfills the conditions for being a *scientia*, and other sorts of non-paradigmatic *scientiae* fulfill these conditions in a partial or less perfect way. One could say, then, that in the *PA* we find an ordered set of notions of *scientia*, which consists of the paradigmatic case and others which more or less perfectly approximate to the paradigm. The advocate of the identity thesis claims that the notion of *scientia* in Aquinas's *Summa theologiae* falls somewhere in the spectrum of notions of *scientia* described in the *PA*.

There is at least a strong *prima facie* case for the identity thesis. In the *Summa* we commonly find the central features of the *PA* notion asserted, often with an explicit citation of the *Posterior Analytics*. *Scientia*, Aquinas tells us in the *Summa*, is about necessary truths.[2] Perfect *scientia* is had through demonstration, and not through probable reasoning.[3] Aquinas tells us that *propter quid* demonstrations reason from the cause, which is prior and better known in itself, to the effect, while demonstrations *quia* move from the effect, which is posterior and initially better known to us but not in itself, to the cause.[4] He writes that each *scientia* is distinguished from others and has its unity from its subject genus, which he calls its formal object.[5] We find in this work the distinction, taken from the *Posterior Analytics*, between superior and subaltern *scientiae*.[6] The condition of doxastic causality – that for *scientia* the apprehension of effects must be through the apprehension of causes – is asserted therein.[7] Indeed, when Aquinas is discussing the nature of and conditions for *scientia* he generally takes his examples from the *Posterior Analytics*.[8] Thus, this argument concludes, the notion or notions of *scientia* in the *Summa theologiae* are simply identical to those found in the *PA*.

Chenu has argued, however, that in spite of these apparent similarities, sacred doctrine is, and Aquinas recognized that it is, not fully an Aristotelian *scientia* as this is described in the *PA*. In an Aristotelian *scientia*, Chenu contends, since one moves from known principles to demonstrate conclusions which are to be known, the epistemic value of a *scientia* is founded upon a complete and unassailable grasp of its principles. Chenu writes:

> "Scientia procedit ex principiis *per se notis.*" Inviolable postulate: the perfect quality of this eminent knowledge which is science is only conceivable and possible if the mind is totally and immediately master of its initial datum; that is, if the statements from which one begins carry in themselves their light, discernible from a consideration of their terms alone, *per se nota.* No appeal [to higher authority], no "docility", but autonomy.[9]

However, Chenu writes, "with faith precisely the opposite conditions hold, of which the first is, in its object, hiddenness and, in the mind, obedience."[10]

According to Aquinas, the principles of sacred doctrine are the articles of faith.[11] The believer cannot immediately grasp or establish by argument the truth of these articles, but can only counter arguments against them. He must accept them as revealed by God.[12] The believer does not have an intellectual vision of the truths to which he assents, for on this earth we cannot grasp the divine essence;[13] we must, then, accept God's revelation as mystery. Chenu's contention, then, is that the imperfect character of the believer's grasp of these principles is incompatible with sacred doctrine being a *PA scientia*, for in such a *scientia* the whole of the *scientia* proceeds from an intellectual grasp of its principles.

Chenu, however, must defend his thesis against what seems to be evidence to the contrary. For when Aquinas discusses the character of sacred doctrine as a *scientia* he seems to recognize these features which distinguish it from the *scientiae* which the *PA* considers, and yet he apparently attempts to argue that sacred doctrine meets the *PA* conditions for being a *scientia*. Aquinas's argument turns on two key notions. The first is Aristotle's notion of subalternation, which we saw above in our discussion of the *Posterior Analytics*. Optics, for example, is subaltern to geometry because at least some propositions which serve as principles in the *scientia* of optics are also conclusions demonstrated in the *scientia* of geometry. The optician assumes that sight is possible because rays emanate from the eyes in cones, and whatever is viewed by rays of greater angles appears larger. Using as principles propositions demonstrated in geometry about the relative size of the angles of triangles of equal bases but of unequal sides, he can show that the nearer quantity is viewed by rays of greater angles, and thus it appears larger. In this way the propositions of geometry are used as principles in demonstrations in optics.

The second notion Aquinas employs is the Christian under-standing of sacred doctrine as a divinely revealed *scientia*. Aside from sacred doctrine, the various *scientiae* humans possess are attained by the exercise of cognitive potencies which they have by nature, and which they apply to the proper objects of these potencies. The proper objects of human cognition are forms existing in matter, and to know these humans have the potency or power to sensibly perceive individuals, to grasp the quiddities of these individuals by their intellect and to reason discursively from premises to conclusions. The various speculative and practical *scientiae*, except sacred doctrine, arise from the application of these cognitive potencies to a certain field of knowledge. In contrast to these *scientiae*, sacred doctrine cannot be attained by the exercise of natural, human cognitive potencies. It can only be had if God reveals certain truths beyond the grasp of natural, human cognition, and if God works in the believer to engender certain virtues by which he can properly receive this revelation. In what follows, I will refer collectively to the *scientiae* based only on natural, human cognitive powers as *merely human scientiae*, in contrast to sacred doctrine, which relies in a special way on divine aid.[14]

Sacred doctrine, Aquinas contends, is a *scientia* subaltern to the *scientia* which God possesses and shares with the saints who behold the divine essence. It does not, therefore, detract from the scientific character of sacred doctrine that we humans on this earth do not fully grasp its principles, for, as the *PA* makes clear, every subaltern *scientia* relies on a higher *scientia* for its principles. According to Aquinas, the subject of sacred doctrine is God and all other things insofar as they are related to God as their beginning or end.[15] Since the divine essence is beyond our grasp in this life, a *scientia* whose subject is God can only depend on divine revelation. The principles of sacred doctrine, then, are the divinely revealed articles of faith to which one assents. As Aquinas writes, although in non-subaltern, merely human *scientiae* indemonstrable principles are grasped "by the light of the natural intellect",[16] nevertheless "there are some [*scien-tiae*] which proceed from principles known by the light of a higher *scientia*. . . . And in this way sacred doctrine is a *scientia*: because it proceeds from principles known by the light of a superior *scientia*, namely, the *scientia* of God and the saints."[17] That is, this *scientia* is a subaltern *scientia* whose principles are taken from another *scientia*, and one had by other subjects, viz. God and the saints, who enjoy the full vision of the divine essence. Furthermore, the principles of the higher *scientiae* are such that their full intellectual apprehension is beyond the powers of those who work in the subaltern *scientia* – namely, we human beings in our earthly existence.

Chenu contends, however, that even when sacred doctrine is viewed as a subaltern *scientia* in this way it is not fully an Aristotelian (i.e. a *PA*) *scientia*, and moreover that Aquinas recognized that it was not. In subalternation as Aristotle understood and applied it to the *scientiae* he knew, such as the subalternation of optics to geometry, the two *scientiae* have different though related subject matters. Whereas the geometrician studies lines *qua* lines, the optician studies lines *qua* visible rays of light. Although the optician employs theorems proven by the geometrician, the difference in subject matter gives optics a different method and independent field of inquiry. It gives the subaltern *scientia* sufficient distinctiveness and autonomy to be a distinct *scientia*. Chenu writes:

In short, this application to a special subject matter, and the addition of a difference which is essential to the subaltern science – but accidental to the subalternating science, constitutes a new epistemological object, which in turn distinguishes a new field of intelligibility, situated ipso facto outside the domain of the superior science.[18]

In sacred doctrine, however, the *scientia* of the Christian believer has the same subject as the superior *scientia* has, and thus it lacks the autonomy which a genuine *scientia* requires. The *raison d'être* of sacred doctrine as a subaltern *scientia* is the cognitive limitations of humans in this life, and not, as in genuine subaltern *scientiae*, the application of conclusions of a higher *scientia* to a new and distinct field of intelligibility.

Chenu believes this is a "serious defect" (*échec grave*)[19] in the scientific character of sacred doctrine, and that Aquinas realized this. In a passage which appears only in some manuscripts of his *Commentary on the Sentences of Peter Lombard*, and which, Chenu contends, Aquinas seems to have inserted in later copyings of this very early work in his career, he calls sacred doctrine "quasi subalternata divinae scientiae."[20] Chenu comments, "The theory of subalternation admirably clarifies the situation, and outlines the structures of sacred knowledge; but it is only a question of a quasi-subalternation, according to St. Thomas's own word."[21] Hence, it can be a *scientia* "only imperfectly."[22]

Another point, which Chenu mentions only in passing but which is worthy of serious consideration, concerns the propositions of sacred doctrine about individuals.[23] As we saw in chapter one, the *PA* stipulates that the propositions of a *scientia* are universal and necessary. Yet the propositions of sacred doctrine concern God, Christ and the particular, contingent individuals and events referred to in Scripture and the Christian Creed. Hence, it seems, sacred doctrine cannot be a *PA scientia*.

The advocate of the identity thesis claims that Aquinas adopted the *PA* understanding of *scientia* in the *Summa theologiae*, while Chenu argues that he knowingly departed from it in a fundamental way. These opposing views can be resolved and sacred doctrine's status as a *scientia* decided, I will try to show, only if we first consider the rather complex doctrines of the *Summa theologiae* about the various sorts of *scientiae* of various kinds of beings. Against this background we can understand the distinctiveness of the *scientia* of sacred doctrine in relation to other human *scientiae*, and yet see it as in accord with the teachings of the *PA*.

2.2 *SCIENTIA* AS AN ANALOGOUS TERM

Problems arise for the identity thesis even apart from any consideration of the central *scientia* of the *Summa theologiae*, sacred doctrine. For in the *Summa* Aquinas speaks at length about various *scientiae* which are certainly not countenanced in the text of the *Posterior Analytics*, and which seem clearly at odds with its analysis. God's *scientia*, for instance, is non-discursive, non-demonstrative, and not distinguished by subject genera. The *scientia* of angels is not based upon sense perception, but on infused ideas; and they know particular things through universal forms. What relationship does the *scientia* of God or angels have to that which is analyzed in the *PA*?

In this section we will consider the *scientiae* possessed respectively by God, angels and humans, and ask about the relationships among them. There are clearly great differences among them, and I will argue that God, an angel and a human being are each said to have *scientia* not in precisely the same sense of the term, but analogously. Still, in spite of differences, I will argue that the *PA* identified central features of *scientia* that are analogously realized in each of these three kinds of being. Thus, although Aquinas certainly goes beyond the analysis in the *PA*, his understanding of these various sorts of *scientiae* retains a deep continuity with the *PA*.

Scientia, as was said in chapter one, is an epistemic virtue or perfection. The *PA* recognized that various *scientiae*, various kinds of epistemic virtues, could be distinguished with respect to their subject matter, their subject genus. Geometry is distinct from arithmetic because the former concerns the genus of spatial magnitude while the latter concerns the genus of number. Indeed, it is only with respect to a difference of the subject genus that the *PA* distinguishes various *scientiae*.

Since *scientia* is an epistemic virtue, though, it might be possible to distinguish *scientiae* in another way. If there were epistemic agents with different cognitive structures and powers, then it would be possible to distinguish *scientiae* with respect to the kind of knower, and not just with respect to the subject matter. If I were locked in a room with a bat, we would both be aware of the shapes and spatial locations of objects in the room, and with respect to those objects, our respective awarenesses would be indistinguishable. But because I am aware of these objects by sight and the bat is aware by echolocation, our respective awarenesses can be distinguished by the way we come to be aware of these objects. Our cognitive perfections of being aware of objects would be distinguished with respect to the way we know, not with respect to what is known.

The *PA*, of course, considered only *human* cognition, and since humans all share the same cognitive structures and powers, it did not distinguish among *scientiae* with respect to the kinds of cognitive agents. In the *Summa theologiae*, however, Aquinas must discuss at length the cognitive structure and powers of God and angels, as well as humans. And because the cognitive structures of these three kinds of being differ fundamentally, he has reason to distinguish *scientiae* with respect to the kind of knowers and not solely with respect to their subject matter. In doing so, I will suggest, he does not repudiate the *PA* analysis of *scientia*, but employs the principles of the *PA* analysis to extend it to cases which Aristotle did not consider at length.

Aquinas's universe is multiform and hierarchical. God is wholly perfect, simple and self-sufficient. In Him all perfections exist in the highest mode, for they exist in God's perfect unity and utter simplicity.[24] He freely created the world so that it would reflect the divine goodness.[25] Since each finite creature can reflect God's infinite

goodness only in a limited way, He made all kinds and grades of
being so that the divine goodness, which is one and simple, might be
most adequately reflected in a plurality of grades of creatures, some
of which are higher and more perfect, some of which are lower and
less perfect.[26] Aquinas's universe, then, consists of a hierarchy of
beings, moving from the wholly perfect and simple existence of the
deity down through angels, humans, brute animals and plants to
inanimate minerals and elements.[27]

The highest places in this hierarchy are occupied by beings
capable of some form of cognition. "Cognitive beings (*cognoscentia*)
are distinguished from non-cognitive beings in this respect: non-
cognitive beings have only their own form; but it belongs to the
nature of cognitive beings to have the form of another, for the
species apprehended is in the one apprehending."[28] Such a being
does not possess the form of, say, a tree by becoming a tree – this
would be to possess the form with what Aquinas calls *esse naturale*.
Rather, it possesses the form in apprehending it, in being cognizant
of it; it possesses it with *esse intentionale*. There are, however, different
ways of possessing a form with *esse intentionale*, and so we find different
grades of cognitive being, each of which possess *esse intentionale* in
more or less perfect ways. The lowest grade is that of brute animals,
which possess only the sensible, individualized form, and do not have
an intellect by which they can grasp the intelligible, universal form.
Our interest here is not in sensible but in intellectual cognition, in
beings who can grasp the intelligible form, and are therefore capable
of *scientia*. These are God, angels and humans, and we will consider
the cognition of each, beginning with human cognition, which,
though it is the lowest kind of intellectual knowledge, is of course
most familiar to us.

Human cognition stands between the strictly sensible cognition of
brute animals and the strictly intellectual cognition of angels. As
Aquinas writes:

The human intellect holds a middle position: for it is not the act of some
organ, but it is nevertheless a certain power of the soul, which is the form of
the body . . . And therefore its proper activity is to apprehend a form
existing individually in some corporeal matter, but not as it exists in such
matter. To apprehend that which is individualized in matter, but not as it
exists in such matter, is to abstract the form from individualizing matter,
which phantasmata represent. And therefore we must say that our intellect
understands material things by abstracting from phantasmata, and through

considering material things in this way we come to a certain apprehension of immaterial things – just as in the opposite way angels apprehend material things through what is immaterial. [29]

The proper object of the human intellect, then, is the quiddity or intelligible species of material things. It comes to apprehend these, however, only through sense perception of particulars. The human intellect is able to abstract from the phantasm, or sense image, the universal form of the thing. The human intellect, then, knows the intelligible species as abstracted from the sensible particular.[30]

Aristotle's analysis of *scientia* in the *PA* was, of course, of *scientia* for human knowers. Human *scientiae*, as we saw in chapter one, concern necessary, eternal and universal causes. They are concerned with the intelligible forms or quiddities of things, not with what is true of them by virtue of being individuals. Human cognition, however, must begin from sense perception of material individuals which are initially better known to us, although they are least known in themselves, or *secundum naturam*. From these the human intellect can abstract the intelligible form of material things, which are its proper objects. One is then able to formulate universal and necessary principles of a *scientia*, and from these one can reason discursively to its conclusions.

Attainment of *scientia* for humans, then, is a gradual and somewhat faltering process in which one moves from sense perception of particulars to abstraction of intelligible form, to universal principles and finally to the conclusions of a *scientia*. In God, however, there is no potency or matter, which is the principle of potency; God is pure act, and as such is utterly simple.[31] Consequently there is in God no process of inquiry or discovery, no abstraction and no reasoning discursively to conclusions, for all of these are the gradual actualization of a potency for knowledge. Moreover, the complexity and distinctions which exist in creatures with respect to the act of understanding are not found in God. Although we may speak about God's intellect and its intelligible species, there is no real distinction between His intellect and the intelligible species by which He knows, nor between His intellect and His substance, nor between God's act of understanding and His substance.[32]

Since God is both the perfect knower and perfectly knowable, Aquinas argues, He understands Himself perfectly,[33] and He knows creatures through His knowledge of Himself: "Similarly, therefore, we must say that God sees Himself in Himself, because He sees

Himself through His essence. And He sees things other than Himself not in themselves, but in Himself, insofar as His essence contains the similitude of things other than Himself."[34] While we know things insofar as they affect our sense organs, God knows all other things as their cause; He knows them as a craftsman knows the works he makes:

> Natural things are the medium between the *scientia* of God and our *scientia*. For we acquire *scientia* from natural things, of which God is the cause through His *scientia*. Hence, as the natural objects of *scientia* are prior to and the measure of our *scientia*, so the *scientia* of God is prior to and the measure of natural things. Similarly, a house is the medium between the *scientia* of the craftsman who made it and the *scientia* of that one who acquires his apprehension from the house which has then been made.[35]

God not only knows His creatures through their essential forms, he knows them, both corporeal and incorporeal, as singular. Since the human intellect can only grasp the universal, immaterial form of things, the human knower only knows individuals through sense perception. God, however, knows individuals in a higher way: "We apprehend what is universal and material through one potency, and what is singular and material through another. But God through His simple intellect apprehends both."[36] Thus God does not abstract the intelligible species from matter, but knows the universal form and the individual through knowing Himself, who is "the existing principle of all principles which enter into the composition of something, whether they are principles of the species or the individual."[37] Furthermore, God apprehends future contingent facts with certainty. God is eternal and hence not measured by time, so He sees all temporal events, past, present and future, all at once and as present to Him, just as we, who exist in time, see contingent events which are present to us.[38] And although He knows variable things as variable, God remains invariable.[39]

Angels, like God and unlike humans, are incorporeal and in this sense simple forms. However, like humans and unlike God, they are not pure act but have both potency and act. Thus the angel is not utterly simple: the angel, its intellect, its intelligible species and its acts of understanding are all really distinct.[40] Since angels are immaterial, they cannot be individuated by matter. Each angel, then, is of a different species and their respective species can be hierarchically arranged according to greater and lesser natural perfection.[41]

Angels are pure intellects, then, without corporeal organs and hence without sense perception, and therefore they cannot come to know by abstracting intelligible forms from sense images. Rather, God infuses the intelligible species into angelic intellects immediately when He creates them: "Superior substances (i.e. angels) are completely free from what is corporeal, subsisting immaterially in intelligible being. And therefore they achieve their intelligible perfection through an intelligible effluence, by which they receive from God, at the same time as they receive their intellectual nature, the species of the things they apprehend." [42] Whereas humans come to discover intelligible forms gradually by abstraction from sense images, angelic intellects are never without the intelligible forms by which their intellects are perfected.[43] Angels higher in the hierarchy of perfection know by fewer intelligible forms each of which extends to more things; lower angels know by a greater number of forms each of which extends to fewer things.[44] Since angels receive their intelligible forms from God, they can, like God, know material individuals by means of them. Thus, "angels apprehend singular things through universal forms, which are nevertheless similitudes of things with respect both to their universal principles and to their individuating principles."[45] Since angels exist in time, they do not know future events as present in the way God does, but they infer them from their knowledge of present events. Thus, they know with certainty those which follow necessarily from their causes, but they can only make probable predictions about those which do not follow of necessity. Since their knowledge of universal causes is more perfect than human knowledge, however, their conjectures about the future are much more reliable than those of humans. However, they cannot know what will occur by chance.[46]

In the hierarchical order of perfection in the universe, Aquinas believes, perfections found in lower creatures exist in higher beings in a more perfect and simple way. And so, since *scientia* is the perfection of intellectual beings, it exists in a more perfect and simple way in higher than in lower beings. When comparing angelic and divine cognition Aquinas writes:

Such is the order of things, that superior beings are more perfect than inferior, and that what is in inferior beings in a deficient, partial and complex manner is in superior beings in a more eminent manner, and in a certain completeness and simplicity. And therefore in God, as in the supreme vertex of things, all things pre-exist supersubstantially according to

His own simple being, as Dionysius says in *On Divine Names*. Among creatures, angels are nearest and most similar to God; hence they partake more fully and more perfectly of the divine goodness, as Dionysius says in chapter four of *On Celestial Hierarchy* . . . Moreover, everything which is in something is in it in the manner of that thing in which it is. Angels are by nature intellectual. And therefore, as God through His essence apprehends material things, so angels apprehend them through the fact that they exist in them through their intelligible species.[47]

While God has *scientia* through His wholly simple and perfect self, then, angels have *scientia* through a greater or lesser multiplicity of intelligible species (depending on their place in the angelic hierarchy), which they receive from God upon their creation. Similarly, while angels know through the intelligible species which they receive immediately from God when created, humans must begin from sense perception of individualized form and abstract from *phantasmata* the intelligible species.[48] Brute animals, who are incapable of intellectual apprehension and *scientia*, are aware only of the individualized form in the sense image.[49]

There are, then, significant differences among the respective *scientiae* of God, angels and humans. Indeed, although each can be said to have *scientia*, Aquinas believes that the expressions which ascribe this perfection are used analogously of these kinds of beings. "It is impossible to predicate something univocally of God and creatures,"[50] he writes. As we have seen, the proper objects of human cognition are the forms existing in material things, which the intellect abstracts from *phantasmata*. Since these are the things we first know, our language was constructed to speak of material things and their attributes.[51] And so for any predicate which denotes a positive perfection, the predicate denotes the perfection as existing in a creaturely manner, and hence a manner which is not absolutely perfect. When we assert the predicate of God we must deny whatever imperfections are involved in our concept, and use it to signify the perfection as existing in God in a higher, more perfect manner.[52] And thus we use the predicate analogously of God and creatures.[53] And so it is when we ascribe *scientia* respectively to God and creatures:

Because perfections issuing from God to creatures exist in a higher manner in God, as has been said above, it must be that whenever some name taken from any perfection of a creature is applied to God, everything which belongs to the imperfect manner proper to creatures must be excluded from its signification. Hence *scientia* is not a quality or habit in God, but substance and pure act.[54]

Similarly, because of the dissimilarity between angels and material beings and their perfections, it seems perfections are also ascribed to angels and humans analogously.[55]

Although we find several discussions of *scientia* in the *Summa theologiae*, then, they do not all treat of the same, univocal notion. The analysis of *scientia* in the *PA*, which we examined and summarized in chapter one, was of *merely human scientia* – that which is accessible to humans by the exercise of their natural cognitive powers. But God's *scientia* is very different. According to the *PA*, human *scientia* is concerned only with universal and necessary, and hence eternal, truths. God, however, has *scientia* of singular, contingent and temporally indexed truths, such as that Socrates is sitting now. Furthermore, in the *PA* the priority conditions required that one come to know effects by demonstrating them from their causes, and the doxastic causality condition required that one's belief in the effect be caused by one's belief in the causes. But divine *scientia* involves neither demonstrations nor one belief causing another, for it is immediate, non-discursive and simple.

So stark are the differences between divine and human *scientiae* that it might seem the constitutive conditions for *scientia* which the *PA* identified are completely abrogated when we come to God's cognition, and thus the *PA* analysis is irrelevant to a discussion of divine *scientia*. Certainly the six conditions for a scientific syllogism which, as we saw in the previous chapter, were central to the *PA* analysis cannot have a place in God's immediate and non-discursive *scientia*. But if there is no commonality among the features and conditions of divine and human *scientiae*, then each is called such in merely equivocal and not analogous senses. If these *scientiae* are called such analogously, as Aquinas explicitly claims they are, there must be more general and fundamental features said of both, though perhaps said analogously. I will argue that there certainly are such features.

As we have seen above, chapter one of Book 1 of the *Posterior Analytics* contains arguments that human *scientia* must come through demonstration. After these introductory arguments, Aristotle in chapter two turns to the pivotal analysis of *scientia*, which is further developed and refined in the subsequent chapters of Book 1. That chapter begins as follows:

We think that we have *scientia* of something *simpliciter* (and not in a sophistical manner, accidentally) when we think (1) we apprehend the cause on account of which the thing is, that it is the cause of that thing, and (2) it is not possible for it to be otherwise.[56]

Aquinas understands Aristotle to state the definition of *scire* here, and believes that the first part of the definition flows from the fact the *scientia* is *perfect* cognition, and the second condition flows from its being *certain* cognition.[57] After acknowledging the possibility that there may be another sort of *scientia* – viz. of indemonstrable principles – he re-asserts the conclusion of chapter one, that "it is clear that we know things through demonstration."[58] Aquinas comments, "the more proper and perfect mode of having *scientia* is what was described above [in chapter one]."[59] Thus, it is on the supposition that human *scientia* is had through demonstrations that the *PA* goes on to consider the six conditions for scientific demonstrations which we considered in the previous chapter. Thus the more specific conditions on a scientific syllogism follow from the definition quoted above, on the supposition that human *scientia* comes through demonstration. Although the more specific conditions cannot apply to divine cognition, the more general and fundamental features can and do apply.

The first fundamental feature of *scientia* is that it is perfect cognition, and hence one must "know the cause on account of which the thing is, that it is the cause." For the human intellect, which reasons discursively, this requires that one have a demonstrative syllogism whose premises state the cause and whose conclusion states the effect. Moreover, the doxastic causality condition requires that one's belief in the conclusion be caused by one's belief in the cause. Since God's *scientia* is wholly immediate and non-discursive, demonstrations can play no role. But although God does not apprehend a cause prior to apprehension of its effect, He nevertheless knows all other things in Himself, their cause.[60] As said above, God knows His creatures as a craftsman knows the things he makes.[61] Thus, in God's non-discursive *scientia*, He knows His effects in their cause.[62] Therefore, the principle of knowing the effect through the cause is preserved in divine *scientia*, although in analogous fashion. For humans it requires that one apprehend a syllogism whose premises state the cause and whose conclusion states the effect, and moreover, one's belief in the effect is caused by one's belief in the cause. For God, all other things, all His creatures, are known immediately and simply in and through His perfect knowledge of Himself, their cause.

The second of the fundamental features stated in the definition is that one has *scientia* of a proposition, p, only if one knows that p is necessary. This follows from the fact that *scientia* is "certa cognitio rei", for "one cannot apprehend with certainty what can be otherwise, therefore it is required further that that of which one has *scientia* cannot be otherwise."[63] Human intellects know directly only intelligible forms and what follows on having such a form. Individuals are known only indirectly, by reflection on the phantasm or sense image from which the forms are abstracted.[64] God, however, Who knows other things as their cause, knows singulars because He is the cause not only of the universal form, but of the matter by which things are individuated.[65] He, unlike humans, knows individuals as such. Moreover, since God exists eternally and outside time, "all things which are in time are present to God from eternity . . . not only because these *rationes* are present to Him . . . but because His intellectual vision is from eternity over all things, as they are when they are present."[66] Thus God has certain, and indeed infallible, knowledge of singular, contingent events. Moreover, as Aristotle writes, "what is, necessarily is, when it is; and what is not, necessarily is not, when it is not."[67] That is, even contingent facts, when they are, have a certain necessity, which is not absolute necessity, but necessity of supposition.[68] Since all contingent events in time are present to God in eternity, they have a certain necessity in God's intellect.[69] In this sense God knows all singular contingent events with a certain necessity, and they can be objects of divine *scientia*.[70]

Much more could be said about the similarities and differences among divine, angelic and human *scientia*, and the above sketch is intended only to provide some examples. However, perhaps this sketch is sufficient to show that the fundamental features of *scientia* identified by the *PA* are not irrelevant when we move to other forms of *scientia*. Although certain conditions in the *PA* clearly apply only to human *scientia*, the more fundamental features from which the more specific conditions flow apply to all these kinds of *scientiae*. The greater cognitive powers of God and angels enable them to realize these features in a higher, more perfect manner, for "superior beings are more perfect than inferior, and what is in inferior beings in a deficient, partial and complex manner is in superior beings in a more eminent manner, and in a certain completeness and simplicity."[71]

Thus, when Aquinas discusses divine and angelic cognition in the *Summa theologiae*, he retains the fundamental features of *scientia* which the *PA* identified, while pointing out how the higher beings realize these in a higher way.[72]

We can now see, I believe, how Aquinas could understand himself to be in continuity with Aristotle's *Posterior Analytics*, and cite this work in support of his views throughout the *Summa theologiae*, even though his treatment of divine and angelic *scientia* goes far beyond anything we find in Aristotle. Aristotle's analysis of *scientia* was, and Aquinas recognized that it was, of *human scientia*. Still, Aristotle does imply, although he does not elaborate, that God possesses *scientia* in a higher and more perfect way than humans do.[73] Aquinas could have understood himself to be developing, in light of both Christian revelation and metaphysical arguments, that which was implicit but undeveloped in Aristotle. Because Aquinas believed in the analogy among various kinds of *scientiae*, when he formulated his account of divine and angelic *scientiae* he could draw on the fundamental features identified in the *PA* and apply them to the higher cognitive powers of these higher beings. Thus, although Aquinas's discussion of divine and angelic *scientiae* went well beyond Aristotle's explicit claims, he could have understood himself to be retaining Aristotle's fundamental principles and to be in continuity with Aristotle's analysis in the *Posterior Analytics*.[74] Aquinas's treatment of divine and angelic *scientiae*, then, was not a repudiation but an extension of the *PA* analysis.

2.3 SCIENTIA AND SACRED DOCTRINE

The account so far considered of various *scientiae* is complex, yet it serves only as background for examining one further twist in Aquinas's notion of *scientia*, which will return us to the central concern of this chapter. The *scientia* of sacred doctrine, the *scientia* in which the *Summa theologiae* attempts to instruct its readers, is a human *scientia*, but one based upon divine revelation. How are we to understand its relationship to the *PA* analysis? Our answer to this question will be in line with the treatment of the previous section. On one hand, the simplistic identity thesis cannot be accepted, for it fails to recognize how Aquinas developed and extended the *PA* understanding of *scientia* in ways not anticipated by that work. But on the other hand, Chenu's thesis cannot be accepted, for it fails to recognize the deep continuity of Aquinas's understanding of the *scientia* of sacred doctrine with the *PA* analysis, and the ways in which that analysis is open to such development. After briefly describing the character of sacred doctrine, I will in what follows argue that Chenu's objections to taking sacred doctrine to be in continuity with the *PA* analysis are not successful.

Although sacred doctrine is accessible to humans and shares many features with other human *scientiae*, it must be distinguished from them, for it cannot be attained by the exercise of natural, merely human cognitive powers of observation and inquiry. It is founded not on principles the unaided human intellect can discover, but on God's revelation of truths beyond the grasp of natural human cognitive powers.[75] Its principles are the articles of the Christian Creed, and assent to them as divinely revealed requires the gift of grace, *gratia*, which engenders the theological virtue of faith. Thus sacred doctrine is "a certain participation in [God's] cognition, and an assimilation to the divine cognition";[76] it is an impression of divine *scientia*.[77] It is therefore a participation in the highest kind of *scientia* by beings of the lowest, most limited intellectual powers.

Sacred doctrine therefore has what we might call a 'mixed' character, in that it is a participation in a higher kind of *scientia* by a lower kind of cognitive being. And it is this mixed character of sacred doctrine that distinguishes it from other human *scientiae* and gives it its distinctive features. As we shall see, some truths of sacred doctrine are of singular things and events of the sort which cannot be known within a merely human *scientia*, but can be part of this *scientia* in which the human individual relies upon God's cognitive powers. Thus this human *scientia* has much in common with the higher *scientiae* of God and angels, and in these respects is superior to merely human *scientiae*. However, an important principle for Aquinas is: "omne quod recipitur in aliquo, recipitur in eo per modum recipientis" – "all that is received in something is received according to the manner of the receiver."[78] Since God's revelation is received by a being of very limited intellectual powers, even when the human person is elevated by God's grace, this reception is in some respects limited and defective. In some respects, then, sacred doctrine is defective in relation to merely human *scientiae* and lacks some of the perfections they have. If we keep in mind the mixed nature of sacred doctrine and the ways in which it differs from other human *scientiae*, we can understand how it can exhibit peculiar features, some of which Chenu points out, and yet still be fully a *scientia*. And, most importantly for our purposes, we can see that the *scientia* of sacred doctrine retains two important features identified in the *PA*: (1) it moves discursively from causes to their effects, in accord with the priority condition; and (2) it strives to meet the doxastic causality condition.

Chenu's argument against taking sacred doctrine as a *PA scientia* begins by emphasizing the tension between faith and the complete grasp of principles required by an Aristotelian *scientia*. He writes: "Science applies all its effort, and finds its cognitive value in the full initial possession of its principles, and it is an evidentness which secures them . . . With faith precisely the opposite conditions hold, of which the first is, in its object, hiddenness and, in the mind, obedience."[79]

Chenu here seems to understand the *PA*'s epistemology in the tradition of the skepticism-driven foundationalism of some modern philosophers. On such a reading, the acquisition of *scientia* within a field begins from an individual's immediate and autonomous grasp of foundational truths. But as we argued in chapter one, this interpretation is misguided, and it fails to appreciate the central notions of apprenticeship, training and submission to authorities in the acquisition of *scientia*. In order that a person may acquire *scientia*, and for what is *per se nota* in itself to become so to him, he must undertake training under experts within a field so that he may acquire the intellectual habits needed for *scientia*.

On the account of the acquisition of *scientia* developed in chapter one, docility and obedience are not opposed to, but are precisely what are required for, the attainment of *scientia*. And it is just this notion of training and apprenticeship which Aquinas exploits when he, quoting Aristotle, attempts to explain the life of faith and the acquisition of the *scientia* of sacred doctrine. In this life, we must submit ourselves to divine instruction and accept God's revelation in the assent of faith so that we may attain perfect apprehension in beatitude, just as students accept the teachings of a master in the acquisition of a merely human *scientia*:

Humans can attain the vision of God only in the manner of one learning from God as one's teacher: as written in John 6:45, "All who [heard] from the Father and learned, come to me." Humans participate in this instruction not immediately, but successively, according to the manner of their nature. Furthermore, everyone who learns in this way must first believe, so that he may attain perfect *scientia*: for, as the Philosopher says, "the one learning must believe." [*De sophisticis elenchis* 1.2, 165b 3] Hence so that humans may come to the perfect vision of beatitude they must first believe God as a student believes his professor who is teaching.[80]

The docility and obedience which sacred doctrine requires, then, are comparable to those required in the acquisition of any *scientia*. The second key notion Aquinas employs in understanding sacred doctrine as a *scientia* is that of subalternation. Chenu, as we have seen, contends that since the subaltern *scientia* of sacred doctrine is without a subject matter which is in any way independent of the superior *scientia*, sacred doctrine can be a *scientia* only imperfectly. It is a "quasi-subaltern" *scientia*, and hence only a quasi-*scientia*.

Aquinas seems to address this issue in the passage which, Chenu claims, was inserted in a later revision of his commentary on the *Sentences* of Peter Lombard, and which Chenu quotes and discusses at length. There Aquinas writes:

One *scientia* can be superior to another in either of two ways: (1) by reason of its subject – as geometry, which concerns magnitude, is superior to perspective, visual magnitudes – or (2) by reason of the mode of apprehension, and in this way theology is below the *scientia* which is in God. For we imperfectly apprehend that which He apprehends most perfectly, and as the subaltern *scientia* assumes some thing from the superior *scientia*, and proceeds by means of those as by principles, so theology assumes the articles of faith which are infallibly established as true in God's *scientia*, and believes them, and through this proceeds to establish further those truths which follow from the articles. Therefore theology is a *scientia quasi* subaltern to the divine *scientia* from which it takes its principles.[81]

Let us for the moment leave aside the final sentence of this passage, which Chenu makes much of, and concentrate on the rest of it. The passage seems to answer the problem which vexed Chenu. God knows Himself and all creation immediately and perfectly, while He remains wholly simple. In this life, we cannot behold the divine essence, and thus cannot share fully in God's *scientia*. However, we can believe certain truths which God reveals, and reason from these to further conclusions. Since our knowledge, unlike God's, is of complex propositions and proceeds discursively, the subaltern *scientia* of sacred doctrine employs a different method, a different way of knowing, from that of the superior *scientia*. Hence, although it has the same subject matter, it differs in method, and thus does have an autonomy with respect to the superior *scientia*. Chenu, however, does not read the passage this way, but empha-

sizes the final sentence, and particularly the word *quasi*. In both
classical and medieval Latin this word can be used adverbially to
bear the sense of "as good as, practically, more or less." Chenu
seems to take it in this sense and as modifying *subaltern*. Hence,
Chenu understands Aquinas to claim that theology or sacred doctrine is only an ersatz subaltern *scientia*.

Chenu's reading, though, makes the passage as a whole difficult to
understand. For in this passage Aquinas asserts that a *scientia* may be
subaltern in either of two ways: (1) by subject matter and (2) by mode
of cognition. He goes on to explain that theology is subaltern in the
second way. Throughout the passage, Aquinas gives us no indication
that the second mode of subalternation, unlike the first, is in any way
defective. Thus it is difficult to understand why, when in conclusion
he states his answer to the question of this *solutio* (viz. "Is theology a
scientia?"), he should suddenly hedge his bets and claim that it is not
fully or strictly a subaltern *scientia*.

Although Chenu's reading of the final sentence is perhaps possible,
there is another much more plausible reading. In both classical and
medieval Latin *quasi* can also bear the sense of "in the capacity of, as,
qua."[82] When Aquinas writes elsewhere that "In any *scientia* some
[propositions] are *quasi* principles and others are *quasi* conclusions,"[83]
he cannot be saying that in any science some propositions are
principles and some are conclusions in only a defective or attenuated
sense. If any and every *scientia* have such quasi-principles and quasi-
conclusions, then any and every *scientia* would only be a quasi-*scientia*
to the extent that it had them. This is certainly not Aquinas's view.
The import of this passage must be that, in any *scientia*, some
propositions are in part of the *scientia in the capacity of*, or *as* principles,
and others are in the *scientia in the capacity of*, or *as*, conclusions.

Similarly, we can take the *quasi* in the sentence in question to have
this sense and avoid the incongruities of Chenu's reading. Thus we
can understand Aquinas to conclude this passage by saying, quite
sensibly, that, given that there are several ways of being a *scientia* (viz.
as a superior *scientia*, or as a subaltern one in either of two ways),
theology is a *scientia* in its *capacity of being*, or *as*, subaltern to the *scientia*
of God from which it takes its first principles. That is, it is a subaltern
scientia in the second way, which is as full and complete a way of
being a subaltern *scientia* as the first way. Thus Chenu's central
argument for his claim about sacred doctrine's defective character as
a *scientia* collapses.

The third difficulty Chenu raises concerns the presence in sacred doctrine of propositions about individuals. *Scientia*, as we saw above, must be of what is universal, necessary and eternal (or, at least, "for the most part"). That which is true of something in this way must be true of it by virtue of its form and common matter, not what is true of an individual *qua* individual. For what is true of something as an individual is true of it by virtue of determinate or sensible matter, which is of a determinate time and place and changeable.[84] Such propositions are therefore contingent and only so "here and now."[85] Insofar as sacred doctrine is of individuals, it seems, it cannot be a *scientia*.

Although Chenu only briefly mentions this issue, it is important to our understanding of sacred doctrine as a *scientia*. I cannot, within the scope of this chapter, discuss this question in all the detail it merits. I will attempt to provide only the outline of a solution, but one perhaps sufficient to show why the presence of propositions about individuals does not undermine the character of sacred doctrine as a *scientia*.

Aquinas raises this objection himself when he discusses whether sacred doctrine is a *scientia*: "A *scientia* is not of individuals. But sacred doctrine concerns individuals, such as the acts of Abraham, Isaac and Jacob and similar things. Hence sacred doctrine is not a *scientia*."[86] To this he responds:

Individuals are propounded in the teaching of sacred doctrine not insofar as it treats them principally, but they are introduced as models for one's life, as in the moral *scientiae*; and also to make manifest the authority of the men through whom comes divine revelation, on which is founded sacred Scripture or doctrine.[87]

Two things about this response are noteworthy for us. First, Aquinas, who in the *corpus* has asserted that sacred doctrine is a *scientia*, recognizes in this response that the *PA* proscription is in some way relevant to this *scientia*. Although, as we will see, his response does not fully resolve the issue of individuals in sacred doctrine, it implicitly accepts that sacred doctrine is fully and genuinely a *scientia*, and thus the principles and conditions of the *PA* are relevant to it. Secondly, his response turns on the important distinction between propositions which are properly intrinsic to a *scientia*, and others which are relevant but only as making evident or clear the intrinsic propositions. Truths about the patriarchs are revealed in Scripture and believed by the faithful, but are intended only to illustrate or support what properly belongs to sacred doctrine. Aquinas explains this distinction at greater length when he discusses the articles of faith, which are the principles of sacred doctrine:

Regarding some things proposed for belief there is faith about them in themselves; regarding others there is not faith about them in themselves, but only in relation to other things. For as in other *scientiae* some things are proposed for themselves, and others to make other things manifest. And because faith is principally about the things which we hope to see in our heavenly home (as said in Hebrews 11:1: "Faith is the substance of things to be hoped for"), what belongs to faith in itself are those things which immediately direct us to eternal life: e.g. the Three Persons, the omnipotence of God, the mystery of Christ's incarnation, etc. And with respect to these articles of faith are distinguished. But some things are proposed for belief in Sacred Scripture not for themselves, but to make manifest the things mentioned above: e.g, Abraham had two sons, a dead man was raised at the touch of Elisha's bones, etc. These are narrated in Sacred Scripture in order to make manifest the divine majesty or Christ's incarnation, and there is no need to distinguish articles with respect to such things. [88]

Aquinas's rejoinder is a satisfactory response to the objection at hand and the examples adduced therein, but it invites a further objection. The subject of the *scientia* is God, and other things insofar as they have their beginning or end in God.[89] One may argue, though, that God is an individual, and the principles of this *scientia* are about God. Hence propositions about an individual are intrinsic to this *scientia*.

Although Aquinas does not explicitly raise and address this objection, a response is not difficult to provide. The *PA* proscription against propositions about individuals is clearly concerned with corporeal individuals, and the difficulty is that truths about them are contingent. Such individuals are composed of matter and form, and while what is true of them formally, by virtue of their quiddity, is universal and necessary, what is true of them by virtue of their individualizing matter is not. Hence, propositions about such individuals *qua* individuals are contingent. God, however, is not corporeal and has no potency at all. Thus, although propositions about God are about an individual in some sense, they are not thereby contingent. Because of the sort of being sacred doctrine treats, it may contain propositions about individuals and still not violate the *PA* requirements.

This response, however, leads us to the heart of the difficulty, for there are, by Aquinas's own admission, propositions intrinsic to sacred doctrine which are about particulars and contingent. Consider *Summa theologiae* 1.46.2, where Aquinas asks "Whether it is an article of faith that the world began." He will respond affirmatively, but in order to establish this he must show both (1) that this doctrine is a divinely revealed proposition proposed for belief by all the faithful; and (2) that it cannot be demonstrated by natural reason without appeal to divine revelation. If (2) cannot be shown, then, though the doctrine may have been revealed and proposed for belief by the faithful, it would be a preamble and not an article of faith.[90] To establish (2), Aquinas argues that the proposition that the world had a beginning in time cannot be demonstrated "from the part of the world," for such a demonstration must begin from a universal quiddity or *ratio*, and "everything, with respect to the *ratio* of its species, abstracts from the 'here and now': because of this it is said that universals are everywhere and always."[91] Thus, Aquinas contends that the beginning of the world in time is an individual event of a kind incompatible with scientific demonstration "from the part of the world." It is, however, an article of faith and a principle of sacred doctrine. It seems, then, that certain contingent propositions about individuals of a sort incompatible with an Aristotelian *scientia* are nevertheless intrinsic to the *scientia* of sacred doctrine. But how can this be, if sacred doctrine is a *scientia*?

In this same article Aquinas goes on to argue that the beginning of the world in time cannot be demonstrated "from the part of the causal agent, which acts through His will." This is because "the will of God cannot be investigated by reason, except concerning those things which God wills absolutely: however, whatever God wills about creatures is not such . . ."[92] Aquinas's point here turns on the distinction between what God wills by absolute necessity, and what He wills in another way. Aquinas holds that God wills His own good by absolute necessity,[93] and He wills all other things insofar as they are ordered to His good. Whatever is necessary for God's good He also wills with absolute necessity. However, God does not will any thing other than God, such as His creatures in this way, for "the goodness of God is perfect and can exist without other things, for other things add nothing to His perfection; it follows that it is not absolutely necessary that He will anything other than Himself."[94] Such things God wills only with the necessity of supposition: "under the supposition that He wills, He cannot not will, since His will cannot change."[95] In this article, Aquinas is arguing that we humans can demonstrate what God wills by absolute necessity, but we cannot do so regarding what He wills by necessity of supposition. Hence, we cannot demonstrate that the world had a beginning in time, nor even that, given only God's existence, He would create.[96] Aquinas concludes, then, that the beginning of the world in time is a contingent event which depends on the divine will, and we humans cannot demonstrate that it occurred.

The proposition that the world began in time, then, is both contingent and a principle of sacred doctrine. Thus this principle of the *scientia* of sacred doctrine seems to be precisely the sort of proposition about the contingent "here and now" which the *PA* prohibits in a *scientia*. It appears that though Aquinas cites the *PA* prohibition against propositions about individuals in the *Summa theologiae*, the *scientia* of sacred doctrine, which is the subject of this work, has a principle which is at odds with it.

To resolve this apparent contradiction it is important to recall the mixed character of sacred doctrine discussed in section 2.2 above. Aquinas's argument in *Summa theologiae* 1.46.2 shows that the proposition in question cannot be demonstrated in, and so cannot be part of, any merely human *scientia*. But, as we have seen, sacred doctrine, though humans can possess it, is nevertheless a participation in God's *scientia*. On a weak reading of this claim about participation in divine *scientia*, Aquinas is simply claiming only that God reveals certain truths, and that divine testimony, as it were, provides merely the grounds for our believing these propositions. We participate in God's knowledge because, through faith, we know some truths which God knows. On a stronger reading, however, not only does God provide the grounds of our belief, but through Christian faith we are able to believe in the manner or mode that God knows these truths. That is, we participate in God's *scientia* not only in knowing *what* God knows, but in knowing *in the way* that God knows it.

Aquinas's remarks on our participation in God's *scientia* in sacred doctrine make it clear, I believe, that the stronger reading is the correct one. God is the formal object of sacred doctrine, and not merely the material object. That is, not only does sacred doctrine treat God, but God is that by virtue of which what can be known in this *scientia* is known. Just as whatever is visible is such by virtue of being colored, so whatever is known in sacred doctrine is known by

virtue of being God, or being ordered to God as its beginning or
end. Aquinas takes this to mean not only that God through revelation
is our source of information, but that in sacred doctrine truths are
known and have their place in this *scientia* in such a way that God
knows them. Although in this life we do not behold the divine
essence and cannot comprehend God's own understanding, nevertheless the status of truths in sacred doctrine is derived from the way
God understands them. Consider, first, the unity of sacred doctrine.
In merely human *scientiae*, we distinguish disciplines which treat
incorporeal beings, such as angels, corporeal beings, such as humans,
and human morals. In sacred doctrine, however, they are treated in
a single, unified *scientia* because this *scientia*, which humans can
possess, considers them according to God's higher cognitive powers.
As Aquinas writes:

Nothing prevents a differentiation of potencies or habits with respect to
matters which together fall under a superior potency or habit, for the
higher potency or habit regards its object under a more universal formal
ratio. For example, the object of common sense is the sensible, including
both the visible and audible: hence, common sense, although it is one
potency, extends to all objects of the five senses. Similarly sacred doctrine,
while remaining one, can consider things which are treated in the various
philosophical [i.e., merely human] *scientiae* under one *ratio*, insofar as they
are revealable by God. In this way sacred doctrine is, as it were, an
impression of divine *scientia*, which is one and simple, yet extends to all
things.[97]

Similarly, while in merely human *scientiae* we distinguish between
speculative and practical *scientiae*, sacred doctrine combines the
speculative and practical, for they are united in God's own knowing.
As Aquinas writes:

Sacred doctrine, as has been said, extends to all those things which belong
to the various philosophical [i.e. merely human] *scientiae*, because of the
formal *ratio* which it considers in diverse things – viz. as they are
apprehensible by the divine light. Hence, although of the philosophical
scientiae some are speculative and others practical, nevertheless sacred
doctrine includes both under itself; as God by the same *scientia* apprehends
both Himself and the things which He made.[98]

Clearly, then, in sacred doctrine, although humans can possess this
scientia, what is considered in it is known, to some degree, in the
manner that God knows it by His higher powers. Human participation in God's own understanding is no doubt imperfect, but in this

scientia which humans can possess, truths have a place according to the way in which God knows them. Regarding the doctrine that the world has a beginning in time, God knows His own will, whether it is willed by absolute necessity or by necessity of supposition, as necessary, for God knows even contingent truths as necessary by necessity of supposition.[99] Moreover, God knows individuals as such, and knows their causes. Hence, when we accept this truth as divinely revealed, we accept it as God knows it. As such, even events which are "here and now" can be known from their causes and as necessary in some sense. And it is as such that the doctrine that the world had a beginning in time can be a principle in the subaltern *scientia* of sacred doctrine. Sacred doctrine differs from the merely human *scientiae* in this way not because it is a deficient or merely a quasi *scientia*, but because in it humans participate, albeit imperfectly, in the highest and most perfect *scientia*, that of God. Because of the greater power of divine cognition, humans have *scientia* of truths of which they cannot have *scientia* in merely human disciplines.

Chenu claimed that sacred doctrine was not, and that Aquinas recognized it was not, fully a *scientia* in accord with the *PA* analysis. I have tried to show that Chenu's arguments for this claim are unsuccessful. Because of sacred doctrine's distinctive character as a *scientia* founded in divine revelation, it has features which are not shared by merely human *scientiae*, such as geometry or optics. Still, I conclude, when Aquinas attempted to understand sacred doctrine as a *scientia* he understood it as in accord with the *PA* analysis. And though Aquinas states or implies that certain features of merely human *scientiae* are not found in sacred doctrine, we can assume, unless we find reasons in Aquinas's texts to think otherwise, that other conditions and features of a *PA scientia* do apply to sacred doctrine. Thus we can suppose that the priority and doxastic causality conditions are relevant to sacred doctrine.

2.4 CONCLUSION

Aquinas's particular genius was in his ability to combine a deep and sincere fidelity to a tradition, whether it be Christianity or Aristotelianism, with subtle but brilliant innovation and creativity. Advocates of the identity thesis are mistaken because they suppose he rather straightforwardly adopted the *PA* concept of *scientia*, and they miss the innovation in his application of this notion of God, angels and sacred doctrine. But Chenu is mistaken because, while he sees Aquinas's innovation with the notion, he fails to appreciate the deeper continuity with the *PA* in Aquinas's fashioning of a *scientia* which is based on divine revelation and consummated in heavenly beatitude.

In this chapter we have seen that although sacred doctrine differs from the merely human *scientiae*, Aquinas was able to understand it as a *scientia* precisely by drawing upon the principles of the *PA* in a creative way. First, he utilizes the notion of apprenticeship in the acquisition of a *scientia*, which, as we saw above, is central to the *PA* analysis. In sacred doctrine, however, Aquinas applies it not to the novice in a speculative or practical discipline who aspires to be an expert, but to Christians *in via*, pilgrims on this earth, who aspire to the vision of God in which Christian beatitude consists. Secondly, he employs Aristotle's doctrine of the subalternation of one *scientia* to another, where the subaltern *scientia* uses for its principles conclusions of the higher *scientia*. In sacred doctrine, however, the higher *scientia* is God's own, which is made known to humans through revelation. And the need for a subaltern *scientia* is not due to the fact that the subaltern discipline has a different though related subject matter, as optics treats visual lines while geometry treats lines abstracted from any matter, but to the fact that humans have limited cognitive abilities to discover and understand the divine truths on which their salvation depends, and that they, unlike God, understand in complex propositions and reason discursively. Thirdly, although the merely human *scientiae* cannot include contingent propositions about individuals, sacred doctrine, as a participation in God's own *scientia*, can, like God, accept contingent truths about individuals as, in some sense, necessary and hence acceptable in a *scientia*.

Aquinas had to go beyond the *PA*, then, to delineate the character of sacred doctrine as a *scientia*. What is important for our discussion in chapter three, however, are the ways in which he retained central features of the *PA* analysis. Although God's own *scientia* is not discursive, human participation in it in sacred doctrine is, and in this *scientia* reasoning proceeds from the principles which have been divinely revealed to conclusions which can be drawn from them. In this discursive *scientia* the priority and doxastic causality conditions hold. And, as we will argue, this shapes Aquinas's project in the *Summa theologiae*.

CHAPTER THREE

'Scientia' and the 'Summa theologiae'

The *Summa theologiae* is the *chef d'oeuvre* of St. Thomas Aquinas. Although all of Aquinas's works are powerful and important, and several are masterpieces, the *Summa theologiae* is his most comprehensive and is thought by most to be his greatest. The sheer organization of such a large amount of disparate material in the four volumes of this work is a remarkable feat. And on any given issue, the *Summa* generally contains the most mature, clear and definitive statement of Aquinas's position. Thus, when there is a dispute about Aquinas's views on some question, debate nearly always turns primarily on one or more passages from this work.

The centrality of the *Summa theologiae* is apparent also from biographical evidence. Most of Aquinas's major theological and philosophical works arose from responsibilities as a student or teacher, or from various controversies of the day, and these situations determined the form of the work in question. The *Sentences* commentary was required of Aquinas as a theology student; the commentaries on Scripture, and perhaps those on the books of Aristotle,[1] arose from his duties as a teacher; the disputed and quodlibetal questions are records of the academic disputations, conducted in a more or less standard form, required or at least expected of Aquinas as a Master at Paris; his polemical works, such as the *De unitate intellectus* and *De aeternitate mundi*, were simply his responses to pressing controversies of the day. Only in the two *summae*, the *Summa contra gentiles* and the *Summa theologiae*, was Aquinas able to break with conventional forms, to cast his thought in a new mold and to compose a systematic work according to what he thought the subject demanded. The *Summa contra gentiles* was a significantly earlier work, written in the early 1260s. The *Summa theologiae* expresses his most fully developed thought and was clearly his most ambitious work, one in which he explicitly claims to have departed from older forms to present the subject in the way it demanded.[2] He labored long over it, beginning the *Summa theologiae* in 1266 and working on it until his death in 1274, when it was left unfinished. And it was the culmination of his efforts to present systematically Christian theology, the subject which his position as a theological Master (*magister in sacra pagina*) at the University of Paris, and his vocation as a Dominican priest, called him to teach.[3] Thus we find in the *Summa theologiae* Aquinas's most mature, most original and most comprehensive treatment of the subject which was his life's work.

In spite of the primacy of this work in the Thomistic corpus, it has, I will argue in this chapter, been widely misunderstood. Scholars have failed to understand the work's fundamental epistemic notion, *scientia*, and so have not clearly grasped Aquinas's intention in writing it. I have tried to elucidate this concept in the previous two chapters, and now I will attempt to discover what light it can shed on the *Summa theologiae* and its presentation of the *scientia* of sacred doctrine.

The *Summa theologiae*, I will argue, is a work of second-level pedagogy, as I explained this notion in chapter one. To the extent that commentators have recognized that the *Summa* is a pedagogical work, they have seen it as a work of first-level pedagogy, and I will begin by arguing against this interpretation. I will then consider the intended audience of the *Summa*, and argue that the work was for very advanced students in theology, who were well suited for second-level pedagogy. Finally, I will argue that we can make better sense of the nature and structure of the *Summa theologiae* on the hypothesis that it is a work of second-level pedagogy, and will conclude by raising some problems for my interpretation which will be addressed in subsequent chapters.

3.1 THE *SUMMA THEOLOGIAE*: AN INTRODUCTION FOR BEGINNERS?

In the prologue to the *Prima pars* of the *Summa theologiae* Aquinas announces his intention in the work as a whole:

Because the teacher of Catholic truth not only must instruct those who are advanced [*provecti*], but also must educate beginners [*incipientes*] (as St. Paul writes in 1 Corinthians 3 [1–2], "Even as unto babes in Christ I have fed you with milk and not meat"), our purpose in this work is to pass on the things which pertain to Christian religion in such a way as is fitting for the education of beginners.[4]

Perspicacious scholars have recognized the importance of Thomas's pedagogical intent in the *Summa*. Chenu writes:

The praise directed toward the *Summa theologiae* throughout the centuries, the technical difficulties encountered in it, the power of the synthesis it contains should not mask the original purpose for which it was written . . . By the author's own avowal, it was dedicated to the instruction of beginners in theology.[5]

James A. Weisheipl writes that in the *Summa* "Thomas wanted to present a comprehensive vision of 'sacred doctrine' for beginners, a handbook suitable for novices."[6] And Leonard E. Boyle suggests that Aquinas began the *Summa* because he felt "practical theology was too much with the Dominican Order and that the 'Fratres communes' and the students in particular . . . were not being allowed more than a partial view of theology."[7]

What sort of instruction is Aquinas attempting to impart in the *Summa theologiae*? In chapter one (pp. 46–49) we distinguished between first and second-level inquiry, and to these correspond first and second-level pedagogy. In first-level pedagogy the student acquires familiarity with the fundamental concepts and principles in the field. The existence of the subject will be proven to him, if this is necessary. And, at this first stage, an instructor would employ demonstrations *quia* which move from truths better known to the student to principles which are better known *simpliciter*. Having acquired a familiarity with the fundamental concepts and grasped the principles, the student in second-level pedagogy would follow the order of scientific demonstrations as defined in the *PA*, moving from causes to effects. The concern at this second stage would be to present material so as to instill the intellectual habits by which the student would readily and correctly consider effects in the field by virtue of their causes. With what sort of pedagogy is the *Summa* concerned?

Since Chenu does not mention any special character to the *Summa*'s pedagogy, it is natural to suppose he means what we, who do not share Aquinas's notion of *scientia*, mean by "instruction for beginners," namely that the work is an initial introduction to the key concepts and basic truths of a field for one unfamiliar with them. Weisheipl suggests this view even more strongly when he calls the *Summa* a "beginner's handbook."[8] And Boyle argues at length that Aquinas "probably had young and run-of-the-mill Dominicans in mind and not a more sophisticated, perhaps university audience when in chiselled prose and in easy, logical steps he put his *Summa theologiae* together."[9] Thus in these writers we find at least the suggestion, and at most the explicit claim, that the *Summa* was intended as a piece of first-level pedagogy – an initial introduction for neophytes to the truths in a field of knowledge. This is, I believe, the standard reading of the pedagogical character of the *Summa theologiae*.

When this understanding is pressed, however, serious problems emerge. For if that is what Aquinas intended, the work seems a spectacular failure. Chenu goes some way toward acknowledging this when he writes that Aquinas perhaps suffered from "some of that illusion which is common to professors as regards the capacities of their students."[10] And Weisheipl writes that though the first part "succeeded admirably," the second and third parts "are far from being a simple introduction."[11] But these admissions, I want to argue, greatly understate the difficulties.

Consider first of all the content of the work. If it is an introduction for neophytes in the field we would expect it to present the key concepts and major issues of Christian theology, but not in all their complexity. What distinguishes an initial introduction is that, though it presents essential concepts, claims and methods within a field, the accounts of especially difficult claims and concepts are simplified, certain qualifications and fine distinctions are neglected, and some objections and disagreements among practitioners in the field are ignored. In place of these we would expect to find concrete examples and analogies drawn from experiences familiar to the student. However, this is not the sort of content we find in the *Summa theologiae*.

Consider, for example, question 85, article one of the *Prima pars*, where Aquinas asks "Whether our intellect understands corporeal and material things by abstraction from *phantasmata*." In this article he distinguishes and briefly describes the sensitive, angelic and human intellects; he presents his view on how humans apprehend intelligible forms by abstracting them from *phantasmata*, or sense images; he distinguishes individualizing and intelligible matter; and he briefly explains what he sees as Plato's error on this question. In the response to the first objection he rejects a crude realism according to which composition in the world must always be mirrored in composition in our intellect for true understanding. In his response to the second objection, he elaborates the distinction between common and sensible matter. In the third response he distinguishes between *phantasmata*, which affect sense organs, and *species intellegibiles* which are impressed on the receptive intellect. In the fifth and sixth responses he discusses the agent intellect, and its role with respect to *phantasmata* and sense perception. The writing is condensed and abstract, and though three examples are mentioned (viz. the color of an apple and the sensations of hot and cold, hard and soft), they are hardly the sort of illustrations which would be of much help to a beginner. And this is only one of 2,669 articles in the *Summa*. Moreover, it is from the first part which Weisheipl says "succeeds admirably" as a simple introduction, rather than from the more difficult second and third parts.

Furthermore, when we compare the *Summa theologiae* with other works of Aquinas, it does not seem related as an initial introduction is to more advanced works. In *Quaestiones disputatae de veritate* Aquinas goes over the same material he treats in *Summa theologiae* 1.85.1, although the questions posed are slightly different. What we have as disputed questions are, of course, the written record of Aquinas's actual disputations at the University of Paris. In such disputations Aquinas, as the disputing Master, would pose the question to be addressed, and it seems that on the first day of the debate the members of the audience, both faculty and students, would pose objections and a bachelor of theology would respond. On the next day, after considering the arguments on both sides, the Master would give his *determinatio* or resolution of the question and his own response to each of the objections. This was then written up and edited by the Master.[12] Thus the *quaestiones disputatae* were the most philosophically and theologically sophisticated presentations to the most sophisticated audience of Aquinas's day.

When we compare *Quaestiones disputatae de veritate* 10.5 & 6 with *Summa theologiae* 1.85.1, we do find that the latter is simplified, but not in the way we would expect for an initial introduction. Because the *Summa* article does not record an actual disputed question, it has fewer objections. (There are six objections in *De veritate* 10.5 and nine in 10.6, while there are only five in *Summa theologiae* 1.85.1.) Many of the objections in the disputed questions are redundant, and in reducing the number Aquinas is no doubt trying to avoid the "frequent repetition [which] generated boredom and confusion in the minds of the members of the audience."[13] Moreover, in *De veritate* 10.6 Aquinas develops his position dialectically by considering and arguing against the "complex variations of ancient opinion."[14] In the *Summa* he presents and argues for his own opinions directly, briefly discussing only Plato as a contrary opinion. He was perhaps trying to avoid the "useless multiplication of questions, articles and arguments."[15] In these ways, then, the *Summa* discussion is simpler. Nevertheless, there is no substantive philosophical or theological point which is part of the exposition of Aquinas's views in the *De veritate* but is not made in the *Summa*. The differences between the works are with respect to the clarity and conciseness of expression, and not to the content of Aquinas's claims and arguments.

When we look at the *Summa contra gentiles* II.77, which treats similar issues, we find its discussion is shaped by Aquinas's dispute with an Avicennian reading of Aristotle. In that article, however, we find no higher level of philosophical and theological content than in the *Summa*. If anything, Aquinas's presentation of his position is less elaborate there.

The content of the *Summa theologiae* is not that of a work gauged for neophytes in a field. The discussion we have considered is not a simplified account for beginners in which important but difficult details have been glossed over; it is, rather, Aquinas's clearest, most precise and most philosophically subtle treatment of these matters. Aquinas does show a concern with clarity, conciseness and elegance of presentation, but his attention does not seem to be directed to beginners.

The structure of the work, moreover, violates Aquinas's own principles for the order of initial discovery and learning. In the *Summa* Aquinas states a pedagogical principle which we saw foreshadowed in the *Posterior Analytics* commentary: "when any effect is more apparent to us than its cause, we proceed through the effect to an apprehension of the cause."[16] This principle is expressed more fully in the commentary on Aristotle's *Physics*:

With respect to the discovery of first principles, [Aristotle] adduces the claim that being better known to us and [being better known] by nature are not the same; rather, those things which are better known by nature are less well known to us. And because this is the natural manner or order of learning – that one moves from things known to us to things unknown to us – thus it is that we must move from what is better known to us to what is better known by nature.[17]

Aquinas begins the *Summa*, however, not with effects which are most apparent to us, but with God, the first cause of all things which is least known to us in this life,[18] but best known by nature.[19] He moves from there to angels, which are also beings better known by nature but less well known to us. Only then does he turn to mundane creatures, with which we are most familiar. This procedure is precisely the opposite of what Aquinas's pedagogical principles regarding initial instruction in a field recommend.[20]

Chenu discusses the structure of the *Summa* at length. Having made the point that Aquinas's purpose was "instruction for beginners," Chenu says that Aquinas sought the proper "ordo disciplinae", the order of learning. Until the thirteenth century, theological treatises took a historical order, the order of salvation history. However, Chenu writes, "at the very moment when, by means of the magnificent Aristotelian inheritance, the notion of science was taking on such vigor in method and meaningfulness, the masters of the first half of the thirteenth century were faced with the problem of applying this notion of science in their theological efforts."[21] Aquinas, Chenu argues, employed the Neoplatonic structure of emanation and return to provide "an order for science, injecting intelligibility into the heart of the revealed datum."[22]

In his discussion, Chenu clearly drifts without explanation from the question of *pedagogical* structure to that of *scientific* structure, and he ends up conflating the two. Views may differ on the proper structure of a science, and they may differ on the proper order for initial instruction of beginners, but certainly these two questions are to be distinguished. Euclid's *Elements* may have achieved the proper structure for geometry, for its deductive structure lucidly displays the logical structure of the science. However, it is far from clear that he thereby hit on the proper way to introduce beginners to geometry. Although we may agree with the scientific structure of the *Elements*, it is far from clear that we should begin a course in elementary geometry with a lecture reciting the definitions, postulates and common notions of Book I. Chenu, however, assuming that Aquinas was interested in some form of initial instruction, and finding the structure of a science in the *Summa theologiae*, is led to confuse the two issues.

Chenu, Weisheipl and Boyle all fail to appreciate fully Aquinas's concept of *scientia*, and how it differs from our cognitive notions. Consequently, they fail to distinguish clearly between first and second-level pedagogy. Realizing that the *Summa* is pedagogical, they naturally suppose that it is pedagogy as we normally understand it, one appropriate to our concept of knowledge. They assume that it primarily involves the discovery of new truths in a field, and do not recognize the need for the intellectual habituation of second-level pedagogy. But when it is understood in that way, the *Summa* is at best odd and at worst incomprehensible. I want to argue that the work is one of second-level pedagogy. Before turning directly to this, though, I shall consider who the *incipientes* and *novitii* were for whom, as the prologue states, the work was written.

3.2 THE INTENDED AUDIENCE OF THE *SUMMA THEOLOGIAE*

In a recent and influential monograph, Boyle has argued that the *Summa* was written not for the students at the University of Paris, as has generally been thought, but for the *studia* and priories in the Dominican provinces.[23] The University of Paris in the thirteenth century, arguably the greatest center of Christian theology which has ever existed, attracted the best minds of Europe for a rigorous and lengthy program of studies. Aquinas lived and taught at the Dominican *studium generale* there, which was the site of study for the most intellectually able Dominican students from all of Europe.[24] Dominicans sent to these general *studia* were destined to go on to become *lectores* or teachers in Dominican priories or in provincial *studia*, or even masters at the universities, and thus were distinguished from those preparing for pastoral ministry.[25]

Boyle argues that the *Summa* was not, as has been thought, written for the intellectual elites at the universities, but for the *fratres communes*, the ordinary Dominican brethren, engaged in the pastoral work of preaching and hearing confessions and for students preparing for such work. The Dominicans, the Order of Preachers, in 1221 received from Pope Honorius the further commission of "hearing confessions and enjoining penances." For this work, study in moral theology was needed, and early Dominicans wrote a number of manuals devoted to practical moral theology. When Aquinas came upon the scene, however, he "may have felt that practical theology was too much with the Dominican Order," and that the brethren "were not being allowed more than a partial view of theology."[26] Aquinas wrote his *Summa* for Dominicans, Boyle suggests, to place their practical moral instruction in a more theoretical, theological context. "By prefacing the Secunda or 'moral' part with a Prima pars on God, Trinity and Creation," Boyle writes, "and then rounding it off with a Tertia pars on the Son of God, Incarnation and the Sacraments, Thomas put practical theology, the study of Christian man, his virtues and vices, in a full theological context."[27]

Boyle's evidence for his conclusions is circumstantial: (1) Aquinas probably began the *Summa* after four years at Orvieto where he first "took his place in the normal stream of the Dominican educational system,"[28] and as a *lector* his task was to instruct Dominicans engaged in pastoral work; (2) Dominican education in the provinces (as opposed to the universities) was focused on an anecdotal moral theology, and Aquinas would probably have felt dissatisfied with its limited scope; (3) the writing of the *Summa* was begun at the *studium* at Santa Sabina in Rome, where, Boyle believes, Aquinas seems to have been given free rein to shape the theological training of students in the Roman province of Dominicans; and (4) the *Summa*, and particularly the second part, seems to parallel the confessional manuals of the time, and so may have been meant to replace them. Boyle himself seems to recognize that evidence of this sort is not wholly compelling, and so only "suggests" a conclusion,[29] and says it is "probably" true[30] or "likely,"[31] or that it is an "assumption [which] is hardly out of the question."[32]

Although Boyle's work is original and suggestive, I think one of its key tenets must be rejected. This is the contention that in the *Summa* Aquinas had "run-of-the-mill Dominicans primarily in mind and *not* a more sophisticated, perhaps university audience."[33] There are several reasons to doubt this claim. First, the considerations of content and structure mentioned above suggest otherwise. Although the articles of the *Summa* are condensed, they are as sophisticated and demanding as anything Aquinas wrote, they address all the most difficult and controversial issues of his day, and the structure of the work is not appropriate for initial instruction. This does not seem to be the sort of work one would write if one's primary audience were those preparing to engage only in the pastoral duties of preaching to, and hearing confessions of, ordinary lay people. Secondly,[34] Boyle correctly portrays Aquinas as very influential in setting the educational policy of his own Roman province. The 1265 provincial chapter put him in charge of establishing and running the *studium* at Santa Sabina in Rome, and the 1272 chapter declared: "We entrust entirely to Friar Thomas d'Aquino the general studium of theology as to place, persons, and number of students."[35] If, as Boyle argues, Aquinas spent several of his most mature years writing the *Summa* for the *fratres communes* in his province, he could, and most likely would, have brought it about that the priories and provincial *studia* began to use the work. Since he spent the years from 1272 until his death in 1274 in the province, he was well positioned to bring it about that the first and second parts of the *Summa*, which were then finished, be disseminated and used in the province's schools. However, there is no evidence that the work was widely used in the province during or immediately after Aquinas's lifetime.[36]

We can make much better sense of the *Summa*, I contend, if we see it as a work intended for a student pursuing a degree in theology, for one aspiring to be a *Magister in sacra pagina*, or for someone at a comparable level. The universities of Paris and Oxford alone were able to confer degrees in theology in the thirteenth century, and Paris was clearly dominant in theology. Moreover, since Aquinas studied and taught at Paris, it would have influenced him. An eyewitness account tells us that Aquinas began the *Summa* after beginning a revision of his commentary of the *Sentences* of Peter Lombard.[37] If this is so, then it is likely that he began the *Summa* after becoming dissatisfied with the limitations a commentary on the *Sentences* imposed. This hypothesis is further supported by the prologue of the *Summa*, which states that the work is intended to break with commentaries, in which "the things which it is necessary for such students to know are not taught according to the order of the discipline, but according to what is required for the exposition of the text."[38] It is most likely, then, that he intended the *Summa* to play the role in the educational system that was comparable to that which the *Sentences* were then playing, albeit unsatisfactorily.

The university student who studied the *Sentences* in Paris would have been well prepared for the *Summa*. He would, first of all, have had extensive philosophical training, and particularly in the works of Aristotle. Before one could commence theological studies, he had to have received the degree of Master of Arts. Traditionally, study in the liberal arts meant the classical liberal arts of the *trivium* and *quadrivium*. The influx of translations of classical works between the middle of the twelfth and the middle of the thirteenth centuries, however, brought about a gradual evolution in the arts course. By 1255 it is clear that the texts lectured on in the Arts Faculty at Paris were those of the Aristotelian corpus, a few writings falsely attributed to Aristotle, and a handful of other works.[39] In Aquinas's mature years, then, study in the arts was primarily the study of Aristotle. A common understanding of Aquinas's Aristotelian commentaries is that they were written for students and faculty in the arts, to guide the reading and teaching of Aristotle's works.[40] If this is so, then these detailed and philosophically challenging commentaries tell us what Aquinas thought a student in the arts should have been taught and should have learned.

The course in the Faculty of Arts was lengthy and rigorous. At Paris, it was five or six years.[41] The first two years were spent listening to lectures and attending disputations, and the next two participating in disputations under the supervision of a master. A minority of students went on to "determine," which consisted in determining or resolving questions being disputed. At this stage, students would also lecture cursorily on assigned texts.[42] Finally, the student could be presented for a license to incept as a master. Although this was not universally enforced, upon graduating as a Master of Arts he was required to lecture for two years on the faculty.[43]

Dominican candidates for theological study were exempt from the requirement of being Masters of Arts,[44] but only because they had completed equivalent studies in their own Dominican *studia*. In 1259 Aquinas, Albert the Great and several other prominent Dominicans were members of a commission which mandated that Dominican *studia* for the arts be set up where they had not hitherto existed, that the curriculum of such schools be brought into agreement with that of the university, and that the method of teaching be through lectures and disputations.[45]

After completing the arts course, a smaller number of highly qualified students would go on to study theology. To become a "Master of the Sacred Page," as one completing the theology degree was called, eight years in addition to the arts course were required.[46] Of this, the first six years were spent hearing lectures; four years were spent on the Bible and two on the *Sentences* of Peter Lombard.[47] After this, if he were 25 or older, the student could petition to be made a bachelor. As a bachelor he gave cursory lectures on the Bible for two years. He then became a bachelor of the *Sentences* – a *Sententarius*, as such a student was called – and he delivered lectures on the *Sentences*.

Here too Dominicans received exemptions due to previous work in their *studia*. Before coming to the university a Dominican would have studied theology for two or three years in a provincial house of studies and for one in a *studium generale*, whether at Paris or elsewhere. Thus when he came to Paris to lecture as a bachelor of the Bible or the *Sentences*, he could begin immediately.[48]

I am arguing, then, that the *Summa* was written for these extremely well prepared and highly capable students who studied, and eventually commented upon, the *Sentences* of Peter Lombard at the University of Paris. These students could have been expected to handle the dense, difficult and copious material presented in that work. Moreover, since our best evidence is that the *Summa theologiae* was written to play a role similar to that which the *Sentences* of Peter Lombard played, it is most likely that it was written for the students who were at the level at which the Lombard's work was to be studied. That is, it was meant to serve as a final, comprehensive course for theology students.[49]

Someone will certainly object, however, that Aquinas would not have referred to such advanced and accomplished students as beginners (*incipientes*) and novices (*novitii*), as he does refer to the intended audience of the *Summa theologiae* in the prologue to the *prima pars*. There Aquinas *tells* us that the work was written for those just commencing the study of theology, and so the interpretation I have argued for cannot be right.

It is not the case, though, that those called beginners are always rank beginners. Words such as *beginner* and *novice* (and *incipientes* and *novitii* in Latin) presuppose a contrast with the more advanced and accomplished, and just what contrast is in question depends upon the context in which these words are used. For example, an aspiring concert pianist about to make his debut with a major orchestra may be called a novice or beginner, though he has been playing the instrument at an extremely high level for years. Such a description is nonetheless apt, for the young pianist is a beginner in comparison with established concert pianists. The designation *beginner* makes sense because the presupposed contrast is between beginning and established concert pianists, not between this pianist and piano players generally. Similarly, it is possible that when Aquinas says that he is writing the *Summa theologiae* for beginners rather than for the advanced, the presupposed contrast is not between advanced students and rank beginners; it is between students, albeit very advanced students, on the one hand, and Aquinas's fellow theological

Masters at Paris, on the other. The former group would have been
very accomplished, would have been studying for a long time and
would not have been far from their inception as Masters. However,
in contrast to St. Thomas Aquinas, St. Bonaventure, Stephen
Tempier, John Pecham and others, they were beginners. When
Aquinas presents arguments in his disputed questions or in his
polemical works, he is engaging in debate with other Masters. So
when Aquinas writes in the prologue to the *Summa theologiae* that he is
writing for beginners and not for the advanced, it is possible that this
means that he is not trying to address disputes with his fellow
Masters, but is attempting to write a work for students who were
nearing the end of their theological studies. And, I would argue, the
nature and structure of the *Summa theologiae* is such that we must
conclude that in fact the "beginners" mentioned are advanced
students, not those just entering upon theological study.

I conclude, then, that Aquinas wrote the *Summa theologiae* as a work
suitable for the pedagogical needs of those very advanced students,
and it was intended as the culmination of their studies before they
took up positions as theological Masters at Paris and elsewhere. But
though I claim that Aquinas wrote the *Summa theologiae* for students at
Paris, I do not want to claim that it was written *only* for theology
students at Paris or Oxford. Although these two universities alone
could confer theological degrees in the thirteenth century, they were
not the only schools of theology. However, these theological universities, particularly Paris, became the model for theological study
elsewhere.[50] The 1259 commission on Dominican education, as we
have seen, brought the Dominican arts curriculum into line with that
of Paris, and established the university system of lectures and
disputations as the proper method of instruction. Although the
educational policy of the Roman province was in flux in Aquinas's
lifetime, and evidence about its nature is scant, it does seem that the
effort was to bring study in the provincial *studia* in line with and up to
the standards of Paris. Thus, although it may be that Aquinas also
had schools in the Dominican provinces in mind when he wrote the
Summa, he hoped that the curriculum there would be comparable to
that in Paris. If that were the case, the *Summa theologiae* could have
been used by them as well.

3.3 THE NATURE AND STRUCTURE OF THE
SUMMA THEOLOGIAE

My contention, then, is that the *Summa theologiae* was intended to play a role in theological education similar to that which the *Sentences* played at Paris, whether the educational institution was in fact the University of Paris, or Oxford, or one of the Dominican *studia*, or any similar institution of theological education. If this is so, then a student would have had extensive preparation before encountering the *Summa*. As Aquinas envisioned it, it is likely that the student would have been through the Aristotelian corpus using Aquinas's commentaries, or at least would have heard lectures in the manner of Aquinas's commentaries. Thus he would, through both hearing and delivering lectures, have had a thorough acquaintance with Aristotelian philosophy, of the ways in which it did and did not accord with Christian orthodoxy, and of the way in which many of its concepts and principles are open to dialectical development in light of Christian doctrine and subsequent philosophical and theological developments.[51] He would, again through hearing and delivering lectures, have had a thorough acquaintance with Christian Scripture. And since lectures on the Bible involved addressing questions and problems of Christian theology, he would have had a sophisticated knowledge of Christian doctrine and theology. Given this wide exposure to philosophy and theology, what more would a student need? What he would need, according to Aquinas, is to grasp the truths of Christian theology, of sacred doctrine, in the right kind of way. What he would need is to have the material presented so that he would grasp effects in virtue of causes, and thus acquire the noetic structure proper to that *scientia*. What he would need is second-level pedagogy, and this, I submit, is what the *Summa theologiae* attempts to provide.

First-level pedagogy, which is in many ways the most prolonged and arduous, would have occurred in the student's course in the arts and in the first four years of theology. In the arts course he would have mastered logic and grammar through the study of Aristotle's *Categories*, *De interpretatione*, *Topics*, *De sophisticis enlencis*, the *Prior* and *Posterior Analytics*, as well as works by Boethius and Priscian. In the physical *scientiae*, he would, through careful study of Aristotle's *Physics*, have learned about, *inter alia*, material substances and their accidents, the four causes and the nature of physical change. Through the study of Aristotle's *De anima*, *De sensu et sensato*, *De*

memoria et reminiscentia and *De animalibus* he would come to know about
the souls of humans and animals, about human action and human
cognition. Through the study of *De caelo et mundo*, *Meteorologia* and *De
generatione et corruptione* he would have been taught about inanimate
nature and about the celestial bodies and their role in the order of
the sub-lunar world. In the practical *scientiae*, through the study of the
Nicomachean Ethics and the *Politics*, he would have considered human
good, action, virtue, happiness (beatitude) and political philosophy.
And in metaphysics, through the study of Aristotle's *Metaphysics*, he
would have learned about being *qua* being and the immaterial
substances, which are God and the intelligences or (as Moses
Maimonides and Aquinas identified them) angels. In all these fields
he would not only have encountered the teachings in each of these
disciplines, but would also have acquired sufficient mastery to
conduct disputations on controversial issues in these fields, and
perhaps even have done some lecturing on key texts.

After first-level pedagogy in the philosophical *scientiae* in the arts
course, the student would then learn the doctrines of Christian
theology by attending lectures on the Bible for four years. These
lectures, though based on the Biblical texts, would have been
substantive theological lectures on Christian doctrine. Through them
the student would have become familiar with these doctrines, and
would have heard lectures on God, the Trinity, creation, the
Incarnation, sin, salvation, grace and so on. In his first four years as a
theology student, then, he would have become familiar with the
concepts and doctrines of Christian theology.

When he was ready to study the *Sentences* of Peter Lombard, then,
he would already have become familiar with the key theological and
philosophical concepts, arguments and claims of Christian theology.
In the ideal case, at least, there would have been little for him to
learn that was new. When Aquinas wrote the *Summa theologiae* to play
the role that the Lombard's *Sentences* had been playing in the theology
curriculum, his primary concern was not to pass on new claims and
arguments, but to take the student through the final stage in the
acquisition of the *scientia* of sacred doctrine. For full *scientia* the
student, having grasped the fundamental concepts, learned the key
claims and acquired the skills of reasoning and disputation, would
need to engage in reasoning from the fundamental causes in this field
to conclusions. This was second-level pedagogy, and its purpose was
to instill in the student a habit of thought, so that his reasoning in the

field would move easily, by second nature, from the fundamental causes to their effects. With this sort of training, when he considered (for example) human beings, he would readily think of them not simply as humans, but as beings which have their beginning and end in God, and as creatures which are finite reflections of the divine goodness. Only when he not only knew that humans were in fact creatures, but had also acquired the ready habit of thought to consider and contemplate them as such, did the student have *scientia* of sacred doctrine. The *Summa theologiae*, I am claiming, is a work of second-level pedagogy which is intended to instill just this habit of thought.

When we view the *Summa* as a work of second-level pedagogy, I contend, it makes much more sense. First, the content of the work is more appropriate for a thirteenth-century theology student who had completed his Master of Arts and four years of Biblical study. The level of sophistication and range of philosophical and theological issues addressed in this work is well beyond what a rank beginner could absorb. However, if the student had gone through the heavily philosophical, Aristotelian curriculum in the liberal arts of the mid-thirteenth century, and had studied, lectured upon and attended substantive theological lectures on the Bible for four years, he would be adequately prepared to take on what we find in the *Summa theologiae*.

Secondly, as we have seen, the structure of the *Summa theologiae* is precisely the opposite of what, in Aquinas's view, first-level pedagogy requires. It seems to accord, however, with what second-level pedagogy demands. This is especially clear in the *prima pars*, in which the discussion moves from God, to creation in general, to a discussion of the kinds of creatures which exist, moving from higher to lower creatures; and it concludes by considering God's conservation and governance of the whole.

Thirdly, to the extent that treatments of questions in the *Summa theologiae* do differ from treatments of the same or similar questions in other works, such as the *Quaestiones disputatae* or the *Summa contra gentiles*, they seem particularly suited to a work of second-level pedagogy. As we saw above in our discussion of *Summa theologiae* 1.85.1 (pp. 81–83), the *Summa theologiae* does not leave out anything essential to the resolution of the question of that article that was found in corresponding passages of the previously composed *Quaestiones disputatae de veritate*. Thus the *Summa*, as was argued above, does not

seem geared to an untrained, unsophisticated audience, as a work of
first-level pedagogy would be. But in the *Summa* Aquinas does
eliminate objections which are either redundant or do not lead to
any distinctively illuminating point, and he also leaves out a discussion of numerous and various opinions of ancient thinkers, something
which is not essential to his response to the question of that article.
The *Summa theologiae*, then, presents Aquinas's resolution of the
question at hand in all its sophistication and subtlety, but free from
extraneous material and repetition. The concern seems to be to set
forth what is essential to the *scientia* in as concise and lucid a manner
as possible. And this interest in clarity and economy of presentation
seems particularly appropriate to second-level pedagogy, for there
one seeks to give a clear and uncluttered view of the whole sweep of
the *scientia*, and particularly of the way its essential claims flow from
its fundamental principles. In the initial discovery of difficult truths,
tangential discussions and a meticulous consideration of objections
are necessary to aid understanding, eliminate confusion and remove
doubts. In second-level pedagogy, however, what one needs is a
perspicuous presentation of the reasoning which leads from principles to conclusion, so that he will begin to think of the subject in this
way. Extraneous or redundant material must be eliminated so that
the structure of reasoning in the *scientia* can be better seen. The
changes we find in the *Summa theologiae* in comparison with the
Quaestiones disputatae seem to be directed to this end.

In the prologue to the *Summa*, Aquinas makes clear that concern
for structure and economy of presentation are what had made him
break with older forms. His dissatisfaction with the currently available works is (1) that they contain a multiplicity of useless questions,
articles and arguments; (2) they fail to treat what is necessary for
scientia according to the *ordo disciplinae*; and (3) the repetition of
material in them produces boredom and confusion in the students.
That is, he does not complain that existing works contain significant
errors, or teach falsehoods, or ignore important material; his com-
plaints all have to do with the fact that they do not present the
material in the right kind of way. In second-level pedagogy it is
precisely *the way* material is taught, the *order of presentation*, which is
crucial. For only when the order of teaching clearly mirrors the
order of causality can one begin to acquire the noetic structure
proper to *scientia*.

Furthermore, we can, on this hypothesis, understand the significance of Aquinas's persistent – even obsessive – concern with the architectonic in the *Summa*. At the beginning of each question Aquinas tells us how that question fits into the larger scheme of the *Summa* and how the individual articles are structured. This may seem an unimportant, idiosyncratically scholastic preoccupation with order, and some writers have felt free to pluck questions and articles out of the context and try to understand them in isolation. But this can only lead to distortions, for, if I am right, then the structure of the work is, in one sense at least, its primary point. Since the concern is with second-level pedagogy, it is precisely the structure which Aquinas wants to communicate to the student, for he hopes thereby to shape the student's understanding.

My claim, then, is that in the *Summa theologiae* Aquinas's primary concern is with second- and not first-level pedagogy. This shift in perspective, I believe, enables us to make better sense of the work. It also gives rise to some important objections, which I will present in the next section. In the remaining chapters of this work I will try to respond to these objections, and we can thereby perhaps acquire a better understanding of the *Summa theologiae* and the *scientia* of sacred doctrine.

3.4 SOME OBJECTIONS

The first objection asks whether Aquinas would have considered a *PA scientia* generally, and not just the *scientia* of sacred doctrine, a practical possibility which might have served as a goal for inquiry. For the stringency of the requirements for a *PA scientia* may lead one to wonder whether we could ever have the apprehension of principles which it demands. According to the interpretation presented in chapter one, for a person to have *scientia* in a field, he must have grasped all the principles of that field; he must also, because they are indemonstrable principles, have apprehended them non-inferentially; and, finally, he must know them better than any conclusions drawn from them in the *scientia*. But for several reasons, the first objection argues, in the merely human *scientiae* this seems such a remote and even unrealizable ideal that it renders this view of *scientia* irrelevant to actual scientific inquiry and training.

For, first of all, given the course of gradual discovery in many disciplines, particularly in empirical sciences, a given individual at a given time in the course of this gradual discovery should not expect to grasp all the principles of a *scientia* adequately. The principles of a *scientia* are immediate propositions, which are propositions in which the definition, or part of the definition, or another immediate attribute is predicated of a subject. It is perhaps plausible that for a mathematical *scientia*, such as geometry, we can identify the relevant immediate propositions and deduce from them all the conclusions of the *scientia*. (Thus it has often been said that Euclid's *Elements* seems to be quite close to the ideal the *Posterior Analytics* offers us, and perhaps served as a model for Aristotle's speculations.) However, Aquinas clearly wants to apply the PA account to natural *scientiae*, such as biology or physics.[52] But the history of science has shown that it is very difficult to arrive at an adequate account of the essences studied in these *scientiae*. Secondly, it seems principles could not be known non-inferentially. In empirical disciplines, an objector may argue, essential definitions and the principles to which they give rise should be viewed as inferences from observational claims about the thing. For example, we infer the essence of water, or cow, or man from a large set of observations about how water, cows and men behave. Therefore, it seems, the essences of these things and the corresponding principles should be viewed as inferences from the observational claims, and thus the principles are known inferentially. Third and finally, some of the observational claims from which, as the objector claims, principles are inferred are conclusions of the *scientia* of which the principle in question is a principle. But, then, the principle could not be better known than the conclusions of the *scientia*, as the doxastic causality condition requires, for it is inferred from some of them. For these reasons, the first objector argues, Aquinas could not have thought that the *PA* notion of *scientia* as we have understood it could serve as an ideal for actual scientific inquiry.

A second objection focuses on the *scientia* of sacred doctrine and its principles, which are the articles of faith. It argues that the previous objection applies *a fortiori* to faith and the principles of sacred doctrine. A common view of Aquinas's account of the epistemic grounds for the assent of faith is that it is based on two sorts of arguments from philosophical theology. First, one constructs or encounters arguments from natural theology which justify the belief that God exists. Secondly, one constructs or encounters arguments that God brought about miracles and signs in Biblical times and in the history of the Church, and that these arguments ultimately justify the claim that what the Church claims as a divine revelation is in fact such.[53] But if this is Aquinas's account, then a Christian's belief that God exists or that God is Triune must be based at least partially on his belief in the propositions which are the premises of these natural theological arguments. However, some of these propositions (e.g. *The world exists*, or *A miracle occurred*) would be conclusions of sacred doctrine, and thus must be derived from its principles, which, according to the *PA*, must be better known than the conclusions. But, it seems, this requirement could never be fulfilled, for the principles are inferred from these putative conclusions.

A third objection argues that Aquinas makes clear that we cannot have *scientia* of the principles of sacred doctrine, and so, it would seem, neither can we have it of the conclusions which flow from these.[54] We can have a full apprehension of the mysteries of faith only when we, separated from our earthly bodies, behold the divine essence in heaven.[55] Thus it seems that, by Aquinas's own principles, he cannot instill the *scientia* of sacred doctrine in his students in this life, as I am claiming he is trying to do in the *Summa theologiae*.

Fourthly and finally, I have claimed that the structure of the *Summa theologiae* moves from causes to effects in a way which accords with second-level pedagogy, and that this is especially clear in the *prima pars*. But, a fourth objector asks, how does the second part, and particularly the *secunda–secundae* fit into this structure? Moreover, there seem to be parts of even the *prima pars* which do not fit into second-level pedagogy. For instance, after the introductory first question, Aquinas considers whether God, the subject of this *scientia*, exists. But according to the *PA*, at the second level of inquiry one must know that the subject exists.[56] Thus, upon a closer, more detailed examination, it is not clear that the structure of the *Summa theologiae* does accord with second-level pedagogy.

3.5 CONCLUSION

I have in this chapter argued against the standard interpretation which takes the *Summa theologiae* as a work of first-level pedagogy. Rather, it was written for very advanced students in theology, to serve as a final, comprehensive treatment of sacred doctrine. That is, it was intended as a work of second-level pedagogy which would present material moving from causes to effects, so that the habits of thought required for *scientia* would be instilled in students.

We have seen, though, that there are objections to the interpretation so far developed. We will give careful attention to these objections in the remaining chapters of this work, and our discussion of them will, I hope, further elucidate Aquinas's understanding of *scientia* and his project in the *Summa theologiae*. In chapter four we will consider the first objection, and look carefully at Aquinas's account of our apprehension of the principles of merely human *scientiae*, and particularly the more problematic physical *scientiae*. We will not be able to discuss these *scientiae* in all the detail they deserve, but I will provide some response to this objection, and this will also provide important background for our discussion of faith. After treating grace and the theological virtues in chapter five, we will in chapter six take up the second objection, and consider Aquinas's account of the assent of faith. Having dealt with these issues, we will be able to return to a consideration of the *Summa theologiae*, and I will attempt to respond to the third and fourth objections raised above.

PART TWO
Intellectus principorum

CHAPTER FOUR

The natural light of the intellect[1]

"The whole of a *scientia*," writes Aquinas, "is virtually contained in [its] principles."[2] We can better understand this important claim if we recall what we said about the principles of scientific demonstration which were discussed in chapter one. The principles from which a conclusion is scientifically demonstrated must be *per se* predications, and they can be such formally, as when a definition or some part of a definition is predicated of its subject (e.g. *A triangle is a figure bounded by three lines*); or materially, as when a proper subject of an attribute is predicated of its attribute (e.g. *Snubness belongs to the nose*); or by intrinsic efficient causality, as when an effect belongs to a subject in virtue of what the subject under consideration is (e.g. *The one who has been slain dies*). Once we have identified the principles and have a perfectly complete understanding of the essences or natures signified by the terms, the conclusions of the *scientia* can, at least ideally, be straightforwardly deduced. It is in this sense that principles virtually contain the whole of a *scientia*: given an absolute and perfect understanding of the principles and all the terms of the *scientia*, the conclusions flow from them by non-ampliative, deductive inference (though of course such an understanding of principles and terms is an ideal to which actual inquiry may only approximate).

Since each kind of *per se* proposition is in some way derived from the definition of the subject or attribute, each is discovered by grasping the essences or quiddities of the things under consideration.[3] As Aquinas writes, "principles known *per se* are those which are apprehended immediately once the terms are understood, because the predicate is placed in the definition of the subject."[4] The potency or faculty by which essences, and hence definitions, are grasped is the intellect, which Aquinas calls the "habit of principles." He writes:

We are properly said to understand (*intelligere*) when we apprehend the quiddity of things, or when we understand these things which are immediately known by the intellect once it knows the quiddities of things, such as the first principles (which we apprehend once we apprehend the terms). Hence intellect is called the habit of principles.[5]

Indeed, because the intellect is that by which we grasp principles, and a *scientia* is virtually contained in its principles, the intellect is called the "principium scientiae", the principle of *scientia*.

Clearly, then, the objections raised at the end of the previous chapter about our apprehension of the principles of a *scientia* must be met by a careful consideration of Aquinas's views of the intellect, and the natural light by which it apprehends essences in the merely human *scientiae*. In many *scientiae*, and particularly in natural *scientiae*, the objector argues, essences are only apprehended with difficulty and after long inquiry. But serious pursuit of a *PA scientia* would seem to require that a full grasp of principles is in sight. Moreover, essential definitions and the principles derived from them are, it is claimed, inferred from certain immediately observable truths. But then these principles would not be indemonstrable. Finally, if principles are inferred in this way, they cannot be better known than the observational claim from which they are inferred. Yet since some of these claims are conclusions of the *scientia* in question, the principles would not be better known than the conclusions which are supposed to be derived from them. How can there be an apprehension of principles in the way a *PA scientia* seems to require? And how are we to understand the intellect by which, Aquinas claims, principles are apprehended?

When Aquinas is discussing the intellect in its first operation, in which it grasps essences or quiddities, he frequently asserts that "the intellect cannot be false."[6] This claim seems rather sweeping and bold, and it is not easy to understand just what it means. Let us label this doctrine of Aquinas, whatever it amounts to, *the doctrine of the indefectibility of the intellect*, or just the *indefectibility doctrine*. There are at least two readings of the indefectibility doctrine. A weaker reading claims that the essential definitions and principles are inferred in some way from observable truths, and that the indefectibility doctrine is compatible with defects in our initial conceptualizations of natural kinds, such that the ideas formed in the intellect's first operation may not correspond to any real essences. A stronger reading denies this inferential account, and denies that this doctrine is compatible with such cognitive defects. The weak reading has won general acceptance by prominent twentieth-century scholars of Aquinas: Etienne

Gilson,[7] Bernard Lonergan[8] and Alasdair MacIntyre[9] have all adopted some version of it. In this chapter, however, I will argue for a stronger alternative. The stronger reading will help us begin to understand Aquinas's views on how a *PA scientia* might be attained, particularly in the more problematic natural *scientiae*.

This chapter will have six sections. First, we will examine more closely just what Aquinas is claiming about the indefectibility of the intellect. Secondly, we will consider and criticize a version of the weaker reading, the one put forward by Bernard Lonergan. Thirdly, I will offer my own interpretation, and, fourthly, I will consider and respond to an objection which will lead to a refinement of my interpretation. Fifthly, we will consider Aquinas's views on some possible epistemic evaluations of the assent to principles, namely, whether the assent is justified and whether it has warrant. Sixthly and finally, we will summarize our conclusions regarding Aquinas's views on the intellect and the apprehension of principles, and we will discuss one final challenge to our interpretation.

4.1 THE INDEFECTIBILITY OF THE INTELLECT

We begin with a brief summary of Aquinas's rather complex terminology and an outline of his account of the structure of human cognition and the role of the natural light of the intellect within it. This will give us a clearer picture of just what Aquinas is claiming when he asserts the indefectibility doctrine.

For Aquinas, the essence (*essentia*) or quiddity of a thing is what makes it the sort of thing it is; it is primarily the substantial form.[10] The essence is a nature (*natura*), though these terms are not co-extensive; Aquinas often refers to accidental forms as natures. A nature abstractly considered is the form with (at least in the case of material forms) what Aquinas calls "common matter" (*materia communis*). Common matter is matter considered abstractly; it is, for instance, the flesh and bones common to all humans, as opposed to *this* flesh and *these* bones of Socrates. The latter, matter taken concretely, Aquinas calls designated matter (*materia signata*). Nature taken abstractly is referred to with abstract terms, such as *humanity*. In contrast, nature taken concretely includes implicitly designated matter, existence, accidents, etc. It is what is predicated when we say "Socrates is a man."

Aquinas also calls nature taken abstractly "nature as such." It is only natures as such that the intellect grasps, and which are described in definitions. This nature as such is, then, what is intelligible and, as the intelligible structure of a thing, it is called the *ratio*. It is the object of abstract thought. This word *ratio* is a difficult one to translate, but I will translate it as *idea*, which accords with Lonergan's translation.

According to Aquinas, human cognition in its natural state begins with and remains tied to sense perception: there must be a *conversio ad phantasmata*, a turning to sense images, if one is not only to form for the first time an idea, such as the idea of triangle, but also to engage in further geometrical speculation about the properties of triangles. Yet human, abstract thought, which is of course more than mere sense perception, also requires the intellect with its natural light.

Aquinas in many places distinguishes between two operations of the intellect, as he does in the commentary on Aristotle's *De interpretatione*:

As the Philosopher says in Book III of *De anima*, the operation of the intellect is twofold: the first operation, which is called the understanding of indivisibles, is that in which the intellect apprehends the essence of each thing in itself; the other operation of the intellect is that of composing and dividing (*operatio intellectus . . . componentis et dividentis*).[11]

In the first operation of the intellect one grasps the essences, or quiddities, of things. And in this first operation there seems to be two stages: in the first stage the receptive intellect receives the intelligible forms which are illumined by the natural light of the intellect in *phantasmata*; having received this determination, in the second stage the agent intellect can form an abstract idea, a *ratio*.[12]

In the second operation of the intellect one engages in *compositio* and *divisio*, positive and negative judgments. Later in the *De interpretatione* commentary, Aquinas elaborates on *compositio* and *divisio* in the intellect:

If we consider what concerns the intellect in itself, there is always *compositio* where there is truth and falsity; for [truth and falsity] are only to be found in the intellect through the fact that the intellect joins one simple conception (*conceptum*) with another. But if the intellect is brought back into relationship with the [extrinsic] thing, sometimes there is said to be *compositio*, sometimes *divisio*. There is *compositio* whenever the intellect joins one conception to another so as to understand the conjunction or identity of the things of which these conceptions are; there is *divisio* whenever one joins one conception to another so as to understand the things as diverse. And because of this, also in verbal utterances, affirmation is called *compositio*, insofar as it signifies conjunction on the part of the thing; and negation is called *divisio*, insofar as it signifies the separation of things.[13]

As Anthony Kenny has pointed out, Aquinas here distinguishes two sorts of *compositio* in the intellect.[14] The first, which we will call *predicative compositio*, is present in both the affirmative judgment that Socrates is sitting, and the negative judgment that Socrates is not sitting; it is also present in the wish and the command, as well as in entertaining the thought, that Socrates is or should be sitting. It is simply that joining of one idea to another which is involved in each of these mental acts. In the second sort of *compositio*, on the other hand, what are "joined," as it were, are the mental synthesis and reality in an affirmation; that is, one not only forms a mental synthesis, but judges that there is some real composition corresponding to it. We will call that second sort *judgmental compositio*. In its complement, *divisio*, one denies the existence of the corresponding composition in a negative judgment. *Compositio* and *divisio* are both forms of assent. Truth and falsity enter into judgmental *compositio* and *divisio* because individual things and their forms may or may not be as they are judged to be.

When Aquinas distinguishes the first and second operations of the intellect, he is using the word *intellect* (*intellectus*) in a more general sense than he uses it elsewhere. In this sense, it is used "commonly" to refer to all cognitive operations,[15] in something like the way the English word *mind* is used. However, Aquinas also uses *intellectus* in a more specific sense – which is its original and more proper sense – to refer to the first operation alone. Using the word in this sense, Aquinas says "the proper object of the intellect is the quiddity of a thing."[16] And, he says, it is from this role that the intellect received its name:

The name *intellect* is derived from the fact that it apprehends what is innermost and profound in the thing: for to understand (*intelligere*) is "to read what is within" (*intus legere*). Sense and imagination apprehend only superficial accidents; only the intellect goes to the interior and essence of a thing.[17]

When Aquinas claims "intellectus non potest esse falsus" – "the intellect cannot be false," he is using *intellect* in its original and more specific sense, to refer to the first operation of apprehending the quiddities of things. And, understood in this way, there is one clear and uncontroversial sense in which the claim is true: in the intellect's first operation, an idea is formed, but there is no assertion about whether the form does or does not exist *in rebus*, in substances in the world. Truth and falsity only enter in the second operation of the intellect, when there is a judgmental *compositio* or *divisio* – an affirmative or negative judgment. But, in the first operation, no false judgments are made because no judgments are made; and thus the first operation of the intellect cannot be false (or true, for that matter).[18] So this indefectibility is not due to being always correct or true, but, rather, to stopping short of judgmental *compositio* or *divisio*, in which thought and reality are "compared" (a "comparatio", as Aquinas says) and assertion is made.[19]

To say that the intellect is indefectible in this sense is, of course, not to say much; it is like saying that the Pope is infallible as long as he makes no claims about God or the world, and even the most anti-Papal Protestant could agree with that. But is there an epistemologically more interesting sense in which the first operation of the intellect is not liable to error? In his commentary on Book III of Aristotle's *De anima* Aquinas suggests there is.[20] There he writes that there are *two* senses in which the first operation of the intellect is not liable to being false: "This intellection [in the first operation of the intellect] is with regard to that about which [the intellect] is not false: not only because what is non-complex is neither true nor false, but also because it is not deceived with regard to what it is (*quod quid est*), as is said below."[21] Later Aquinas further explains the sense in which the intellect cannot be false, and is indeed true, in this second way: he writes, "the intellect in understanding what is non-complex is true insofar as it is assimilated [*adaequatur*] to the thing understood."[22]

It seems, then, that Aquinas wants to say that not only is the first operation of the intellect indefectible in the sense of being neither true nor false by stopping short of judgments about the world, but also, more positively, it is in some sense "always true."[23] For the sake of convenient reference, let us label the former doctrine the doctrine of the *infallibility of the intellect,* and the latter the doctrine of the *veracity of the intellect.* Thus what we have labeled Aquinas's indefectibility doctrine is actually a conjunction of two doctrines: the infallibility and veracity doctrines of the intellect. The sense of Aquinas's infallibility doctrine seems unproblematic; but what does Aquinas mean in claiming that the intellect is always veracious?

4.2 THE LONERGAN READING

Before arguing for our strong reading of this doctrine, we will consider one prominent advocate of a weaker alternative, Bernard Lonergan. Lonergan is formidable not only as an interpreter of Aquinas, but also as a thinker in his own right, and his reading of Aquinas is bold and in many ways illuminating. Considering his account will both help us see the difficulties with a weaker reading, and will, by providing a contrast, enhance our understanding of the stronger alternative.

According to Lonergan, what emerges from the first operation of the intellect, which he calls "direct understanding," are simply hypotheses. On the level of direct understanding, he says, there are two types of events: first, there is insight into phantasm, which is expressed in definition; second, he writes:

There is the coalescence or development of insights which provide the hypothetical synthesis of simple quiddities. On the reflective level [which is the second operation of the intellect which ultimately issues in judgments] these hypothetical syntheses are known as hypothetical; they become questions which are answered by the *resolutio in principia*.[24]

What is hypothetical, however, is not simply what is unasserted, but something which, in the absence of evidence yet to be gathered, there are not sufficient grounds for asserting; most hypotheses eventually end up in the dust-bin of bright ideas which did not work out. Thus the ideas formed in the first operation of the intellect, it seems, may frequently fail to correspond with the actual essences of existing individuals.

In the second operation of the intellect, which Lonergan calls "reflective understanding," ideas formed in the first operation, or direct understanding, are evaluated:

We may infer that the reflective activity of reason, returning from the synthesis of intelligibilities to its origin in sense and in naturally known principles terminates in a reflective act of understanding, in a single synthetic apprehension of all the motives for judgment, whether intellectual or sensitive, in a grasp of their sufficiency as motives and so of the necessity of passing judgment or assenting.[25]

In reflective understanding, then, the intellect considers the ideas formed in direct understanding in light of their basis in sense experience and in naturally known principles, and sees whether there is a sufficiency of motives for judgment which will render such judgment necessary. Before such judgment is made, however, there is no assurance that our ideas correspond to the quiddities of things. Thus, Lonergan claims, it is only in the second stage of reflective understanding that the intellect participates in the Divine Light: "We read that human intellectual operation is perfected in two manners, by intelligible *species* and by intellectual light; in virtue of the former we have our apprehensions of things; but in virtue of the latter we pass judgment upon our apprehensions."[26] It is because our intellectual light participates in the Divine Light that we know the forms which God created. If this only comes into play in reflective understanding, then at the level of direct understanding there is no particular assurance that ideas formed here correspond to quiddities in the world. Thus, we may come to see that ideas formed in the first operation of the intellect are of no real essence, and must be abandoned. Thus Lonergan adopts the weaker reading.[27]

If Lonergan accepts the weaker reading, how does he understand Aquinas's claim that the intellect in its first operation is veracious? Although Lonergan does not discuss the passage from the commentary on the *De anima* in which Aquinas talks about the veracity of the intellect, Lonergan's answer to this question seems clear. In its first operation, the intellect forms ideas, but as yet the question of their correspondence with the actual essences of things is not raised. At this stage, thoughts do not refer to individual things and their forms in the world, but are simply of the mind's own conceptions: as Lonergan says, "as yet one knows not the thing, but the idea of the thing."[28] So there is no question of these being true or false in the sense that "Socrates is snub-nosed" may be true or false; ideas cannot correspond, or fail to correspond, to the mind's objects. As Lonergan writes, it is only "the second operation of the intellect . . . [that] introduces the duality of idea and thing and makes the former the medium in and through which one knows the latter."[29] Only in this second operation, then, is there a question of the correspondence between our thought and individual things and their forms, and so of truth properly so called.

Nevertheless, consider the expression, "A bachelor is an unmarried male." There is certainly a sense in which this is true. But, Aquinas may be saying, this and expressions like it are not true in the sense that "Socrates is snub-nosed" is true; these expressions are true in virtue of expressing the content of some single idea. Such statements express the content of one's ideas and, insofar as they do so, are true. The distinction here between these sorts of statements and thoughts corresponds to the analytic/synthetic distinction, at least in some sense of those terms. And the distinction between these two sorts of truth reflects the different sorts of criteria for the truth of the respective kinds of statements.

If this is the distinction Aquinas is concerned with, then we can see why thoughts are, at the stage of the intellect's first operation, on one hand, neither true nor false, and on the other, always true. They are neither true nor false in the sense synthetic statements are, for they do not raise the question of correspondence with individual things and forms which are the proper objects of the intellect. Nevertheless, truth for such thoughts depends upon the content of one's ideas. The intellect, however, does not make mistakes about its own contents; it infallibly knows its own ideas. Consequently, with respect to such thoughts the intellect is always veracious.

Despite its initial plausibility, Lonergan's reading is fatally flawed, I will argue, because it cannot make sense of Aquinas's distinction between *complexa* and *incomplexa*, complex and non-complex conceptions of the intellect. To see this, let us examine this reading more carefully.

As we have seen, the Lonerganean reading invokes the analytic/synthetic distinction. Lonergan's passing remarks on the issue do not pin down any precise notion of analyticity which we might attribute to Aquinas, but perhaps we might turn for illumination to Kant, who first formulated the distinction in these terms. Kant seems to have offered two different criteria for analyticity. One is logical, and according to it a predicate which can be deduced by the laws of logic from what is immediately contained in some concept is analytic. According to this criterion, rather esoteric logical consequences of more obvious definitional truths, though these remain quite unknown to a subject, are analytic. Thus this logical criterion will not be of use to the Lonerganean reading, for the doctrine of veracity demands that the intellect is "always true" with regard to such analytic judgments; but certainly one could be in error about esoteric logical consequences of more obvious definitional truths. The second criterion is psychological; according to it, "A is B" is analytic only if the idea of B is contained in the idea of A in such a way that anyone who has completely grasped the idea of A could not think of A without B. So, "human beings are rational" is analytic just if it is the case that anyone who has completely grasped the idea of human being cannot think of a human being who is not rational. This criterion does seem to serve the purposes of the Lonerganean reading, since for anyone who has competently grasped the idea in question, the intellect would be "always true" about analytic judgments.

Although the psychological criterion of analyticity is perhaps vague and needs refinement, it is sufficient for our purposes. For I will argue that regardless of how it may be refined, it cannot serve to make sense out of what Aquinas says about the veracity of the intellect. For, first of all, Aquinas tells us that the intellect in its first operation is *intellectus incomplexorum* (understanding of what is non-complex). These *incomplexa* are the proper objects of the under-standing, and it is the understandings of such which are always veracious. On the other hand, he tells us, "Among those intelli-gibilities in which there is truth and falsity, there is then a certain joining (*compositio*) of what is understood, that is, of the things under-stood, as when some unity comes to be from many."[30] In the latter, the apprehension of what is complex, "the intellect joins (*componit*) many previously separate non-complex elements (*incomplexa*) . . . and makes from them a single understanding . . ."[31] These intellectual apprehensions, in contrast, are sometimes true and sometimes false.

Since non-complex understandings are the proper object of the intellect, and since it is with respect to these that the intellect is veracious, it seems that the Lonerganean reading must hold that what is part of a non-complex understanding may be predicated of the idea analytically (in the psychological sense). But is this correct? Aquinas goes on to describe the sort of non-complexity which the objects of the first operation of the intellect have. It is unity or indivisibility *secundum speciem*:

As for what is indivisible – not quantitatively but as a species – the soul (*anima*) understands it in an indivisible instant of time and with an indivisible part of the soul. . . . And although what is indivisible as a species is divisible in its parts, nevertheless the soul understands divisible parts accidentally – not insofar as they are divisible either with respect to that which is understood or to the time, but insofar as they are indivisible . . .[32]

Thus, what is part of an idea in a non-complex manner is part of it *secundum speciem* or essentially. On the Lonerganean interpretation, then, whatever is part of the essence must be predicated analytically of the idea in question.

Clearly, though, this is false. First of all, Aquinas frequently tells us that parts of an essence are unknown to us.[33] On the notion of analyticity under consideration, however, nothing analytically true of some subject could be unknown. Secondly, Aquinas tells us that when parts of an essence are unknown to us, we must employ some proper accidents in definitions. In such cases, these proper accidents would be predicated analytically of the subject. However, what is accidental to an essence, whether properly or not, is not part of the essence and hence not part of the non-complex understanding.

It does not seem that there is any understanding of the analytic/synthetic distinction which can make sense of the veracity doctrine and which accords with Aquinas's distinction between what is indivisibly connected with an idea and what is not. This, I submit, is because the latter distinction is equivalent to the distinction between what is essential and what is not, and when Aquinas draws this distinction, he is speaking of *real*, and *not nominal*, essences. Only if essences in Aquinas were nominal essences, essences insofar as they are known and defined by us, could the distinction under consideration hope to correspond with the analytic/synthetic distinction. But this is not how Aquinas uses *essentia* and *accidentia*.

The Lonerganean reading also suffers from an inability to make sense of much of what Aquinas says about the veracity doctrine. We turn now to develop the stronger reading of veracity. Further problems with the weaker reading will become evident as we proceed.

4.3 THE STRONGER READING OF THE VERACITY OF THE INTELLECT

In Aquinas's main argument for his claim that the intellect's first operation is always true, he compares this operation of the intellect to sense perception, arguing that the former is always veracious in a way analogous to that in which the latter is. According to Lonergan's weaker reading of veracity, the first operation of the intellect is veracious because it does not concern the relationship between thought and its objects in the world, but simply its own ideas. Thus, on this reading, the veracity of the intellect is due to the privileged access a subject has to his own ideas. As we move to sense perception, then, we would expect Aquinas to focus upon claims whose truth does not depend upon the object of sense, but upon the subject's own internal sensings, to which he has a privileged access. Candidates for such claims would be those like the one expressed by the Chishol-mian "I am appeared redly to."[34] This claim is incorrigible because whether it is true depends only upon internal factors, not upon external objects of visual perception.

However, when we look at Aquinas's arguments, we find he is saying something quite different. The argument is essentially the same in the commentary on the *De anima* and in the *Summa*, but is more fully presented in the latter work. There Aquinas writes:

> The senses are not deceived about their proper objects. For example, sight is not deceived concerning color – except when, as may happen, in an incidental way there is an impediment of the organ; as, for instance, in the case of feverish persons, the sense of taste judges sweet things to be bitter, because of the fact that the tongue is filled with bad humors.[35]

Clearly, the veracity here cannot be because the reports in question are only of subjective seemings; these reports are just as true for someone with a fever, but Aquinas says his perception of taste is not veracious. The veracity here is with respect to the proper object; in the case of sight, these are the colors of things in the visual field. Sight is veracious in the sense that by it, given that the organ is healthy and that there is sufficient light, one perceives the actual colors of things, sight's proper object.

In support of this claim Aquinas offers a general argument which applies not only to sense perception, but to any cognitive potency:

> The reason for this [veracity of sense perception] is obvious. For each potency, as such, receives an intrinsic, non-incidental ordination to its proper object (*per se ordinatur . . . ad proprium objectum*). But whatever has this sort of ordination is always the same. Thus, as long as the potency remains intact, its judgment concerning its proper object is not defective (*non deficit*).[36]

The presupposition of this argument seems to be that cognitive potencies are directed to gathering information about the world. The critical feature of potencies which are always veracious is that they always act in the same manner, barring the loss of the potency, as when sight or hearing is lost through damage to the corporeal organ. Apart from such impediments, error enters only in the case of potencies which are under the control of the will, and can act sometimes in one way, sometimes in another. Sense perception acting always in the same way invariably achieves its cognitive ends.

Applying this to the intellect, Aquinas writes: "The proper object of the intellect is the quiddity of a thing. Thus, the intellect is not deceived concerning the quiddity of a thing (given that we are speaking of what is intrinsic and non-incidental to [the quiddity])."[37] Thus it is not, as the weaker reading suggests, that the first operation of the intellect is veracious in correctly grasping its own ideas. Rather, it correctly apprehends the quiddities or essences of those things to which it has access through sense perception.

These passages suggest that Aquinas's doctrine of the veracity of the intellect makes a strong epistemological claim: just as sight, given a healthy organ, correctly perceives the colors of things in its visual field, so the intellect in its first operation apprehends the quiddities, the real essences of sensible things. This stronger reading of veracity is well supported by *lectio* 11 of *In De anima*, which contains one of Aquinas's most extensive discussions of the veracity of the intellect.

There Aquinas, in commenting on Aristotle, contrasts the first and second operations of the intellect. The second operation is expressed in a complex judgment which is either true or false: "[Aristotle] says that the statement by which the intellect says 'something about something,' as happens in affirmation, is always either true or false."[38] As said above, such a judgment involves both predicative *compositio*, the joining of discrete ideas in thought, and some assent; that is, the subject either takes an affirmative attitude in judgmental *compositio*, asserting that the mental synthesis exists in reality, or takes a negative attitude in *divisio*, denying such a correspondence. Such mental states are said to be true or false with respect to the *content* of the mental attitude; that is, they are veracious or fallacious with respect to a mental predication understood (according to Aquinas) as corresponding, or not corresponding, to what is.

As we have seen, truth and falsity cannot enter into the intellect's first operation as they do into the second operation, for in the former there is as yet no judgment; in the first operation there is no mental attitude of judgmental *compositio* or *divisio*, which refers one's understanding to the individual things and their forms which are the proper objects of the intellect. Still, although in the first operation the subject does not refer his understanding to the objects of understanding, his intellect in understanding can be said to correspond with such objects. As Aquinas writes of the first operation of the intellect:

But nevertheless, although this non-complex intelligibility itself is neither true nor false, nevertheless the intellect in understanding this [intelligibility] itself is true insofar as it is assimilated to the thing understood. And thus

[Aristotle] adds that the intellect – "which is of this very 'what it is' [*quid est*] insofar as this is of something the 'what it is to be' [*quod aliquid erat esse*]" (that is, insofar as it understands what a thing is [*quid est res*]) – it [i.e. the intellect] is always true, and not insofar as it apprehends something about something.[39]

The thing understood here, I submit, is the essence of that which has been perceived by the senses. The intellect in understanding is assimilated (*adaequatur*) to it insofar as its idea corresponds to this form, insofar as the essence is grasped in the idea. As Lonergan tells us, the term "quod quid erat esse" is generally used by Aquinas "with special reference to the ground of essential definition, namely, the formal cause, so that at times it almost is, or simply is, the formal cause."[40] The formal cause as the ground of essential definition is not in the intellect, but in the individuals with the form in question. The first operation of the intellect is true, then, in that its ideas correspond to the essences of things. Let us say that when the intellect is true with respect to a certain idea in this sense it is *directly true*.

As I am interpreting Aquinas, then, he is claiming that the intellect's first operation is always veracious in the sense that it is always directly true with respect to its ideas. That is, he is making the strong epistemological claim that the ideas of natural, essential kinds which the intellect forms spontaneously in its first operation, invariably correspond to the essences of things with whose *phantasmata* the intellect is presented. "Hence the intellect is never deceived in thinking what human being is (*quid est homo*)," as Aquinas writes.[41] Of course, in the pre-judgmental stage of its first operation, the intellect does not understand or affirm that its apprehensions correspond to the essences of things; as Aquinas writes, "the intellect [is true] in thinking what something is: but not because it thinks or affirms the truth."[42] That is, although the intellect does not understand its own understanding to be true, nevertheless, from the third-person point of view, the intellect in apprehending a quiddity can be said to have a true understanding of the essence.

4.4 AN OBJECTION AND A RESPONSE

On the account so far formulated, the intellect's apprehension of principles seems wholly unproblematic: it simply has the ability, by its natural light, to apprehend the essences of things perceived by sense perception, and from this it is a short step to asserting the propositions which are the principles of the various *scientiae*. There is, however, an obvious objection to my stronger reading. Aquinas himself recognizes and discusses cases of imperfect and incorrect apprehensions of natural essences: he mentions our ignorance of the respective essences of flies,[43] bees[44] and fire;[45] he says that because essences are often unknown to us, we must use accidents in place of substantial differences in our definitions;[46] and, when our grasp of essences is deficient, we must use fallible discursive reason in coming to a full grasp of the essence.[47] It seems that, contrary to my claim about the veracity of the intellect, Aquinas thinks that our grasp of quiddities is liable to error.

Although I have so far spoken of the "stronger reading" as a single set of interpretive claims, it is necessary now to distinguish various versions of it. The passages just cited do undermine what we might call the *strongest version of the stronger reading*, which claims that the intellect in its first operation fully and perfectly intuits the essences of all natural, material things which are perceived by the senses. Such a reading is both highly implausible in itself and at odds with Aquinas's texts. But then what sense can we make of the claim about the intellect's veracity?

I want to claim that while the intellect is veracious in that it is competent to distinguish essences and classify individuals according to their essences – "to cut the world at its joints," if you will – it is often, at least initially, unable to specify the whole of the essence, or even the parts of the definition. On this interpretation, reasoning about ideas formed in the intellect's first operation is not employed somehow to establish the correspondence between these ideas and real essences, but to move from an imperfect to a full grasp of the essence. This interpretation we can still label the *strong version of the stronger reading* of the veracity doctrine, or just the *strong reading*.

Aquinas tells us that our intellect moves from an incomplete to a complete actuality, from a more universal, vague grasp of an essence to a less universal, definite grasp.[48] Before we arrive at the complete actuality of "perfect *scientia*," there is often "imperfect *scientia*" in which "we have *scientia* of things indistinctly and with a certain amount of confusion."[49] Aquinas explains:

It is manifest that apprehending (*cognoscere*) something comprised of many, yet without having a proper awareness (*notitia*) of each of those of which it is comprised, is to apprehend something with a certain confusion. And one can apprehend not only the whole universal (in which parts are contained potentially) but also the integral whole in this way: for in each case the whole can be apprehended with a certain confusion, that is, without apprehending the parts distinctly.[50]

Thus our initial grasp of an essence is sufficient to have an idea, to identify individuals of that essence and make competent judgments about them. And indeed, such judgments issue in *scientia imperfecta*. Yet one is unable to state what all the essential properties are.

In his commentary on the *Posterior Analytics* Aquinas states that in imperfect *scientia*, although the whole of the essence is not apprehended, something of it is, as, for example, "if we apprehend that human being is on the basis of the fact that human being is rational, while not yet apprehending the other attributes which complete the essence of human being."[51] When one has a grasp of some part of the essence in this way, one grasps the essence partially and is in potency to a full apprehension.

It is important for us to appreciate, however, what the imperfect idea is *not*. It is not, for some essential attribute, the idea of whatever has that attribute. In the case of thunder, for instance, the claim is *not*:

(1) The definition of *thunder* is "any noise in the clouds."

This would not be an idea of *thunder* at all, for, as Aquinas says, "not every noise in the clouds is thunder."[52] If the cognitive grasp in question is to be the idea of thunder, then it must be an idea of the property *being a noise in the clouds* as *part of* a yet-to-be-discovered essence. This would involve a presupposition that there is some essence yet to be discovered, and some way in which that essence is signified. The idea must be that expressed by:

(2) The definition of *thunder* is "*a certain sort* of noise in the clouds" (*quaedam sonam in nubibus*).[53]

I am taking the "certain sort of" as a reference to the as-yet-not-fully-known essence. The reference would seem to be in virtue of the instances of the properties which are taken as part of the essence; the phrase in question refers to their underlying cause. As he says in an analogous case, when speaking of using proper accidents in place of unknown essential properties, the proper accidents are used in the definition as "effects of the substantial forms, and as making these forms manifest (*manifestant eas*)."[54] That is, they are used to identify demonstrably the underlying essence which is to be discovered.

As the reader may recognize, I am attributing to Aquinas an

externalism for concepts or, better, a *conceptual externalism*. Conceptual externalism, which is current in philosophical literature, asserts that the individuation of at least some of our concepts not only depends on what is "in our mind" (as we have access to this through introspection), but also depends on the environment.[55] Returning now to the objection raised above, we can see that our initial grasp of quiddities may fall far short of full understanding: one may only apprehend part of the essence and remain ignorant of many or most essential properties. When this occurs, one's understanding may be expressed in a sort of nominal definition in which proper accidents stand in place of essential differences, as signifying the essence which is their cause. When we have such an imperfect grasp, we must employ discursive reasoning to come to a full grasp of the essence. However, in spite of such imperfect apprehensions, Aquinas may still claim that our ideas, our *rationes*, do in fact correspond to the essences causally responsible for the *phantasmata* considered by the intellect, and so do correspond to the essences of things in the world. And thus the natural, essential kind of classifications which the intellect spontaneously forms does, in fact, correspond to the real essences of what one perceives; our intellects in their first operation do "cut the world at its joints." This claim is not trivial, for it assures us that in a given scientific field we have identified and have some grasp of the essences which can be the objects of further inquiry, and the source of the principles of that *scientia*. Thus the power of the intellect and its natural light is such that after our initial apprehension of an essence, although we may have more to learn about these essences, we have a good, initial purchase on the principles of merely human *scientiae*.[56]

4.5 JUSTIFICATION AND WARRANT

We have seen, then, that although one may not fully grasp the essences of things, nevertheless ideas formed in the intellect's first operation do correspond to real essences, and one does grasp some part of the essence. In the intellect's second operation, one understands one's own mental apprehension as in some way corresponding to what actually exists. As Aquinas puts it, "[truth] follows the operation of the intellect to the extent that the judgment of the intellect is about a thing insofar as it is. For it is known by the intellect insofar as the intellect reflects on its own act, not simply insofar as it knows its act, but insofar as it knows the proportionality [of its act] to the thing . . ."[57] The second operation, then, issues in a judgment on the basis of what was apprehended in the first operation. If an essence is perfectly grasped in the first operation, the judgment formed in the second operation is a principle of a *scientia*, such as *Man is a rational animal*, or *Triangle is a figure bounded by three lines*. If the apprehension in the first operation is incompletely or imperfectly apprehended, the second operation issues in the judgment such as *Thunder is a certain noise in the clouds*, or *Eclipse is a certain blockage of light*. The latter judgments are not as yet principles of a *scientia*, but they constitute an important first step in the discovery of principles. Since they are instances of what Aquinas calls imperfect *scientia*, we can call them *imperfect principles*. We will call fully apprehended principles *perfect principles*.

We can now raise certain questions about Aquinas's views regarding the epistemic evaluation of these sorts of judgments. Are such judgments justified? If so, how? Do they possess the positive epistemic status of knowledge, or something similar? Answering these questions is not easy, for, first of all, there is a good deal of confusion in contemporary discussions as to what these terms of epistemic evaluation mean, and before we can answer these questions we must identify some more or less precise sense for them. And secondly, Aquinas does not raise these questions with corresponding Latin terms, and so we must infer his position from what he does, or does not, say. We will deal with each of these difficulties in turn.

The concept of justification in epistemological discussions has a long and complex history, and the word is now used by various authors in different and not always clearly distinguished senses.[58] In this discussion my use of the term will be based upon what I think is a commonsensical notion. In ordinary contexts, when we are asked about a person's justification for his belief that a proposition, p, is true, we are generally asking for that person's *reasons* or *grounds* for believing p. These are the reasons or grounds that the person is aware of, which serve as the basis on which he assents to p.

When people are asked about their justification for a belief in this sense, they may give either of at least two kinds of answers: they may claim that the belief in question is basic or that it has inferential justification. Let us begin with inferential justification. When asked about their justification for a belief, people may offer other beliefs they have from which they inferred (in some way) their belief that p.

For example, Mr. Jones believes the 7:00 am bus will be late, and he believes this because he has been taking that bus daily for the past two months, and it has been at least 10 minutes late every day of those two months. In this case Jones's belief that the bus will be late today is inferred from his beliefs about the tardiness of the bus on each day for the past two months. And so Jones's justification for the belief about today's bus consists of certain other beliefs Jones has together with the inferential relationships they bear to the belief in question.

In another sort of case, one may need no other beliefs as grounds for one's belief that p. For under certain conditions, a person can form a belief which is its own justification, without being inferred from or based on other beliefs. For example, Ms. Smith may form the belief that it is chilly outside. But she does not infer the belief that it is chilly from other beliefs in this situation, she just knows it. We can say this belief, and others like it, are *basic* for Smith.[59] It is not the case, of course, that this belief would be basic no matter how or when it was formed. For example, if it is formed when Smith knows she is chilled from a fever, her belief that it is chilly outside would not be held as basic. When one claims that a belief is basic, it is usually because it is formed under certain conditions – e.g. Smith's body temperature is normal, she has gone outside, she is attentive to the air temperature, etc. When one claims that a certain belief is basic, then, the justification may include reference to a set of conditions such that, when a person forms this sort of belief under these conditions, it is basic for her.

Of course, the justifications which people offer for their beliefs may be open to criticism and defective in some way. If Jones has only taken the 7:00 am bus once, and is basing his belief that it will be late today on his knowledge that it was late just once, we would say his belief is unreasonable. Though Jones may offer this as a justification for his belief, his belief is unjustified. Let us say that a belief is *justified* if its justification for the belief is unimpeachable, according to some specified standards for justification. Of course, in the history of philosophy various philosophers have offered various accounts of the proper standards of justification, but we need not go into these. For the illustrative purposes of the present discussion I have in mind the often implicit and perhaps imprecise ones which guide our epistemic evaluations of beliefs in ordinary contexts.

Furthermore, according to ordinary standards of justification, it may be that a person is in fact justified in believing p and that p is false. If the bus has been at least 10 minutes late every day for the past two months, then Jones is certainly justified in believing that it will be late today. But it may be that, unknown to Jones, every once in a while the bus driver decides to throw his passengers off by being impeccably punctual, and he plans to do so today. He will come at 7:00 am sharp and leave 30 seconds later. In this case, Jones is justified in believing that the bus will be late today, though it will be precisely on time.

Let us turn now from justification to knowledge. For a long time in philosophical discussions it was more or less assumed that to know that p is just to have a true, justified belief that p. With Edmund Gettier's famous counter-examples,[60] and others which he inspired, most agree that having a justified true belief is not sufficient for knowledge. Various and sundry alternative accounts of the necessary and sufficient conditions for knowledge have been offered in recent years, but it is not necessary for us to go into these for present purposes. Let us simply acknowledge that S's knowing that p may require more than that p be true and S be justified in believing p, and let us call the conditions for knowledge, whatever they are, *warrant*. And let us say that one who has met these conditions with respect to some belief that p *has warrant* for this belief, and hence knows that p. According to a more traditional account of warrant, in addition to the truth of a belief, what was required for knowledge were solely truths to which the subject had special epistemic access – those which he could know by reflection alone. These are forms of *internalist accounts of warrant for knowledge,* or just *internalism.* More recent accounts have seen warrant including factors to which the subject has no special epistemic access, and which he need not even be aware of in order to know the proposition in question. A subject knows p, various philosophers have claimed, just if the cognitive processes which produced the belief that p are "reliable,"[61] or his belief "tracks the truth,"[62] or his belief is "caused (or causally sustained) by the information that [p],"[63] or if it was produced by cognitive faculties adapted to the subject's cognitive environment when these faculties were functioning properly.[64] There may be conditions (apart from the condition that the belief in question is true) for a subject knowing something to which, when he knows, the subject has no special epistemic access as to whether or not they are met; and he may be completely unaware of whether or not they are met. Because this sort of account of warrant includes conditions which are in this way external to the awareness of the knower, they are called *externalist accounts of warrant*. This sort of externalism about knowledge is not to be confused with conceptual externalism, which we discussed in the previous section. Thus I will refer to it as *epistemic externalism*, as opposed to the conceptual externalism discussed above.

We can now ask about Aquinas's views on the epistemic evaluation of judgments about perfect and imperfect principles – judgments made in the second operation of the intellect on the basis of quiddities which are wholly or partially grasped in the intellect's first operation. According to Lonergan's interpretation, the justification of these judgments is of the inferential sort. As he writes, judgments in the second operation are made only after "a synthetic apprehension of all the motives for judgment, whether intellectual or sensitive, in a grasp of their sufficiency as motives . . . ."[65] Thus, it seems, such judgments are inferred from a set of beliefs about sense experience and intellectual principles; their justification for Aquinas would then refer to other beliefs from which they are inferred.

I have argued above against the plausibility of Lonergan's understanding of the competence of the intellect in its first operation. Furthermore, there is no compelling textual evidence for Lonergan's understanding of the evaluative and inferential role of the second operation of the intellect.[66] I want to claim that the assertions of perfect and imperfect principles in the second operation of the intellect are basic assertions or beliefs. Presented with certain *phantasmata*, one spontaneously forms an idea in the intellect's first operation, and in the second operation the intellect is moved to make a non-inferential judgment. Such judgments are justified as basic.

Turning now to warrant, some further distinctions are needed and some new terms must be introduced. As described above, a belief has warrant just if it fulfills the conditions for knowledge. We have argued, however, that among Aquinas's epistemic terms there is no wholly unproblematic correlate for *knowledge*, and so it would be foolish to ask whether certain judgments have warrant. Aquinas does, however, recognize certain positive epistemic states. Regarding perfect principles we have *scientia* of the sort appropriate for principles (as opposed to *scientia* of conclusions of demonstrations, which was discussed in chapter one).[67] Regarding imperfect principles we have a positive epistemic state which Aquinas refers to with at least three pairs of terms: *cognitio/cognoscere*, *notitia/noscere* and imperfect *scientia*/imperfectly *scire*. It would perhaps be least confusing to refer to the apprehension of imperfect principles as *notitia*.[68] Thus, although we cannot ask about Aquinas's views on warrant for knowledge, we can ask about them regarding warrant for *scientia* and *notitia* respectively.

Eleonore Stump has argued that Aquinas was an epistemic externalist regarding warrant for certain positive epistemic states. "For Aquinas," writes Stump, "human knowledge [i.e. *notitia*] is a function of our using the cognitive capacities God created in us as God designed them to be used in the world God created them to be used in."[69] I am in broad agreement with Stump that these sorts of conditions are included in warrant for *notitia* of imperfect principles, and I want to extend this to *scientia* of perfect principles. Warrant for *scientia* of perfect principles, then, includes the conditions that the proposition believed is true, that it is in fact a principle (as they are defined in the *PA*), that the subject is justified in believing this proposition – which in this case means he assents to the principle as basic. But, what is more, he would have to meet something like the following conditions: (A) S's cognitive faculties were well designed by God to arrive at the truth with regard to the matters in question in the environment in which S finds himself; and (B) S's belief was formed and is held as a result of the proper operation of these faculties. *Notitia*, as we have seen, is an imperfect *scientia*, for one does not fully apprehend the principle, but grasps only part of the essence. Warrant for this state, though, is similar. For one to have *notitia* the proposition believed must be true; part of the essence, which is imperfectly understood, must be predicated of the subject; the belief must be justified as basic; and his belief must fulfill something like conditions (A) and (B) above.[70]

I say that "something like" conditions (A) and (B) is necessary because I do not think that Aquinas was more precise in formulating his own views about warrant for these positive epistemic states. Aquinas was never pressured by the philosophical debate of his day to make his position explicit and argue against alternatives. (For this he would have had to consider some of the unusual and even bizarre brain-in-a-vat counter-factual cases common in contemporary epistemological debates.) Thus he was never led to make his views on the conditions for the positive epistemic status of *scientia* or *notitia* fully explicit and precise. Nevertheless, I think it is sufficiently clear from what he does say that something like the epistemically externalist conditions listed above are necessary for *scientia* of principles and *notitia* of imperfect principles respectively.

4.6 INTELLECT: THE PRINCIPLE OF 'SCIENTIA'

We began this chapter with several questions about whether and how one could apprehend principles, particularly in the study of natural things, as is required for a *PA scientia*. Could one expect to apprehend all the principles of a natural *scientia*? Could one know them non-inferentially? Could one know them better than one knows the conclusions of a *scientia*? We are now in a position to begin to answer these questions. In its first operation, the intellect by its natural light is able to grasp the essences of the material things which are within the competence of human cognition, and in its second operation the intellect assents to the immediate principles of a *PA scientia*. Although initially the apprehension of certain essences may be partial and imperfect, nevertheless we can be assured that our ideas of essences do in fact pick out real essences, and that they enable us to assert at least imperfect principles, which are an important first step toward the discovery of perfect principles. In response to the first question, then, we can say that on Aquinas's view, one has reason to believe that careful observation of a genus of material beings within the competence of human cognition could put him well on the way to apprehending the principles of that *scientia*. Regarding the second question, we can now see that although ideas formed in the first operation of the intellect emerge from sensible *phantasmata*, essential definitions and principles are not inferred from immediately observable truths by some tentative and fallible abductive or theoretical inference. Hence, principles can be known non-inferentially. And, regarding the third question, we can now see that since principles are not inferred from judgments about what is apparent to sense perception, but are grasped by the intellect which is always veracious with respect to its proper object, the quiddities of perceptible things, the principles can be better known than, or at least as well known as, the conclusions of the *scientia*.

We find a summary of Aquinas's solution (which Aquinas believes was also Aristotle's solution) to some of these problems in his commentary on the final chapter of the *Posterior Analytics*. This chapter completes the work by taking up a question which was raised in the opening chapters, but immediately set aside. As we have seen, the *Posterior Analytics* began with the claim that "all teaching and all intellectual learning come about from already existing knowledge."[71] But in chapter three Aristotle argues that since demonstration can neither be circular nor regress infinitely, there must be indemonstrable principles which, it seems, do not proceed from pre-existing knowledge. In chapter two Aristotle alludes to another sort of *scientia* which is not *scientia* of the conclusion of a demonstration, but this is not investigated.[72] It is only in the final chapter that, as Aquinas writes, "[Aristotle] shows how the first common principles of demonstration are apprehended."[73]

Much of the chapter and Aquinas's commentary on it are concerned with a puzzle: it seems awareness of principles can neither previously exist in us nor be acquired. It cannot be that we already have it, but it is in some way hidden, for "those who apprehend principles have a more certain apprehension than that which comes through demonstration."[74] Yet conclusions of scientific demonstrations are very well known, for *scientia* of these requires that one knows the proposition could not be otherwise. Thus it does not seem that one can apprehend the immediate principles, which must be better known than any conclusion, and yet be unaware of it. On the other hand, it does not seem that apprehension of principles can come to be when it did not exist before. As said in chapter one, all learning is from pre-existing cognition, and so, if the apprehension of principles comes to be, it comes from some pre-existing awareness. But whatever is derived is less certain (*certus*) than the pre-existing cognition from which it is derived. The apprehension of principles, however, must be the most certain, for, according to the doxastic causality condition, it must be the cause of all other apprehension in the *scientia*. Hence, apprehension of principles can neither pre-exist in us nor be derived from any other apprehension.

The resolution of the puzzle lies in recognizing that "it is necessary that there is in us from the beginning some cognitive potency which clearly exists prior to the apprehension of principles; but it is not such that it is more powerful with respect to certainty than the apprehension of principles."[75] This pre-existing cognition, from which apprehension of principles emerges, is sense experience, which, as said above in our discussion of the operations of the intellect, precedes the apprehension of quiddities. From sense perception comes memory of various sense images, from memory and reasoning comes experience, from experience comes the universal "resting in the soul" – the reception of the universal form in the receptive or passive intellect – and from this, by the operation of the active intellect, emerges the universal *ratio* or idea which is the "principle of art and *scientia*."[76] The *ratio* is the principle of *scientia* because once one has grasped it, whether perfectly or imperfectly, one's intellect in its second operation asserts the immediate principles, whether perfect or imperfect, from which the whole *scientia* flows. Apprehension of a principle does emerge from pre-existing cognition, then, for it arises from sense perception, which gives rise to memory, which gives rise to experience, which gives rise to the reception of an intelligible form in the receptive intellect, which gives rise to an abstract idea formed by the active intellect, which gives rise to assent to principles. Clearly, however, apprehending a principle in this way does not emerge from a better-known, pre-existing cognition in the way that apprehension of the conclusion of a demonstration does. The derivation of immediate principles from pre-existing cognition is of a different sort. As Aquinas concludes, "neither does there exist in us a habit of principles as 'determined' and complete; nor does it come into being from some better known pre-existing habit, as the habit of *scientia* is generated in us from previously apprehended principles; but, rather, the habit of principles comes to be in us from pre-existing sense perception."[77]

Aristotle called this process which leads to the apprehension of principles ἐπαγωγή, and this was rendered *inductio* in the translation Aquinas used. It is not, of course, induction in the sense this English word *induction* has come to have in philosophical contexts. It is, rather, the process by which the intellect, by its natural light, abstracts from *phantasmata* a universal idea, and from this one asserts a principle. Although this apprehension is part of and even the foundation of a *scientia*, it is not properly called *scientia*, for *scientia* is discursive. Aquinas calls it *intellectus*, intellect, and he claims it does give us the certain apprehension of principles which a *PA scientia* requires: "No genus of cognition other than intellect," he writes, "is more certain than *scientia*. For, clearly, the principles of demonstration are better known than the conclusions of demonstration, as was stated in book one."[78] Thus, the *PA* concludes, "intellect will be the principle of *scientia*, because it is clear that through intellect the principles of *scientia* are apprehended."[79]

What we have said so far is important for understanding Aquinas's attitude toward the possibility of a *PA scientia*, but it is, as was stated above, only the beginning of an answer to the questions which have been considered. We have discussed only the initial apprehension of principles, which, as we have seen, may be imperfect and generate only what we are calling an imperfect principle. We have not addressed the question of how one moves from an imperfect to a perfect apprehension of principles. This movement is very important for the acquisition of merely human *scientiae*, but we will not be able to examine it in this work, for we must turn to Aquinas's account of our apprehension of the principles of sacred doctrine, the *scientia* which is our primary concern.

Nonetheless, although our discussion of the apprehension of principles in merely human *scientiae* has been limited, we have argued that Aquinas's doctrine of the veracity of the intellect makes a strong epistemological claim: although we may only imperfectly apprehend essences, nevertheless ideas of natural kinds formed in the first operation of the intellect invariably correspond to real essences. Although Aquinas may have thought that scientists of his time only imperfectly understood the respective essences of, for example, earth, air, fire and water, he nevertheless believed they should be confident that these classifications corresponded to real essences. This claim, then, exhibits a high degree of what we might call epistemological optimism about our ability to apprehend essences and principles.

An objector may argue, however, that Aquinas's epistemological optimism is implausible and excessive. Modern empirical science has had great success in discovering the essential micro-structures of natural elements. This has led us to see that pre-scientific classifications of natural kinds, which are based on ordinary observation, do not always correspond to classifications according to real scientific essences. It may have seemed to Aristotle and Aquinas, for instance, that air was a kind which had a single, natural essence, but modern chemistry has shown that there is no such essence, that a variety of amalgams of gases which share only certain salient features are called air. Indeed, for many natural entities modern chemistry has shown not only that through ordinary observation we are unable to grasp all the essential properties of a thing (something which Aquinas recognized), but also that our classifications based on these observations do not always correspond to real essences (something which our interpretation claims Aquinas did not appreciate). But to attribute to Aquinas this sort of epistemological optimism is to attribute to him a great deal of epistemological naivety. Though he did not have the benefit of modern science, he was or should have been astute enough to recognize its possibility. Thus, the objection concludes, either our interpretation of Aquinas is wrong, or we must judge him to be seriously benighted on epistemological issues.

Let us consider first the former suggestion, that our interpretation is wrong and Aquinas did in fact recognize the possibility of revision of our conceptualization of natural kinds in virtue of the discovery of micro-structure. This seems manifestly wrong, for Aquinas rejected the possibility of unobservable natural things or parts of natural things. Speaking of terrestrial bodies, which are corruptible, as opposed to incorruptible celestial bodies, he writes in his commentary on Aristotle's *De anima*, "all corruptible bodies, being either simple elements or compounds of elements, necessarily have tangible qualities [i.e. sensible to touch]."[80] And in the commentary on the *Physics* he writes, "it is not possible that there should be certain parts of flesh or bone which are non-sensible because of smallness."[81] Aquinas, then, seems not to have recognized the possibility of the non-observable theoretical entities which modern science takes to constitute the essential micro-structure of many natural kinds. Thus, Aquinas certainly did not anticipate the possibility of conceptual revision in light of discoveries about micro-structure.

We turn now to the latter suggestion in the objection above, that we should consider Aquinas's epistemology benighted and below par. This seems wrong for two reasons. First, the recognition of non-observable, theoretical elements in virtue of which observable properties are explained did not come easily or quickly in the emergence of modern science. The gradual acceptance of such non-observable entities and properties was a long and intellectually arduous process.[82] We cannot consider Aquinas benighted because he failed to anticipate scientific developments several centuries ahead. Secondly, even though Aquinas's epistemology must be revised in significant ways, there is much in it which can be preserved. As mentioned above, his externalism for *scientia* and *notitia* is similar to Alvin Plantinga's recent account of warrant for knowledge. Although we cannot here discuss possible revisions of Aquinas's epistemology, it seems that in light of recent developments in epistemology, there is much in it which is valuable and illuminating. The prospects for formulating a viable Thomistic epistemology, I believe, are very good, though much work needs to be done.

Although the preceding discussion does not answer all questions about our apprehension of the principles of merely human *scientiae*, it does help us to begin to see how Aquinas thought one could attain *scientia* as the *PA* describes it in these fields. But it also serves to prepare us for a discussion of our apprehension of the principles of sacred doctrine through faith. For, as I will try to show in chapter six, the operation of the intellect in virtue of the light of faith is analogous to its operation by virtue of the natural light of the intellect. However, before we can discuss faith, we must consider in chapter five grace, which makes faith possible, and the theological virtues, among which faith is numbered.

Grace, theological virtues and gifts

Our concern in this and the following chapter is with Aquinas's understanding of the nature of faith, and whether someone with faith can apprehend the principles of sacred doctrine in a manner which would make *scientia* possible. In the *Summa theologiae*, when Aquinas introduces the theological virtues, one of which is faith, he writes:

Human beatitude or happiness . . . is twofold. . . . One is proportionate to human nature, and this a human being can attain through the principles of his nature. The other is a beatitude surpassing the nature of a human being, which a person can attain only by divine power, through a certain participation in divinity.[1]

In this passage, as in many similar passages in the corpus, we find a cluster of interrelated notions: nature and natural principles or potencies, the beatitude proportionate to human nature and that which exceeds natural human powers, and the divine help or grace which God may give so that an individual may attain this higher beatitude. If we are to understand faith, we must understand these key notions. In this chapter, as preparation for our discussion of faith in chapter six, we will consider: (1) nature and natural principles, (2) God's action in natural actions, (3) the obediential potency – a creature's capacity to be moved by God apart from its natural principles, (4) natural and supernatural human goods and (5) grace and the theological virtues.

Some of these topics are among the most controversial for, and most extensively commented on by, scholars of Thomas Aquinas. However, since this chapter is preparatory for the next chapter's examination of faith, we will not treat the issues to be addressed in all their detail and complexity. We will attempt to give a summary of Aquinas's views which will be satisfactory for the discussion of faith in the following chapter.

5.1 NATURE AND NATURAL PRINCIPLES

In *Summa theologiae* III.2.1 Aquinas sketches the etymology and distinguishes the senses of the term "nature" (*natura*).[2] *Natura* (Aquinas thinks) was derived from *nascendo* (being born) and was first used to signify the generation of living things. It then was used to signify the principle of this generation. And, then,

> because the principle of generation in living things is intrinsic, the term *nature* was further extended to signify any intrinsic principle of motion; thus [Aristotle] says in the second book of the *Physics*, "nature is the principle of motion in that in which it is *per se* and not accidentally."[3]

Because the end of a thing's generation is its essence, *nature* then came to signify the essence and also the definition which expresses the essence. It is in this last sense that we have used *nature* above to refer to the quiddity of a thing.

Since we are now concerned with the natural movements or changes of a thing, we are concerned with the third sense listed above, nature as the principle of motion and rest in the thing. For this sense, Aquinas quotes Aristotle's definition and refers to the second book of the *Physics*. There this definition is elucidated by isolating several words and phrases and commenting on each.[4] Aquinas notes, first of all, that the principles are diverse in diverse natures: in light and heavy bodies, there are potencies for movement up and down respectively; in animals, there are active potencies for self-movement. Secondly, the principle is one of both movement and rest (*principium motus et quietis*). *Movement* here is to be taken in the broad Aristotelian sense, which includes any change from potency to act, whether this is change of place, generation, sensation or even the non-physical change involved in understanding. In saying that the principle is of both motion and rest, Aritotle's point is that the principle is not only of the movements or changes in a thing, but of the thing coming to rest when it reaches the proper terminus of its movement. Thirdly, Aquinas notes that the principle is intrinsic, it is *in eo in quo est*. In this respect natural things differ from artificial things, for the movement of the latter requires an artificer as an extrinsic cause. In his commentary on the *Posterior Analytics*, as we have seen, Aquinas says that what occurs through such an intrinsic cause occurs *per se*: "when the subject or some part of it is the cause of that which is attributed to [the subject], this [attribution] also signifies *per se*.″[5] In the *Physics* commentary, as a fourth and separate point, he says that the principle must be *per se et non per accidens*. Under this heading, he makes the additional point that the *per se* cause, the intrinsic principle, cannot be accidentally so, as when the doctor happens to be the one who heals himself. The accidental nature of the doctor's self-healing is evinced by the fact that he heals *qua* doctor, but is healed not *qua* doctor, but *qua* patient. In natural movement, the intrinsicalness of the principle is not accidentally so, and there is not this duality of descriptions of what moves and is moved: when fire moves upwards, it is *qua* fire that it both moves and is moved.

A fifth point Aquinas makes is that the principle is primitive (*primo*). We have seen this term in our discussion of the *PA*, where it is said that in the premises or principles of demonstration the predication must be primitive. There primitiveness is introduced as a further restriction on *de omni* and *per se* predications, and it is illustrated with the claim *Isosceles has three angles*. While having three angles is a necessary or inseparable attribute of an isosceles triangle, it is not as being isosceles, but as being *triangle* that a figure has three angles. When certain attributes belong to whatever possesses a generic form, they are said of them *primitively* in virtue of the generic, and not the specific form.

The above point is not readily applicable to the example used in the commentary on the *Physics*, for that does not involve a generic and more specific form. Aquinas writes:

[Aristotle] then adds "primitive" because even though nature is a principle of motion of composite things, nevertheless it is not [such] primitively. Hence that an animal moves downward is not due to the nature of animal insofar as it is animal, but is due to the nature of the dominant element.[6]

What is his point here? As with the isosceles/triangle case he is distinguishing, I believe, between potencies which belong to something in virtue of its nature and those which, though they are necessary attributes of things with such a nature, do not belong by virtue of the nature specified. For Aquinas, animals are in some sense composites of matter and form. The operations which belong to an animal in virtue of having this nature are self-movement, sensation, generation and increase.[7] So, only those potencies which contribute to these operations are attributable primitively by virtue of the soul. The tendency to move downward, however, since it does not itself contribute to these operations, is not attributable primitively in virtue of the soul. This is so even though the tendency to move downwards is a necessary attribute of animals. Consequently, the tendency to move downwards, though a necessary attribute of animals, is attributed primitively in virtue of the matter of the animal's body, and not its soul. Generally, then, a potency is attributed primitively to what has a given nature only insofar as it contributes to the operations proper to that nature. Potencies which do not so contribute, though they may be necessary attributes of things with a given nature, are not said primitively of them by virtue of that nature.

We find, then, the following progression toward further specificity in Aquinas's exposition of the definition of nature. Nature is of the genus of principle. The principle is intrinsic, and not extrinsic, as we find in artifacts; it is not accidentally intrinsic, as when the patient being healed happens to be the same as the doctor healing; and it is the principle not of any and every movement to which the subject is inclined (as, for example, downwards movement in the case of animals), but only of those movements which are involved in the operations proper to such a nature.

In the above discussion, we have spoken of the potencies which a subject has by virtue of its nature. These we will call the *natural potencies* or *principles* of the subject, and the movements which arise from natural potencies or principles we will call *natural motion* or *movements*. These natural potencies arise from the nature of the thing, but are distinct from it.[8] In diverse natures, of course, they are diverse: fire, for instance, has a natural potency to move upwards; animals have natural potencies for sensation and self-movement.

5.2 DIVINE ACTION IN NATURAL ACTIONS

That we exist, and what we are within the natural order established at creation, are God's freely given gifts to us. Grace, as we are using the word, is some further gift, a supernatural endowment over and above what God gives in creating and sustaining the natural order. To understand this second, further gift, we must set forth at least in broad outline this natural order and the ways in which God acts in the operations of creatures within it, for it is only over and against the divine actions and effects within this natural order that the supernatural gift of grace can be understood. Aquinas's views on

God's actions in the natural operations of creatures are set forth in several places, the most clear and thorough of which are *Summa theologiae* 1.105.5 and *Quaestiones disputatae de potentia* 3.7. Although there are some differences between these presentations, we can extract from them key features of Aquinas's abiding view on divine action in the natural movements of creatures.

God can be said to act in some creature's action insofar as God can be said to be in some way the cause of that action. Of course the word *cause* in the previous sentence translates Aquinas's *causa*, which in turn translated Aristotle's αἰτία, which, as is well known, is said in four ways: it can designate (1) the material, (2) the formal, (3) the efficient, or (4) the final cause. It is under the headings of the final three causes that Aquinas in *Summa theologiae* 1.105.5 discusses the ways in which God can be said to be a cause of natural actions of creatures, and thus can be said to operate in these natural operations. Matter and material causality are not relevant to a discussion of divine operation, for matter is not a principle of action, but is merely receptive of it; God, as pure act, has no intrinsic passive principle.

The two modes of divine causality which Aquinas first discusses are placed under the heading of formal causality. First, God brings into being every creature with its particular nature and proper potencies. But God does not simply bring creatures into being; Aquinas contends that creatures would cease to exist if God did not sustain them in being. In his *De potentia* discussion, Aquinas writes:

In this way God performs all the actions of all creatures, because He gave to natural things the powers through which they can act, not only as the one generating gives power to the heavy and the light, yet does not conserve it as well; but [God also acts] as one continuously holding the power in being. For He is the cause of the power which has been bestowed, not only as the one generating [is the cause], but also with respect to being. So God can be said to be the cause of action insofar as He causes and conserves natural powers in being.[9]

So God is the cause of the actions of creatures insofar as He (1) creates and (2) sustains them in their substantial existence. Though Aquinas discusses these under the heading of formal causality, it is not that God is the substantial form of creatures, but that as their creator and sustainer of their existence, He is the cause of the coming to be and enduring existence of creatures with such substantial forms.

Thirdly, God is the cause of the actions of creatures insofar as He moves them to action. As Aquinas writes: "In the third mode one thing is said to be the cause of the action of another insofar as it moves another to act; which [mode of causation] is not understood as the bestowing or conservation of the active power, but as the application of the power to action."[10] Such "application of power to action" is always for some good which is the end of the action, and this is accomplished in distinct ways in cognizant and non-cognizant creatures respectively. As Aquinas writes:

> In one way, as the agent itself to [its] end, as in the case of a human being and other rational creatures; and to such things it belongs to apprehend the idea (ratio) of the end, and of the means to the end. On the other hand, something is said to be moved or to be put in action because of an end, as an action or direction to an end by another; as in the case of the arrow which has been aimed moved to a target by an archer, who apprehends the end, but not the arrow.[11]

In the latter case, that of non-cognizant creatures, God acts both as an efficient cause moving creatures to their end, and as final cause. In the former case, that of self-moving, cognizant creatures such as human beings, God acts only as final cause. We will consider first the way God moves as efficient cause – the third way in which God acts in the operations of creatures – and subsequently His moving as final cause – which includes both the fourth and fifth ways. The exposition of the third, fourth and fifth ways in which God acts will require a somewhat extended discussion of Aquinas's understanding of natures and causes in the natural world. This digression however will be helpful not only in treating the matter at hand, but also as background for the subsequent discussion of obediential potencies and grace.

As illustrative examples of the natural movements of non-cognizant creatures, let us look at Aristotelian simple bodies.[12] In On Generation and Corruption Aristotle identifies three principia of corporeal bodies: (1) prime matter, (2) the contraries and (3) the four simple bodies. Prime matter is of course the substratum which does not exist apart, but which underlies substantial change. The contraries are the two pairs of opposed qualities which are the distinctive qualities of bodies qua bodies: (a) hot and cold and (b) moist and dry. The fundamentally simple bodies are constituted by a distinctive set of contraries: fire (hot and dry), earth (cold and dry), air (hot and moist) and water (cold and moist). The simple bodies are not the air, fire, etc., which we normally find in nature; they are similar, but purer in their kind.

As we saw in the previous section, for any thing with a nature there are certain natural potencies and natural movements. Aquinas, however, distinguishes several ways in which a movement may be called natural, one of which occurs whenever something is moved by supernatural grace. Yet even within the natural order which is distinct from supernatural grace, there are two ways in which a movement may be said to proceed from such an intrinsic, natural principle, and hence two distinct senses in which some movement may be said to be natural (*secundum naturam*).

Consider the four simple bodies. By virtue of their natures, earth and water, the heavier bodies, have a tendency to move toward the center; earth, the heavier of the two, tends to move closest to the center and water, the lighter, moves next nearest the center. Fire and air, on the other hand, tend to move toward the limit; fire, the lightest, moves nearest the limit and air, the heavier, moves to the position next nearest the limit. In one sense of *natural*, any movement of, say, water to the position near the center is natural to it. Such movement is natural in the sense that it is in accord with what Aquinas calls the *particular nature* of the thing: "for a particular nature is called such according to the order of a particular cause to a particular effect."[13] Aquinas's point here is that a movement is in accord with the order of the particular nature if it is in accord with its natural potencies *considered individualistically*, i.e., apart from anything else which may causally influence it. In the first sense of *natural*, then, a movement is natural if it is in accord with the thing's nature considered individualistically. We can call such a movement or potency for such a movement *individualistically natural*.

Natural things are not only self-moved, however, they are also moved by other agents, and while some of these movements are not natural, some are. When the movement of a natural thing is not in accord with its natural, passive potencies, the movement is not natural, but is what Aquinas calls *violent* (*violentus*).[14] By this he means not that the thing is moved by vehement or destructive force, but simply that it has no intrinsic, natural potency to be moved in this way. When, for instance, water is propelled gracefully upwards by the pumps of the fountains in Trafalgar Square, it is a violent motion.

In many cases, however, movement by an extrinsic agent is

natural. When water is moved upwards by the moon at high tide, for example, it is not a violent but a natural movement. This is because water, along with every other terrestrial, corporeal creature, has a natural passive potency to be moved by celestial bodies. As Aquinas writes:

> If . . . [the effect resulting from the victory of the agent over it] is not contrary to the natural disposition of this subject, there will not be the necessity of violence but of the natural order . . . as occurs . . . in the alternation of lower bodies by the celestial bodies; for there is a natural inclination in lower bodies to receive the influence of higher bodies.

Thus when a thing has a natural, passive potency to be moved by another, the movement is natural, and we can call the mover an *extrinsic natural cause*. Of course, such movement is not natural according to the particular nature of the thing; it is not indivdualistically natural. Rather, it is natural, says Aquinas, "secundum naturam universalem", according to the *universal natural order*.[15] The universal natural order is the order of causes to effects in the natural processes of the world. For ease of reference we will call this order the *UNO*. And so in a second sense of *natural*, Aquinas calls a movement natural if it is in accord with the UNO. We will call such a movement or potency for such a movement *UNO natural*, and we will call a nature as considered within the UNO a *UNO nature*.

When we ask whether God acts in the natural actions of creatures in general, and, in particular, whether He acts in the movements of non-cognizant creatures by moving them to act, it is *natural* in the sense of *UNO natural* which is presupposed. And, in light of the preceding discussion, we can understand how God acts as the efficient cause of the operations of non-cognizant creatures. The celestial bodies are inanimate and moved in their cyclical movements by intellectual substances, and are ultimately moved by God Himself.[16] The celestial bodies, in turn, move corporeal bodies, such as the four simple bodies, to attain their good by acting in accord with the UNO. But any secondary causes, such as the celestial bodies, act only by virtue of their primary cause, which is God. Hence, God acts in the operations of corporeal bodies as the prime mover moving them through intermediary, secondary causes to engage in their proper UNO-natural operations.

Non-cognizant creatures, then, act for an end, but they do not move themselves toward that end; rather, they are directed to the end they cannot themselves apprehend by their extrinsic natural causes, and ultimately by God. For this reason, Aquinas says, "The whole of non-rational nature stands to God as instrument to the principal agent."[17] Human beings, on the other hand, are lords of their actions, and so are moved to their good in a different way.[18] The human will cannot be moved to act by another creature directly, in the way corporeal entities can be moved, but only indirectly, as understood. That is, it can be moved to act by another creature only insofar as that creature is understood as a good or end,[19] or insofar as it is conducive to the attainment of such an end.[20] As such, an object moves the will through the intellect when it is apprehended as good or as a means to the good, and thereby it stirs the will. No creature, however, whether corporeal or non-corporeal, can directly impress itself (i.e. not insofar as apprehended as an object of the will) on the intellect or move the will.[21] God alone can do this.[22]

Although God is able to move the human will directly, He does not do this in the UNO. When a human agent acts within the UNO, Aquinas claims, God moves as final cause. If we are speaking of actions directed to the full vision of the divine essence, the supernatural good for humans, or to the contemplation of God naturally known, which is the pre-eminent natural good, it is clear how God moves human beings to act as final cause. Yet what of human actions which have as their ends other goods, such as knowledge, or health, or social interaction, which are part of the natural human good? How, when these goods are sought, is God the final cause? And, indeed, how is God the final cause of morally bad actions, in which the end sought is not genuinely good?

Aquinas sometimes speaks as if the actions of creatures have God as their final cause insofar as creaturely ends are somehow instrumental for realizing the divine good.[23] Let us say that some end is a *merely instrumental* good if it is good only insofar as its attainment is conducive to attaining some further good which is good in itself. It does not seem that creaturely goods in general, and the human good in particular, can have God as their final cause only in the sense that they are merely instrumental goods conducive to some divine good. First of all, it just seems patently false that whenever humans seek knowledge, health or social intercourse, they are choosing these merely as instruments to the realization of the divine good. Secondly, Aquinas's position is that these basic goods are intrinsically good, and not only insofar as they contribute to some further good.[24] But if this is so, how can God be the final cause when human beings seek these goods?

I believe we can distinguish two ways in which, in Aquinas's view, God can be said to be the final cause of all human actions. First, he suggests that an individual can be said to seek God insofar as he seeks any good, whether genuine or only apparent. He writes, "since every operation is for the sake of some real or apparent good, and nothing either is or appears to be good except insofar as it participates in some similitude of the highest good, which is God, it follows that God Himself is the cause of any operation as its end."[25] Aquinas says here, as he does throughout his writings, that mundane goods are similitudes (*similitudines*) which participate (*participare*) in the divine good. Such terms clearly have Platonic and Neoplatonic roots, as Aquinas himself says in *Summa theologiae* 1.6.4 ("Whether all things are good by the divine good"). There he reviews what he understands as the Platonic view, that something said to be good is truly said to be such insofar as it stands in the proper participatory relationship to the exemplar, the *per se* good. He does not of course accept this view because it countenances subsistent, separate forms of natural things. Yet he accepts that God through His essence is good and plays a role played by Platonic exemplars: "From the first being and good [viz. God], which is such through its essence, everything can be said to be good and to be insofar as it participates in [the first being and good] in the manner of assimilation, albeit remotely and deficiently."[26] Creatures, then, are said to be good insofar as they are similitudes which participate in what is good through its essence, God. Yet, as Aquinas adds, they are nevertheless intrinsically good by virtue of their forms: "Nonetheless each and every thing is called good by the similitude of the divine goodness inhering in it, which is formally its own good by which it is denominated."[27]

Given this Platonic, or quasi-Platonic, understanding, we can see how God can be said to be the final cause of actions whose end is some mundane good, such as non-theological knowledge. I pursue knowledge of, say, physics because knowledge is good. It can be said, then, that what I pursue is goodness, which is exemplified by my possessing this knowledge. As Aquinas writes, "If . . . nothing is inclined to anything as an end except insofar as that thing is good, it must therefore be that the good as good is the end."[28] If my end is the good as good, then it can be said that I act for goodness itself when I seek some particular good. But if this is so, then, though what

I seek is an imperfect similitude of the exemplar of goodness, never-theless I can be said to seek goodness itself. But since God is goodness itself, the exemplar of all that is good, I can be said to seek God in such actions, at least implicitly.[29] It is in this way that we can understand how Aquinas moves from the claim "nothing . . . is . . . good except insofar as it participates in some similitude of the highest good" to the conclusion "it follows that God Himself is the cause of the operation as its end."[30] And in this sense God is the final cause of my actions not only when I act for what is genuinely good, but even when I act for what is only an apparent good;[31] for even then one seeks the good as good.

And, indeed, in this sense God is the final cause not only of human agents, but of all creatures. For all creatures, whether cognizant or not, can be said to tend toward the good as good when they seek their proper natural end, and thus they can be said to tend toward goodness itself, which is God. In this sense, God is the final cause of the natural operations not only of cognizant creatures, but of all creatures. And this is the fourth way in which God acts in the operations of creatures.

There is also a second sense in which Aquinas understands God to be the final cause of all human actions. The end of the divine will is none other than the divine goodness.[32] The end of God's creating, then, is His own goodness. But since God is wholly perfect, His goodness cannot be served by adding something to Himself, but only in bestowing the divine goodness on creatures,[33] each of which receives this imperfectly and each in its own way:

God, who is the first agent of all things, does not act as if He acquires something by His action, but as if by His action He bestows – because [God] is not in potency so as to be able to acquire something, but is only in perfect act, because of which He can impart.[34]

Thus, although any human good is an intrinsic good, its attainment also serves the divine goodness insofar as it is part of the profusion of that goodness.

It seems to be this second sort of divine final causality that Aquinas discusses further in the *De potentia* passage. There he notes that where there is an order of causes, there is an order of effects which corresponds to it. Where we find such an order, Aquinas writes:

Nor can the secondary cause [have any influence] through its own power on the effect of the primary cause, although it is an instrument of the primary cause with respect to that effect. For the instrument is in some way a cause of the effect of the principal cause, not through its form or its own power, but insofar as it participates somewhat in the power of the principal cause through its being moved.[35]

He illustrates this with a brief reference to the example of an artisan wielding an axe. Elaborating Aquinas's example, let us consider the artisan who, not long before Aquinas came to Paris, carved the figure of Christ in the Last Judgment scene above the central portal of the Cathedral of Notre Dame de Paris. His axe, when it meets with the stone with sufficient force, has the potency of chipping it. It does not, however, given just any force, have the potency to carve a figure of Christ in relief; for this it is necessary that a skilled stone-mason wield the axe. However, because the axe serves as the stone-mason's instrument it can be said, in some sense, that it carves the figure. (An archaeologist on a dig near the Cathedral may announce that he has found the axe which carved the figure of Christ on the central portal.)

The end or good proper to each creature is that which is attainable through the exercise of its potencies. God has ordered all creation, though, to attain a universal good, which is the divine end, the profusion of divine goodness. Just as an axe cannot carve a figure in stone without the skill of the artisan, so a creature cannot play a role in attaining the universal good without God's ordering of creation. Insofar as creatures do attain this universal good, they rely on God's power and are God's instruments. Nevertheless, they can be said to attain the universal end, just as an axe can be said to carve the figure of Christ. Since the universal end is the divine end, which is God, God can also in this sense be said to be the final end of all creaturely operations. This, then, is the fifth way in which God acts in His creature's actions.

To sum up, we have considered five modes in which God acts in the merely natural operations of creatures. Under the heading of formal causality, (1) God creates the substantial forms of creatures, and (2) He sustains these creatures so informed in existence. Under the heading of efficient causality, (3) God is the prime mover of non-cognizant creatures as their efficient cause. Under the heading of final causality, (4) God is the final cause as the end of a creature's natural appetite for its proper natural good, and (5) God is the universal end which creatures tend toward as instruments of divine power. However, though Aquinas carefully enumerates the various modes in which God acts in creaturely operations, he is just as interested in defining and defending the autonomy of creatures *vis-à-vis* God. As he writes:

> I respond that some understood that God operates in any operation of anything in the sense that no created power has any affect on things, but God alone immediately effects all; e.g. fire does not heat, but God in fire, and similarly regarding all things. This, however, is impossible.[36]

Because God is creator and sustainer of all creatures (modes (1) and (2) described above), He is the primary cause of their existing and continuing to exist with the forms they have. The substantial forms of creatures are the principles of their proper potencies.[37] So because God is responsible for the forms creatures have, He is responsible for the potencies they have. Furthermore, God moves creatures to their proper end (modes (3) and (4) described above), and they can be said to tend toward the universal good as instruments of the divine power (mode (5)). Yet, although God acts in these ways in every action of a creature, nevertheless the creature retains a certain autonomy. Consider a human being. Given that he has his UNO nature, no further act of God is needed so that he has the various potencies he in fact has; these flow from his nature. Secondly, the exercise of a particular potency on an occasion is due immediately to the creature, and not to God. In these ways, creatures in general and human agents in particular retain their causal autonomy in their proper, UNO natural activities.

5.3 OBEDIENTIAL POTENCY

When God acts within the UNO-natural operations of creatures, He acts within the natural order which He established at creation. He can and does however act outside this order, as when He parted the Red Sea, healed the man born blind and, indeed, when He gives supernatural grace. And all creatures have what Aquinas calls an obediential potency (*potentia obedientialis*, or sometimes *potentia obedientiae*) to be moved in this way. This notion of obediential potency is critically important in Aquinas's account of grace, and as prelude to our discussion of grace we turn now to Aquinas's notion of obediential potency.

Aquinas's notion of an obediential potency became an important one and has been extensively discussed by theologians in the centuries since Aquinas wrote. Aquinas's own remarks about it, however, are relatively few. Indeed, most of what he has to say is found in brief responses to objections to the claim that God can move things outside the natural order. It is through a consideration of these objections and their responses that we can come to grasp Aquinas's understanding, such as it was, of obediential potency.

Aquinas's question was whether God's movement of creatures outside the UNO was violent and unnatural. As we have seen in the previous section, a thing's motion is UNO natural just if it is moved by that thing's own active potencies for movement or in accord with its passive potencies to be moved by another within the UNO. A thing's motion is violent with respect to the UNO order if it is moved by another for which it does not have a passive potency to be moved within the UNO. Since God's miraculous movement of a creature is outside the UNO and so not in accord with the passive potencies of the creature to be moved within the UNO, it seems it is violent and unnatural.

Consider for example the movement of water upwards in the parting of the Red Sea, at least insofar as the event is portrayed in the Book of Exodus. Water moved upwards when the Red Sea was parted, but it was moved neither by itself, nor by any celestial body, nor by any principle acting within the UNO: God moved it as a special effect outside the UNO.[38] But if this movement of water in the Red Sea was not according to the UNO, was it not violent? Was it not against the water's nature, which God gave it when He created it?

In his response to this problem in *De potentia* 6.1.ad 1 Aquinas reminds us that although the upward movement of water at high tide is against the nature of water individualistically considered, it is nevertheless moved by a more universal cause (viz. the moon), for which it has a natural passive potency, and according to a more universal order of nature. Thus, though it is contrary to a certain particular order of nature, it is not contrary to nature *simpliciter*. So it was with the parting of the Red Sea. Aquinas writes:

Just as . . . through a celestial power something can come to be against this particular nature, and this is nevertheless not against nature *simpliciter*, because it is in accord with universal nature; so by the power of God something can come to be against the universal nature which is from celestial power. Nevertheless this will not be against nature *simpliciter*, because it will be according to the most universal nature, which is considered with respect to the order of God to all creatures.[39]

Aquinas here responds to the objection by introducing a *third* sense of *natural*. The miraculous event, though not in accord with the UNO, is natural in that it accords with the *most universal natural order* (MUNO), the order of all creatures to the will of God.

Aquinas makes clear that it is the MUNO which is prior and most fundamental, for it is by virtue of this order that the universal and individualistic natural orders were established as they are. As he writes elsewhere, the causes of the UNO are to be understood as secondary causes of God, but causes by which God is by no means constrained:

Because [God] is not subject to the order of secondary causes, but this order is subject to Him (as proceeding from Him not by necessity of nature, but by freedom of the will – for He could have established another order of things) . . . [God] can also act apart from this established order, when He wills.[40]

The causes of the UNO are secondary causes through which God normally achieves His effects in the world. But the divine will, on which these secondary causes depend, is not constrained by them; God can achieve His effects in different, special ways when He wills it.

The special movement of creatures by God, then, is *supra naturam* insofar as it is above the order of particular and universal nature; but it is not *contra naturam*, for it is in accord with a prior, and more fundamental, order, the MUNO. We will call such movements and potencies for these movements *MUNO natural*. If such movements are in fact natural and not violent, the creature must possess some natural, intrinsic principle which disposes it to such movement. It is here that Aquinas introduces the notion of obediential potency. In addition to the UNO-natural passive potencies creatures have to be moved by other creatures, they have a MUNO-natural potency to be moved by God: "and this is called the obediential potency, according to which any creature obeys the Creator."[41] All creatures have such an obediential potency to be moved in whatever way God wills:

For as from water or earth something can come to be by the power of the celestial bodies which cannot come to be by the power of fire, so from these [elements] something can come to be by the power of a supernatural agent which cannot come to be by the power of any natural agent. And in accord with this we say that in the whole of creation there is a certain obediential potency, in virtue of which every creature obeys God in receiving in itself whatever God has willed.[42]

A difficulty with this notion of obediential potency arises from Aquinas's understanding of the natural good for creatures. According to Aquinas, a creature attains its good through the actualization of its natural potencies. So, the good for any creature consists in the proper exercise of its natural potencies, and the failure to exercise such potencies would result in a failure to realize fully its natural good. But if this is so, then it would seem that, because of their obediential potencies, most creatures fail to realize their natural good, and they fail to do so because God does not act. The actualization of the obediential potency of a given creature depends upon God's special action outside the UNO. But, though He can, God does not act to realize the obediential potencies of most creatures: God could have, for instance, parted every body of water there is, but (as far as I know) He only parted the Red Sea and the Jordan River.[43] Therefore it seems that, because the obediential potencies of most creatures are unactualized, not only do they fail to achieve their natural good, but God is responsible for this failure.

In response to this objection Aquinas says that though a creature who fails to actualize its natural potencies falls short of its natural good, this is not the case for potencies which are obediential: "A certain . . . potency is strictly obediential in the sense that something is said to be in potency to those things which God can do in it above nature, and if such a potency is not reduced to act, it will not be an imperfect potency."[44] Although God created creatures so that the actualization of UNO-natural potencies is required for the realization of their UNO-natural good, this is not so for obediential potencies.

In summary, God can move creatures outside the UNO as He wills. Though such movement is above the UNO (and thus *supra naturam*), it is not against nature *simpliciter* (and thus not *contra naturam*), for it is in accord with a prior and more fundamental natural order, the MUNO, the order of all creatures to the divine will. All creatures were created with an intrinsic, formal, passive potency to obey God's will, and this is what Aquinas calls an obediential potency. But to say that there are such obediential potencies, and that God can move creatures *supra naturam*, is not to say that such movements occur, or what sorts of movements occur. In order to understand why and how God moves human beings *supra naturam*, we must consider the natural and supernatural goods or beatitudes of human creatures.

5.4 THE NATURAL AND SUPERNATURAL GOODS

Of all the controversial areas touched on in this chapter, that of the natural and supernatural goods and their relationship to one another has been and is one of the most difficult and controversial; this is attested to by the staggering amount of scholarly work in the area. However, since the following outline of Aquinas's views is intended to prepare immediately for a discussion of grace and ultimately for a discussion of faith, I will avoid many of the difficulties and controversies and mention others only in passing.[45] Our concern is with giving a general sketch of Aquinas's views on the natural and supernatural good for humans.

The natural good for a human being is specified in the principles of practical reason, which Aquinas also calls the precepts of natural law. The first principle of practical reason is: "Good is to be done and pursued, and evil is to be avoided" (*Bonum est faciendum et prosequendum, et malum vitandum*), and assent to this principle arises from the intellectual grasp of the *ratio boni*, the idea of good. In addition, there are other subordinate, more specific principles of practical reason which specify kinds of goods to be pursued or done and contrary evils to be avoided.

It is certainly a misunderstanding to suppose that the first principle of practical reason is first because the subordinate principles are somehow derived or deduced from the first principle alone. Germain Grisez points out that in *Summa theologiae* I–II.94.2 Aquinas presents the structure of practical reason as analogous to that of theoretical reason.[46] In theoretical reason the first principle is the principle of non-contradiction, assent to which arises from a grasp of the *ratio entis*, the idea of being. That is, one who has grasped the notion of being has grasped that something cannot be and not be at the same time and in the same respect, and this understanding is expressed by the principle of non-contradiction. This principle is first not in the sense that others are derived from it, but in the sense that all other principles presuppose it. Similarly, the first principle of practical reason is first in the sense that all others presuppose it and the *ratio boni*.

The fundamental principles of practical reason, the precepts of natural law, do not straightforwardly specify that certain sorts of actions are to be performed or are not to be performed. Rather, they specify the sorts of goods that are to be pursued by action. In

Aquinas's ethics we find a clear distinction between *goods* to be pursued, which the first principles of practical reason make known, and *norms*, developed in the light of these primary principles, which concern actions to be performed and to be avoided. We can call the goods specified in the first principles the *basic goods* which are to be realized in human life. These basic goods include such things as the preservation of life, procreation, the rearing of children, sociability, knowledge and (natural) religion. Only upon grasping these as goods does one formulate prescriptions that such ends are to be pursued, and that such and such actions, which enable one to attain or participate in a certain good, are to be performed. The emphasis in Aquinas's ethics is on positive precepts which specify how these goods are to be realized in an individual's life. And Aquinas's view is quite compatible with there being a diversity of ways in which various individuals realize the basic goods in their lives.

The natural law, of course, prescribes that the natural human good is to be pursued in human endeavors. As we saw in the last section, for any nature there are principles or potencies proper to that nature, and there is a good – the good of the thing generated – which is attained through the proper exercise of these potencies. The good which a human being may attain through the proper exercise of his strictly natural potencies is what Aquinas calls *imperfect beatitude*. Since imperfect beatitude is attainable through the exercise of potencies one has simply in virtue of having a human nature, it is said to be "proportionate" to human nature: "One beatitude is proportionate to human nature, which a human can of course attain through the principles of his nature."[47] This natural good, imperfect beatitude, consists in the realization of, or participation in, the basic goods mentioned above. In several passages Aquinas seems to suggest that there is an order among these goods, with the highest one being the operation of the highest human potency – viz. intellectual understanding – with respect to the highest object – viz. God.[48] As McInerny points out, however, this good is preeminent but by no means exclusive.[49]

Participation in these basic goods is the highest good attainable by natural human endeavors, but not the highest good possible; this is why Aquinas calls natural human beatitude imperfect. Imperfect beatitude involves a contemplation of God merely as the source and goal of all things, but all the time God in His essence remains unknown. Perfect beatitude, on the other hand, consists in contem-

plation of God with a perfect apprehension of His essence. And
when we attain this perfect contemplation of God, we even become
participants in the divine essence:

Another beatitude surpasses the nature of a human person, and this a
human being can attain only by divine power, according to a certain
participation in divinity. As is said in 2 Peter 1:4, through Christ we have
been made "sharers in the divine nature."[50]

The divine help required is, first of all, some gifts (*gratia*) of God, and
it is had only through the economy of Christian salvation. Such gifts
are the primary concern of the following chapter and will be
discussed at length there. Secondly, there must also be the raising of
the body by God in the afterlife. We turn now to consider the gifts or
graces through which we can attain perfect beatitude.

5.5 GRACE

Some of the most momentous, profound and contentious disputes in
the history of Christian theology have centered on the interrelated
notions of grace, human freedom and the justification of the sinner.
In the patristic period, the most important controversy was between
Pelagius and Augustine. Pelagius understood human nature, human
freedom, the moral law, the example and doctrines of Christ and the
forgiveness of sins all to be grace. But apart from these, he claimed, a
person receives no further help from God to do good, for any further
strengthening of the will or intellect would be incompatible with
human freedom. Augustine strenuously opposed Pelagianism, and
held that grace is a collection of gifts really distinct from nature and
natural perfections, that it is wholly gratuitous and not due to human
efforts, and that it is necessary in order for a human person to do
good. Grace is not incompatible with the exercise of free will,
Augustine thought, but it heals the will and enables one freely to
choose and achieve the good.

Pelagianism was decisively condemned by the Council of Ephesus
in 431, and in the medieval period Aquinas inherited and developed
a broadly Augustinian understanding of grace. Aquinas's account,
which we will summarize in the following pages, set the terms for
subsequent theological discussions, but it did not end controversies.
Many disputes have emerged about grace, freedom and justification,
and often each disputing party has claimed its position is the most

faithful to Aquinas. We will not go into these controversies, but, as we have been doing throughout this chapter, we will present an outline of Aquinas's position sufficient to enable us to treat the assent of faith in chapter six.

According to Aquinas, then, the theological virtues of faith, hope and charity direct us to the perfect, supernatural beatitude which consists in the apprehension of God's essence, and the genesis and exercise of these theological virtues is possible only through grace. The grace in question is what Aquinas calls "elevating grace," for it directs us to supernatural beatitude, an end beyond merely human powers. For a fuller presentation of elevating grace, we will also consider other sorts of graces which contribute to the justification of the sinner.

In the *Summa theologiae* I–II.110.1 Aquinas resolves an ambiguity present in the work of earlier writers by distinguishing three senses of *gratia*, which we are translating as *grace*. Grace, "according to the common way of speaking" (*secundum communem modum loquendi*), has three senses: it can refer (1) to the love (*amor*) or esteem (*dilectio*) one person has for another, or (2) to some gift the lover gives to the one loved, or (3) to the gratitude which one who receives such a gift feels toward the giver. Let us distinguish these with the labels $grace_1$, $grace_2$, and $grace_3$. As Aquinas points out, $grace_1$ is the cause of $grace_2$, and $grace_2$ the cause of $grace_3$. Aquinas's use of *gratia* in his theological discussion is derived from this ordinary sense, but he notes important differences. In human relationships, the love one person has for another arises from some good or goods which the lover discovers in the object of his love. In the case of God's love for creatures, however, any creaturely good proceeds from God's benevolent will, and so God's love does not arise from some good He finds in creatures. Thus the love or esteem of God ($grace_1$) for creatures is not brought about by, but brings about all creaturely goods, and so all such goods are $graces_2$. And, though we could speak of a distinct $grace_3$ as well, Aquinas rarely uses the word in this sense in theological contexts, and so we shall ignore it in this discussion.

As characterized so far, *any* and *every* creaturely good is a $grace_2$ which proceeds from divine $grace_1$. Aquinas, however, draws an important distinction between two sorts of divine love on the basis of two sorts of creaturely good: "One [love is] common, by which '[God] loves all things that exist' (Wis. 11:24) . . . and in accord with it natural existence is bestowed on creatures. Another love is special, by which He draws the rational creature above the condition of His nature to participation in the divine good."[51]

As the quotation points out, the distinction between common and special grace is related to the distinction between natural and supernatural good for human beings described in section 5.4. The natural good for a human person consists in the realization of the ordered set of basic goods. This is attainable through the proper exercise of one's UNO-natural potencies. As we saw in section 5.2, divine action is needed for the exercise of even such UNO-natural potencies: for any such action, God must act insofar as He (A) created the human race (the first mode of divine causality listed in 3.1), (B) sustains creatures, matter and substantial form, in existence (the second mode), (C) is the final cause of the action (the fourth mode), and (D) directs that action, like every creaturely action, to serve the universal good (the fifth mode).[52] Thus in this common sense of *grace* God's grace is needed for any UNO-natural human action, and what is received may be called grace$_2$.

The supernatural good for human beings, the perfect vision of the divine essence, cannot be attained through this sort of common grace and the exercise of UNO-natural potencies. Since the supernatural good is not in proportion to UNO-natural human powers, its attainment requires some further help, some further gift from God. This further gift is special grace$_2$, and it flows from a special grace$_1$ of God. It is this special grace which is our concern in what follows.

Aquinas, in the great majority of cases, uses simply *gratia* to refer to this special grace. Moreover, when he uses *gratia* he is generally referring to grace$_2$, and not grace$_1$. So, in what follows, we shall use simply *grace* to refer to special grace$_2$, unless otherwise indicated.

After the fall of the human race from paradise, the proximate effect of special grace is the justification of the impious; its ultimate effect is the attainment of perfect beatitude. In this context, "justice is said to be in the sense that [the term] signifies a certain rectitude of order in the interior disposition of the human person; that is, insofar as the highest in a human is subject to God, and the lower powers of the soul are subject to the highest – viz. to reason."[53] The various sorts of grace which result in the justice or rectitude of a person can be divided into two broad categories. First, there are those graces by which a person is moved immediately to act, and those by which virtues are instilled. Secondly, there are those graces which result in the elimination of a person's culpability and render his actions meritorious.[54] Since our concern is with theological virtues, we will ignore the second category.

Of the first category, several kinds may be distinguished. One broad category is *gratia gratum faciens*, or *sanctifying grace*, which is that by which the receiver is himself brought to justification. It consists of both *gratia sanans*, or curative grace, and *gratia elevans*, or elevating grace. By the first, one is healed of the corruption due to sin and acquires virtues necessary for natural, imperfect beatitude; by the second he acquires virtues necessary for supernatural, perfect beatitude. We shall consider each of these kinds of sanctifying graces in turn. In contrast to sanctifying grace, there is *gratia gratis data*, freely given grace. This consists of the gifts given to one person for the sanctification of another, such as the ability to perform miraculous healings or predict future events. Freely given grace is not directly related to our concerns in this work, and we shall ignore it in the following.

5.6 CURATIVE GRACE

We look first, then, at curative grace in preparation for a discussion of elevating grace and the theological virtues, which are our main concern. Curative grace heals those suffering the effects of sin, and sin is of two sorts: (1) the actual sins of an individual for which he alone is culpable; (2) the original sin committed by Adam and Eve for which all their descendants are in some way culpable. In *Summa theologiae* 1–11.85.1 ("Whether sin diminishes the good of nature"), Aquinas considers the effects of both these kinds of sin. First, he says that sin does not destroy or diminish our human nature and its potencies. This would be literally to destroy us as human beings, which sin does not do. The original sin of Adam and Eve did, however, completely destroy the "gift of original justice," which human beings enjoyed in the pristine state. This original justice was the perfect subordination of lower to higher powers of the soul, and of reason, the highest power, to God.[55] It was the state of moral and intellectual rectitude which was the terminus of justification of the impious, though for Adam and Eve this was originally instilled from the start, and did not involve turning from an earlier state of sin. It was not due to UNO nature, but was a supernatural gift of grace.

The loss of this original justice was a grave consequence of sin, but its loss cannot have diminished our UNO-natural good. As a special grace, it was something over and above UNO nature; and the good of an individual's UNO nature remains intact whether or not he receives or loses some further grace. Moreover, if God's creation of UNO nature is not defective (and Aquinas certainly thinks it is not), this UNO nature, with or without the further grace, should be adequate for an individual to attain the corresponding natural good. However, Aquinas says that without grace a person cannot not sin either venially or mortally.[56] Thus sin must bring about some impairment of an individual's UNO-natural good. This impairment consists in a second harmful consequence of sin, the diminishing of what Aquinas calls "the very inclination to virtue."[57] Just what this natural inclination to virtue is is an issue important for an understanding not only of curative grace, but of elevating grace and the theological virtues as well, so a more careful look is in order. Although there are such inclinations in both the appetitive and intellectual powers,[58] our concern in the next few paragraphs is only with inclinations for the moral virtues and in the appetitive powers. It is the appetitive powers which are primarily corrupted by sin and more in need of curative grace,[59] and it is these that Aquinas focuses upon in his own discussion of curative grace.

In the *Nicomachean Ethics* Aristotle wrote, "neither by nature . . . nor contrary to nature do the virtues arise in us; rather we are adapted by nature to receive them, and are made perfect by habit."[60] Of this natural aptitude for virtue Aquinas wrote, "there exists in us a natural aptitude to acquire [moral virtues] – that is, insofar as there is in us by nature an aptitude to obey reason."[61] This natural aptitude of appetitive powers is not itself the steady disposition which Aquinas calls a *habitus*; presumably the inclination is not sufficiently strong or steady[62] to be a *habitus*. It belongs more to a potency than a *habitus*.[63] Aquinas does, however, call it an "inchoate *habitus*"[64] and a "seed of virtue."[65] It seems, then, to be a sort of rudimentary inclination of a human potency to act well. Let us call such an inchoate *habitus* a *rudimentary inclination to virtue*.

Inclinations of appetitive powers admit of degrees; they can be strong or weak. When Aquinas says that one's rudimentary inclinations to virtue are diminished but not destroyed through sin, his point is simply that this inclination is weakened through sin:

From the fact that something is inclined to one of two contraries it must be that its inclination to the other is diminished. Hence, since sin is contrary to virtue, from the very fact that a human person sins, the good of nature, which is an inclination to virtue, is diminished. [66]

Aquinas frequently distinguishes the integral state of nature, which Adam and Eve enjoyed before the fall, from the corrupt state of nature, to which those who live after the fall are subject. The distinction, with respect to the acquisition of virtue, cannot be made with reference to the possession or lack of original justice, for, as was said, this was a supernatural grace and not a state *of nature*. It is with respect to the relative strength or weakness of the rudimentary inclinations to virtue that the states are distinguished. [67] In the integral state of nature, one's rudimentary inclinations to virtue were strong and avoidance of sin, both venial and mortal, was a practical possibility. The corrupt state of nature is that state in which one's rudimentary inclinations to virtue, though not entirely destroyed, are greatly weakened. In this state, a person cannot consistently avoid not only venial, but also mortal sin. Since the inclination of the lower appetites to obey reason is reduced, though one may resist the sinful inclination of such an appetite on occasion, one cannot do so consistently over an extended period of time. [68] Similarly, in the corrupt state of nature, reason lacks a sufficiently strong inclination to be subject to God. Thus, though a person can avoid mortal sin on occasion through premeditation, he eventually falls into sin when vigilance is lacking, and especially when unexpected circumstances present themselves. [69]

Consequently, "in the state of corrupt nature the human person is deficient even with respect to what is possible according to nature, and he cannot fulfill the whole of such good through natural principles." [70] Clearly, however, the natural virtues are required for justification of the impious. Curative grace, then, is required for this justification. [71]

The reception of such curative grace involves reception of certain *habitus* – a habit. [72] Aquinas recognizes two broad sorts of *habitus* or habits: (1) those directed in the first place to a certain form or nature (e.g. the humors of the body may be disposed to health or beauty); and (2) those directed to a certain sort of activity (e.g. generosity is a habit for generous actions). We will be concerned only with habits of the second sort. Such an activity-directed habit is an intermediate state between mere potency for an act and its performance. Scrooge, for example, before that fateful Christmas Eve had a mere potency for generous actions, though he was not at all likely to perform any. After that night, he not only had a mere potency for acts of largesse but was steadily disposed to perform such acts in appropriate circumstances. It is this sort of steady disposition that Aquinas calls a habit.

A habit, for Aquinas, is not only of the appetitive potencies, but also of the cognitive. One who cannot speak French nevertheless has a mere potency for speaking it. However, when he learns it he acquires a steady disposition to speak French, when he wants to do so.

Virtus can more or less adequately be translated as *virtue*. It is a habit by which one is steadily disposed to act well.[73] A human potency is open to many actualizations, and one can have a habit for many sorts of actions. A virtue is a habit for the right sort of action. There are not only moral virtues, by which the appetitive powers are well disposed, but also intellectual virtues, by which the cognitive powers are disposed for the right action for such a potency. A virtue is said primarily and simply of one who has a good will, and thus uses all his faculties well. It is said secondarily and *secundum quid* of one who does not have a good will, but who possesses, for example, a certain intellectual habit which perfects the operation of that intellectual potency considered in itself. A person may have a full understanding of nuclear physics, but use this knowledge to make nuclear bombs for irresponsible tyrants. Because such an intellectual virtue can be used badly in this way, it is only a virtue *secundum quid*.

Returning to curative grace, Aquinas regularly distinguishes two sorts: "grace can be understood in either of two ways: in one way, [it is] the divine help by which [God] moves us to will and act well; in another way, it is the habitual gift divinely implanted in us."[74] The first we will call *actual grace*; it consists in a certain actualization of some potency by God, as when God moves the will of an evil person to desire good. The second we will call *habitual grace*; it consists in the infusion of virtuous habits. A person is healed from the corruption of his nature through the reception of habitual grace. But before he can receive that, he must receive actual grace preparing him for the reception of habitual grace: "In order that one prepare himself for the reception of this gift [of habitual grace] . . . we must presuppose some gratuitous help from God who moves the soul inwardly, or inspires the proposed good."[75] That is, one first receives the actual grace of God moving one to will the good. Subsequently, the natural virtues are infused as habitual graces. In this way, a person acquires the natural virtues required for justification.

When God does move the will of a person to desire the good through actual grace or when He infuses habits, Aquinas is clear that the giving of grace is not without the person's free choice.[76] Just how Aquinas understood the compatibility of free will and grace is a difficult and controversial question, and we will not go into it here. It was the subject of a protracted and vehement dispute in the sixteenth and seventeenth centuries between the Molinists and Bañezians, both of whom claimed to be faithful to Aquinas's position.[77] It suffices for our purposes to remember that, for Aquinas, the justification and sanctification of a person is not without his free choice.

5.7 ELEVATING GRACE, THEOLOGICAL VIRTUES AND GIFTS

Gratia sanans, then, consists in the actual and habitual graces by which one comes to possess and act in accord with the moral and intellectual virtues. These virtues are directed to the end which corresponds with the nature a human being has according to the UNO. Let us call these virtues, whether infused or otherwise acquired, *merely human virtues*. With the acquisition of these merely human virtues God is known and loved as the source and end of creation. *Gratia elevans*, on the other hand, brings a person to know and love God as He is in Himself. Since such a knowledge and love of God is beyond the powers of UNO nature, we can only progress toward this end through a grace elevating us beyond that UNO nature. Elevating grace, then, consists in the actual and habitual graces by which we come to possess the virtues of faith, hope and charity. These we will call the *theological virtues*, for they are infused by God, they direct one to God as He is in Himself, and they are revealed in Scripture.[78]

Let us briefly recall the nature of the merely human virtues. The potencies a human being possesses as rational are not determined to one actualization, but open to many. What we are calling the rudimentary inclinations to virtue of a human being are the inclinations of his potencies to action in accord with his natural good or end. Though their strength can be diminished by sin, they are never fully lost nor can they be acquired *ex nihilo*; rather, they are due to UNO human nature. A habit (i.e. an activity-directed habit of a potency) is a steady disposition for a certain sort of actualization of that potency. A virtue is a habit for an action in accord with the good of the given nature. Such virtues can be acquired through one or many actions or they can be infused by God.

Aquinas frequently explains the nature of elevating grace and theological virtues by comparing them with the merely human virtues. But it is the *contrasts*, I believe, which are more illuminating than the similarities. I will try to illustrate his account of the theological virtue, then, by noting some of the more significant contrasts with the merely human virtues.

A first contrast is that, whereas one who acquires the merely human virtues and acts in accord with these virtues *ipso facto* attains the corresponding beatitude, this is not the case for the theological virtues. When one acquires the merely human virtues and these lead one to virtuous actions, one has thereby attained the end corresponding to UNO human nature, which consists in the realization of the ordered set of basic goods discussed above. However, no matter how much one grows in faith, hope and charity in this life, one does not thereby enjoy the beatific vision; although the rectitude which consists in the acquisition of the theological virtues is necessary for the enjoyment of perfect beatitude, it can only be enjoyed when God grants it after this life to one who has these theological virtues.

A second dissimilarity concerns the potency and the rudimentary inclination to virtue. In the case of the merely human virtues, as we saw above, one has by UNO nature a rudimentary inclination toward each virtue. Because this inclination is due to one's UNO nature, Aquinas calls it a natural inclination to virtue and a natural principle. Though this inclination is weakened through sin, it is never entirely destroyed.[79] When one acquires a virtue one, as it were, builds upon this inclination so that there emerges a steady disposition for virtuous actions. But this is not the case for faith, hope and charity:

Because such [perfect] beatitude surpasses what is proportionate to human nature, the natural principles of a human being, from which one proceeds to act well according to what is proportionate [to his nature], are not sufficient to direct the human person to [perfect] beatitude . . . some principles must be divinely added to the person by which he can be directed to supernatural beatitude, just as through natural principles he is directed to a connatural end . . . And such principles of the soul are called theological virtues.[80]

When one acquires faith, hope and charity, then, one does not move simply from a rudimentary inclination to the steady disposition. New inclinations, new *principia*, are necessary.

In the last sentence of the passage just quoted Aquinas says that the infused rudimentary inclinations (*principia*) are called theological virtues. It seems, then, that if we compare the way in which a person is ordered or directed to his supernatural end with the way in which he is ordered to this natural end, the analogues of the theological virtues are *not* the various merely human virtues, but the *rudimentary inclinations* to such virtues. The reason for this becomes clear when Aquinas discusses what he calls the "Gifts of the Holy Spirit." The theological virtues are infused active principles insofar as they are dispositions for self-moved actions. And though they are directed toward a higher object (viz. God in Himself) than the merely human virtues, they are less perfectly possessed: "for [a theological virtue] is possessed as something imperfect; for we imperfectly know and love God."[81] In the case of faith, for example, it is apprehension of God as He is in Himself, and thus is superior to natural knowledge of God through His effects; but it is imperfectly possessed by us in this life, for it does not include a full grasp of the divine essence. And, as Aquinas says, "that which imperfectly possesses some nature or form, or power, cannot act through itself, unless it is moved by another."[82] So, for example, a medical student, though he can handle some cases, cannot handle them all without the help of his instructor. Similarly, since the theological virtues are imperfectly possessed they do not on their own steadily dispose a person to the appropriate acts; thus they are considered simply rudimentary inclinations.

The further moving principle which is required for faith, hope and charity is the indwelling Holy Spirit: "in reason's order to the ultimate, supernatural end, to which it moves insofar as it is in some way and imperfectly formed by the theological virtues, the movement of reason itself is not sufficient, unless there is also added the promptings and movement of the Holy Spirit."[83] The indwelling Holy Spirit is not, of course, a grace in the sense we are using the term, for it is not a created effect in the person but the uncreated deity. There are, however, certain graces which dispose a person to be readily moved by the promptings of the Holy Spirit, and these are called *Gifts of the Holy Spirit* (*dona Spiritus Sancti*): "the Gifts of the Holy Spirit are certain habits by which a human person is perfected to obey readily the Holy Spirit."[84] There are seven such Gifts and each of them corresponds to one of the theological virtues.

We can see, then, that though Aquinas often explains the theological virtues by analogy with the merely human virtues, the former have a distinctly different structure. Simply by virtue of his UNO nature a person has rudimentary inclinations to virtue, and the mere virtues are acquired habits in accord with such inclinations. In the case of theological virtues, however, the *infused virtues are rudimentary inclinations* which become steady dispositions through the promptings of the Holy Spirit and the Gifts, each of which is a habit to be moved readily in accord with such promptings. As Aquinas says:

> In place of natural principles God confers on us theological virtues, by which we are directed to a supernatural end . . . Hence it must be that to these theological virtues there correspond divine habits caused in us, which are related to the theological virtues as the moral and intellectual virtues are related to the natural principles of the virtues [i.e. rudimentary inclinations to virtue].[85]

The Gifts, of course, differ from the merely human virtues in that they are not dispositions to self-moved actions, but they are passive dispositions to be moved by the Holy Spirit.

Let us say, then, that a third dissimilarity with merely human virtues is that theological virtues do not of themselves have the strength and steadiness of a habit, but must be supplemented by certain Gifts of the Holy Spirit if we are to acquire these qualities. Although we list this as a single dissimilarity, it is meant to mark the very different structure of merely human and theological virtues: while the former are self-sufficient habits, the latter are infused rudimentary inclinations to virtue which must be supplemented by the Gifts to become steady dispositions. Since this is so, a person can have a theological virtue but lack the corresponding Gifts. Indeed, one who has faith and commits a mortal sin thereby loses sanctifying grace and loses the Gifts,[86] but he need not thereby lose faith; he still may have what Aquinas calls "unformed faith."[87] In what follows, however, when we speak of theological virtues we shall assume, unless otherwise indicated, that these are supplemented by the corresponding Gifts and the promptings of the Holy Spirit.

So far we have spoken of grace as simply the infused virtues, which are habitual graces, and the actual grace which is the effect of God moving the will. This certainly accords with Aquinas's use of *gratia*.[88] However, when Aquinas asks "Whether grace is the same as virtue" in *Summa theologiae* I–II.110.3, he distinguishes the infused habits from the "higher nature" from which they arise and by which they are directed. As usual, he compares this with the merely human virtues, and he begins by citing Aristotle's definition of virtue: "virtue is a certain disposition of the perfect; and I call perfect that which is disposed according to nature." Aquinas goes on:

It is clear from this [definition] that the virtue of each thing is called such in virtue of its relation to some pre-existing [nature]: namely, when each thing is disposed in a way befitting its nature. But it is clear that the virtues acquired through human acts . . . are dispositions by which a human being is fittingly disposed with respect to the order by which he is a human being; whereas the infused virtues dispose a human person in a higher manner, and to a higher end: hence, this must also be with respect to a higher nature.[89]

Thus the reception of the theological virtues presupposes the reception of some determination of a human being so that he has a "higher nature." This does not, of course, mean that he ceases to be a human being and takes on another substantial form; Aquinas is clear that the reception of this higher nature is an accidental attribute of the soul.[90] Nevertheless, though it is a habit it is not one whose subject is a potency and which in the first place is directed to some activity. The soul, rather, is its subject;[91] and not by virtue of some of its attributes, but "according to its essence." Through it, a person attains a certain participation in the divine nature: "through the nature of the soul one participates according to a certain similitude in the divine nature, through a certain regeneration or new creation."[92] Just as wood, while remaining wood, can participate in the nature of fire, so the human soul, while remaining human, can participate in the divine nature.[93]

This grace which is a determination in the soul is prior to the virtues, for it is their source and principle.[94] Aquinas speaks of the light of this grace (*lumen gratiae*), which is something distinct from the theological virtues and is their rule and measure:

Therefore, just as the natural light of reason is something distinct from the acquired virtues, which are ordered to this natural light, so also this light of grace, which is a participation in the divine nature, is something distinct from the infused virtues, which are derived from that light and ordered to it.[95]

In the person with merely human virtues, the appetitive powers are subject to natural reason, which is in turn subject to God, and which grasps the proper ends and discerns the proper means to them. Such virtues, then, enable one to live according to the rule and measure of the light of natural reason.[96] In the case of theological virtues, a higher light is needed, which arises from this grace in the soul through which we participate in the divine nature. This is the *lumen gratiae*, a light "higher" than that of natural reason. The theological virtues enable us to live according to the rule and measure of this "higher" light.[97]

This, then, is the fourth difference between the merely human and the theological virtues. The former are such as to be directed by the light of natural reason, and natural reason directs toward the end which corresponds to UNO nature. The latter are such as to be directed by a "higher" light, the *lumen gratiae*, and this directs one toward the higher end of perfect beatitude, that end which corresponds to the "higher" nature which is a participation in the divine nature.

5.6 CONCLUSION

This has been a somewhat condensed summary of Aquinas's intricate and highly nuanced account of natural actions in the universal natural order and God's action in these natural actions, obediential potency, natural and supernatural beatitude and grace and the theological virtues. It will serve as background for the discussion of the assent of faith in the next chapter.

One general point has, I hope, become clear in the course of the preceding discussion. This is that, for Aquinas, a real and fundamental transformation in a person is wrought by grace. As St. Paul wrote, "if any is in Christ, he is a new Creation; the old one has passed away, behold, the new one has come."[98] Aquinas did not think of this as inflated religious rhetoric; he took it and statements like it with utter seriousness and applied his genius to making philosophical and theological sense out of them within the framework which he found in Aristotle and developed. Failure to appreciate just how seriously Aquinas took the transformation brought about by grace will lead to a fundamental misunderstanding of his thought. Indeed, many misinterpretations of Aquinas have, I think, been due to such a failure.

Two specific aspects of this general point are relevant to interpreting Aquinas on the theological virtue of faith. First, the differ-

ence between one person without a certain merely human virtue and
another with it is not the same as that between one without and
another with a theological virtue such as faith. Though a miserly
man may not be generous, he nevertheless has it within him to be
generous; he could undertake to perform works of generosity and
gradually begin to acquire the proper virtue. Thus, though he may
lack the virtue of generosity, he nevertheless has the *capacity* to be
generous.[99] This is not the case with the theological virtues, for the
man without grace lacks any inclination to these virtues and lacks the
higher nature and light of grace by which such virtues are measured
and ruled (*ordinare*). Thus, such a person not only lacks the virtues of
faith, hope and charity, he lacks even the *capacity* to acquire them. It
is only with the advent of grace that he acquires this capacity.

A second point is that the theological virtues and their acts cannot
be accounted for fully by merely human nature and its potencies.
The theological virtues require that a person be transformed so as to
acquire a "higher nature" which is distinct from UNO human
nature, and to acquire as the source and measure of the theological
virtues a light of grace which is distinct from the light of natural
reason. If the acts of theological virtues could be accounted for in
terms of merely human nature and the light of reason, then reference
to the higher nature and light of grace would be otiose.

As we turn to the theological virtue of faith, the significance of
these conclusions will, I hope, become clear.

CHAPTER SIX

The light of faith

As intellect is the principle of *scientia* in the merely human disciplines, so faith is the principle of *scientia* in sacred doctrine, for it is through faith that we apprehend the principles of sacred doctrine – the articles of faith.[1] In this chapter we will examine Aquinas's view of faith, and ask whether we can, through faith, have an apprehension of principles which makes the *scientia* of sacred doctrine possible. Thus, as with the discussion of our apprehension of the principles of the merely human *scientiae*, we will be interested in what the justification for our assent to the principles of sacred doctrine is, and what its warrant is. I will argue that our apprehension of the principles of sacred doctrine through faith is in many ways analogous to our apprehension of the principles in the merely human *scientiae*: as to justification, it is basic; and as to warrant, Aquinas held an externalism of a sort which involved conditions similar to those we find in apprehension of principles through the natural light of the intellect. Faith and intellect differ, however, in that the assent of faith results from the proper operation of the light of faith that comes through grace, and not through the proper operation of the natural light of the intellect that we have by nature.

My reading of Aquinas on faith is at odds with standard interpretations in the recent literature, and I will begin by arguing that these standard views are wrong. After a brief summary of some of the obvious and less controversial features of Aquinas's view of faith, we will consider two accounts of the nature and justification of faith. We will first consider what will be called the *naturalistic interpretation* of Aquinas on the assent of faith, for it puts great emphasis on arguments which appeal to the natural powers of the intellect. Subsequently, we will turn to the *voluntarist interpretation*, for it puts emphasis on the command of the will as opposed to strictly intellectual considerations. The deficiencies of naturalism and voluntarism will help us to see what is needed for a more adequate interpretation, and in the next section I will go on to argue for my interpretation. Finally, I will consider the important question of the role of the will in faith.

In many contemporary discussions *to have faith* means simply "to believe that God exists." For Aquinas the belief that God exists not only does not constitute faith, it is not, strictly speaking, even a part of faith. So before considering the naturalist, or any other, interpretation of Aquinas on faith's justification and warrant, we must say something about how he understood the nature of faith.

Although the interpretation of some of Aquinas's claims may be controversial, it is at least clear that he makes the following claims. The formal object of faith is simply the first truth, which is God; the material object is God and other things insofar as they are related to God.[2] The human intellect, however, considers what is utterly simple, God, through considering what is complex.[3] Thus faith consists in believing certain propositions, which are the articles of the Creed.[4] Aquinas insists that we cannot have perfect *scientia* of the articles of the Creed in this life,[5] for that would require a complete understanding of the divine essence, which is beyond us on this earth.[6] Certain other propositions which are not articles of the Creed, such as *God exists* and *God is one*, can be demonstrated by a demonstration *quia* – a demonstration which proceeds from effects to causes – and of these propositions one with a demonstration has *scientia quia*, while they are believed by way of an assent of faith (*per modum fidei*) by others who have not encountered or cannot understand the demonstration.[7] These latter propositions are not articles of faith but preambles of faith (*preambula fidei*).[8]

Propositions believed as part of faith are believed on the basis of divine authority.[9] They are believed with as firm a conviction as if one had *scientia* of them.[10] This assent is due to a command of will,[11] and it is meritorious.[12] Corresponding to the "inner act of faith," the assent just described, there is an "outer act of faith," which is public confession on certain occasions of what one believes as part of faith.[13] Faith is an infused, theological virtue, as is clear from the discussion in the previous chapter, and as such it requires grace. Furthermore, as a theological virtue, it directs its possessor to the supernatural end of perfect beatitude.

6.2 THE NATURALIST INTERPRETATION

What then is Aquinas's account of the justification for the assent of faith? Several prominent contemporary philosophers of religion have endorsed a certain line of interpretation of Aquinas on this issue, which I will call the *naturalist interpretation* (and abbreviate *NI*).[14] The NI holds that Aquinas thought that, at least in the case of some persons, the individual assents to the articles of the Christian Creed because he accepts a cluster of arguments from natural theology. Such a person first is convinced, by metaphysical arguments of natural or philosophical theology, that God exists. Subsequently he believes on the basis of testimony and other evidence that there were miracles and signs in Biblical times and in the history of the Church. From these beliefs he is led to the conclusion that God has made revelations in history, and that the essence of these revelations is contained in the Christian Creed as this is defined by the Church. Thus the individual assents to the articles of the Creed because he accepts, first, proofs of philosophical theology which purport to show that God exists, and second, arguments from testimony of miracles and signs from Scripture and the history of the Church that what the Church claims to have been God's revelation is in fact such, and hence is to be believed. Let us call this cluster of arguments the *arguments from the evidence of credibility* or just *credibility arguments*. The evidence they adduce we will call *credibility evidence*. As we are taking the NI, the assent of faith is justified for Aquinas because the individual assents on the basis of these credibility arguments, which are that person's justification for his assent.

I will go on to raise a series of objections to the NI. The first and perhaps the second are not likely to trouble the naturalistic interpreter a great deal; they are raised so that this interpretation may be further elaborated. However, the later objections are more serious.

An objector may complain that the person with faith does not have *scientia* of the propositions to which he assents; he has not fully understood the divine essence and thereby immediately grasped the truth of these propositions. Yet the assent of faith is supposedly firm and without doubt. It seems, then, either that the firmness of this assent is arbitrary and irrational or that the individual is able to grasp the truth of the propositions.

The naturalistic interpreter can respond to this by directing our attention to Aquinas's distinction between full *scientia* and other sorts of cognition. As we have seen, for Aquinas *scientia* is knowledge which arises from an immediate grasp of the truth of principles or from demonstrations from such principles. Yet I may come to the firm conviction that a proposition is true without grasping its truth in the way of *scientia*. I may come to believe it on the authority of another though I have not established its truth on my own. This kind of apprehension is even compatible with failing to understand the content of the proposition, as when a person believes that photons are posited by Planck's theory even though, being a wash-out in physics, he only has the most rudimentary grasp of Planck's theory and what photons are. Similarly, though our understanding of the propositions of the Creed is very limited,[15] and though we do not have full *scientia* of them, nevertheless we still may believe that these propositions are true with firm conviction and in a non-arbitrary manner.

A second difficulty arises from the fact that the NI as so far presented cannot hope to be an account of the assent of most Christian faithful. Most of the Christian faithful in Aquinas's time were not only unable to make competent judgments about rather complex metaphysical and historical arguments, they were illiterate and could not even read the arguments of philosophers; thus they could not come to assent by way of accepting the credibility arguments. With regard to this issue the naturalistic interpreter will simply point to the qualification in the above formulation of this interpretation, that assent is on the basis of credibility arguments "at least in the case of some persons." The NI distinguishes – as Aquinas distinguished – between those who have the education and intellectual sophistication to understand and make competent judgments about these arguments and those who do not. Let us label the former class the *sophisticates* and the latter the *simple*. Given the NI's presupposition that the justification of assent of faith comes from arguments which appeal to natural reason, the most plausible account for justification for simple believers is that their assent arises from accepting the testimony of the sophisticates that God exists and has revealed what is contained in the Creed. That is, the simple person of faith believes a (or some) sophisticate(s) who affirm(s) that God exists and that God has revealed the articles of the Creed as the Church teaches these. He believes this because he believes that the sophisticate has sufficient evidence for his beliefs, though he need not know what this is, or even be able to understand it.

The NI, then, must give one account of the justification of the sophisticates and another of the simple. But the difficulty here for the NI is that, as far as I know, Aquinas never says that the simple must hear or believe the testimony of the sophisticates regarding the credibility arguments. This is somewhat surprising, for most Christians in Aquinas's day would have been simple believers. It is difficult to explain why Aquinas did not say more about the justification of their faith.

Perhaps the naturalistic interpreter can make a cogent response to this and perhaps he cannot. In what follows, however, I will leave the question of the faith of the simple and focus on that of the sophisticates. If the NI is right, the justification of the simple is in some way derived from or dependent on that of the sophisticates, and the NI suggests that Aquinas concerned himself with the latter. Hence, if the NI cannot be defended on the question of the faith of the sophisticates, it certainly cannot be defended on the question of the simples' faith. In the subsequent discussion, then, when I speak of a believer or prospective believer it will be a sophisticated believer of whom I will be speaking.

A third objection, which concerns the *naturalist* character of the NI, is more serious. As suggested above, the credibility arguments are meant to appeal to the UNO-natural intellectual powers of a person who is sufficiently perspicacious and intent on seeking the truth. This seems clear from the writings of advocates of this interpretation. Terence Penelhum, for instance, argues from what Aquinas says of the faith of devils to his view on human faith, and concludes that Aquinas clearly opts for the view that "the believer does have enough evidence to convince him beyond reasonable doubt."[16] Thus, although grace is needed for assent without reluctance, the prospective believer "will not need it because of any inconclusiveness in what he hears."[17] That is, he may need grace to move the *will*, but not the *intellect*. John Hick wonders "whether these *preambula fidei* [i.e. the credibility arguments] are held to be rationally compelling, so that *anyone who examines them and who is not prejudiced* [italics mine] against the truth must acknowledge them, or whether, on the contrary, some degree of faith enters into acceptance."[18] Although Hick does not find Aquinas clear on the matter, he eventually opts for the former disjunct, that the credibility arguments are compelling to anyone who has natural intellectual powers and is not prejudiced. Obviously, no special illumination is required for this. Alvin Plantinga begins his brief discussion of Aquinas with a discussion of his general account of UNO-natural knowledge in general, and then goes on to apply this to the assent of faith; and he says that this assent to the articles of faith is not irrational because "we have *evidence for* the conclusion that God has proposed them for our belief."[19] Clearly the suggestion is that this evidence appeals to the UNO-natural intellect.

At the end of the last chapter two points were made about the difference between theological virtues and what we are calling merely human virtues. First, in the case of a merely human virtue, such as knowledge of French, although one may lack the virtuous habit, any person without some special defect has the capacity to acquire it; he can move to Paris or enroll in a French class. But in the case of a theological virtue a person without elevating grace lacks not only the habit but also the capacity to attain it; until elevating grace is bestowed, there is nothing he can do which of itself will bring him to faith. The second difference is that, for a merely human virtue, the corresponding act can be explained in virtue of UNO-natural potencies and principles. For a theological virtue, however, new principles, new rudimentary inclinations and different causes of the steady disposition must be introduced. But according to the NI the credibility arguments are such that any person of normal intelligence who understands them will be moved to assent, and his assent can be explained in virtue of UNO-natural intellectual powers alone.

The need for new principles for the assent of faith is not only clear from Aquinas's general discussion of the theological virtues in *Summa theologiae* I–II; he also makes the point explicitly in his discussion of faith. In *Summa theologiae* II–II.6.1 ("Whether faith is infused by God") Aquinas writes:

But with respect to . . . the assent of a human person to those things which belong to faith, two causes can be considered. One is that which leads externally: as a miracle which is witnessed, or the persuasion of another human leading [one] to faith. Neither one of these is a sufficient cause, for of those who witness one and the same miracle, or hear the same speech, some believe and some do not. And therefore we must posit a further interior cause, which moves a human being internally to assent to what belongs to faith. . . . For because a human being who assents to what belongs to faith is elevated above his nature, it must be that this occurs in him from a supernatural principle moving internally, which is God. And therefore faith, as regards the assent of faith (which is the principle act [of the theological virtue] of faith), is due to God moving internally through grace.[20]

In this passage Aquinas says that certain credibility arguments have a role in moving one to assent, though what this role is is not entirely clear from this passage. What is clear is that such arguments are not sufficient to move the UNO-natural intellect to assent; grace is required. Yet according to the NI the credibility arguments are sufficient.

The objection to the NI, then, is that it fails to account for Aquinas's repeated and explicit statements about the necessity of grace. Penelhum is the only one who addresses this problem. He writes, "if [as Penelhum holds] the believer has, or can have, evidence sufficient to establish conclusively the authority of whoever speaks to him, then even though he may need grace to enable him to accept what it says *without reluctance*, he will not need it because of any inconclusiveness in what he hears."[21] Penelhum's suggestion is that grace is needed for the will to command assent without reluctance, but no grace is needed in the intellect. But this suggestion is unsatisfactory on two grounds. First, no further powers or principles beyond those of the UNO nature are needed in order for the will to command assent to propositions which are within its power to apprehend, but which one may be reluctant to acknowledge. If such acts of will did require something beyond UNO nature, then we would need grace to grasp truths about even mundane, material objects which we were reluctant to grasp (e.g. an unwelcome moral truth). Aquinas says, however, that grace is not needed to apprehend truths about mundane matters.[22] Secondly, Aquinas speaks of the *lumen fidei*[23] which, along with the *lumen prophetiae*, is a *lumen gratiae*.[24] This is an infused light of the intellect,[25] a grace, and is necessary for the assent of faith. Penelhum's suggestion fails to account for this infused light *of the intellect*.

Another serious objection to the NI is that Aquinas says repeatedly that the conclusions of arguments of natural theology are significantly less certain than the beliefs of faith. In the *Scriptum super libros sententiarum*, a very early work, Aquinas writes: "And to the objection that one is not most certain in this doctrine, we say this is false: for one assents more faithfully and firmly to what belongs to faith than [one does] even to the first principles of reason."[26] And in the *De veritate*, regarding the firmness of the conviction of the assent

of faith, he says "faith is more certain than all understanding and
scientia . . ."[27] Since the first principle of theoretical reason is the
principle of non-contradiction, these passages imply that the faithful
hold the articles of faith with greater conviction than the principle of
non-contradiction. If this is Aquinas's view, then it is clear that no
proposition believed on the basis of credibility arguments can attain
the required degree of certainty. In his more mature works,
however, Aquinas does not, as far as I know, make such a strong
claim for the certainty of the assent of faith. Nevertheless, he does
write in the *Summa*:

> With respect to matters having to do with divinity human reason is most
> deficient: a sign of this is that philosophers, who through investigations of
> natural reason study human affairs, have fallen into many errors and have
> contradicted one another. Therefore, so that there would be indubitable
> and certain cognition about God among humans, it was necessary that
> divine matters be passed on to them in the manner of faith, as something
> said by God, who cannot lie.[28]

This passage clearly implies that the beliefs of faith are held with
greater certainty than the conclusions of arguments of philosophy
and natural theology. Yet if, as the NI has it, one is moved to faith by
the credibility arguments, the resulting beliefs are held on the basis
of such philosophical and theological arguments.[29]

Another difficulty for the NI is that Aquinas seems to deny that the
articles of the Creed can be established by any sort of argument. In
the first question of the *prima pars* of the *Summa*, which serves as a
kind of preface to the whole work, article eight is headed "Whether
sacred doctrine is argumentative." The doctrine he refers to is sacred
doctrine, which is the *scientia* of revealed, Christian theology whose
first principles are the articles of faith. If these first principles of
sacred doctrine can be established by arguments from credibility
evidence, we would expect Aquinas to give some indication of this
role of argumentation here. Instead he explicitly denies that the
articles of faith can be straightforwardly established by discursive
argument: "This doctrine does not argue to prove its principles,
which are the articles of faith; but from these one proceeds to
establish something else . . ."[30]

The advocate of the NI may respond that Aquinas is here making
only a formal point about the kind of demonstrations that are
possible in sacred doctrine: sacred doctrine, like any other *scientia*,
does not prove its own principles, the articles of faith, though there

may be proofs for them outside the *scientia* (as the principles of optics can be proven in geometry, but not in optics). However, it is clear from the remainder of the corpus of this article that Aquinas's point cannot be this merely formal one. His argument is based on an analogy between what he calls the philosophical *scientiae*, which are all the *scientiae* not based on revelation, and sacred doctrine, which is so based. Among the former, Aquinas acknowledges, a subaltern *scientia*, such as optics, "neither proves its principles nor disputes with those who deny them, but leaves this to the higher *scientia*." But because metaphysics is the highest of the philosophical *scientiae*, it cannot refer disputes about its principles to a higher *scientia*, but must take them up on its own. Though it cannot prove its principles, it can dispute with one who denies them, but only if the opponent concedes some of its principles. Otherwise it cannot dispute with him, but can only resolve objections brought against those principles.

Sacred doctrine, Aquinas writes, is in the same position as metaphysics regarding its principles:

Hence Sacred Scripture [i.e. sacred doctrine], since it does not have a superior *scientia*, disputes with one denying its principles by arguing, if the adversary concedes something of that which has been divinely revealed (as we dispute with heretics through the authority of sacred doctrine, arguing from one article against those who deny another); but if the adversary believes none of the things which have been divinely revealed, there remains *no other way to prove the articles of faith through arguments*; it is possible only to resolve objections, if any are brought forward against faith.[31]

The point here is clearly that the parties concerned must believe something of revealed truth before discursive arguments for articles of faith can be adduced. But if Aquinas thinks this is so, clearly he cannot also believe that credibility arguments can move a normal, unbiased but unbelieving person to assent to the articles of faith, for these arguments would then constitute a "way to prove the articles of faith through arguments."

The above objections adduce some passages and doctrines of Aquinas which the NI has not accounted for and seems unable to account for. Now I want to turn to some passages which advocates of the NI have adduced in support of their interpretation. I will argue that these not only fail to provide support for the NI, they support its denial.

Penelhum finds "an unresolved tension between Aquinas's insistence that the propositions of faith are not established conclusively and his insistence that the assent to those propositions is a rational assent."[32] But in *Summa theologiae* II–II.5.2, he thinks, Aquinas "commits himself unequivocally to the view that the evidences of the authority of the Church [i.e. the credibility evidence] are such as can compel assent,"[33] and such assent, he suggests, is the genuine assent of faith. In this article, Penelhum believes, Aquinas is faced with a class of beings – devils – who have faith, but who assent with a bad will and without the help of grace. Thus a devil is "convinced solely by the strength of the evidence."[34] Penelhum concludes that evidence for assent to the articles of faith must be sufficient for the human believer as well, although he believes willingly:

If the believer and the devil differ only in the presence of absence of merit, and this is the result of the disposition of their respective wills, then *either* the devil does not have enough evidence to convince him beyond reasonable doubt, *or* the believer does have enough to convince *him* beyond reasonable doubt. Thomas clearly opts for the second alternative. But if the believer has, or can have, evidence sufficient to establish conclusively the authority of whoever speaks to him then even though he may need grace to enable him to accept what it says *without reluctance*, he will not need it because of any inconclusiveness in what he hears.[35]

Penelhum, therefore, endorses the NI, the position that the credibility evidence is sufficient to bring about assent in one who considers it impartially and carefully in the light of the UNO powers of the intellect. A good will and grace are needed only to bring about willing and meritorious, as opposed to grudging and unmeritorious, assent.

Penelhum's reading of *Summa theologiae* II–II.5.2 is highly problematic. First, the considerations offered above against a naturalist interpretation of Aquinas generally tell against a naturalistic reading of this article. Secondly, while Penelhum wants to understand Aquinas as *likening* the devils' assent to that of humans, in this article he seems more concerned to *distinguish* them. Thirdly, the attempt to see Aquinas as likening the devils' assent to human assent is very odd given that, as we saw in chapter two, angelic beings (among which are devils, the fallen angels) have different and greater cognitive powers than humans, and have a different and superior access to information. Penelhum seems to recognize that his reading does not fit with much of what Aquinas says, for he admits to finding an "unresolved tension" in Aquinas's writing on this issue.[36]

A non-naturalistic, alternative reading of this article is much more plausible. The article addresses the question: "Whether there is faith in devils." The answer to this question is not in any doubt for Aquinas, since a passage from the Letter of James in Scripture, which Aquinas cites in the *sed contra* of this article, unambiguously asserts that they do: "Show me your faith apart from your works, and I by my works will show you my faith. You believe that God is one; you do well. Even the demons believe – and shudder."[37] The real question is *how* the devils, who by their sin have lost the gift of grace, can have faith. Aquinas's response is to distinguish the faith of devils from that of Christian believers. He writes:

The will's moving the intellect to assent can happen in two ways. In one way, from the order of the will to good; and believing in this way is a laudable act. In another way, the intellect is convinced by the considerations which are presented that what is put forward is to be believed, but it is not convinced through evidentness of the thing itself [which is believed]. . . . It is to be said, therefore, that among Christ's faithful faith is laudable according to the first mode. And faith is not present in devils in this way, but only in the second way.[38]

There are, then, two ways in which the will can move the intellect to the assent of faith. The first of these is laudable and is found in the Christian faithful; the second is not and is found in the devils. The first is due to the "order of the will to the good"; the second is due to the fact that "the intellect is convinced . . . that what is put forward is to be believed." The first then is due to the desire for the good; the second to the compulsion of evidence on the mind. In his response to the second objection of this article Aquinas tells us explicitly that the devils' faith is due simply to the influence of credibility evidence on their UNO-natural intellects, but human faith is not:

Faith which is a gift of grace inclines a human being to believe in accord with some affection for the good, even if it is unformed. Hence faith which is in devils is not a gift of grace; rather, they are to a greater degree forced to believe from the perspicacity of the natural intellect.[39]

That the evidence is sufficient to convince the UNO-natural intellects of devils but not humans, as Aquinas clearly indicates it is, is due to the fact that devils have greater natural cognitive abilities. Aquinas describes these in *Summa theologiae* 1.64.1. Truth is apprehended (*cognoscitur*) by a intelligent creature either by nature or grace, and since grace in this operation can be twofold, apprehension (*cognitio*) comes in three ways: (1) through purely natural cognition, (2) through a purely theoretical or intellectual graced cognition and (3) through an affective graced cognition quickened by desire and issuing in love for God. The third of these was destroyed in the devils when they fell from blessedness, but the first remains intact and the second remains in a diminished form.

Regarding the first, natural cognition, the devils have greater abilities to apprehend an incorporeal God because they are incorporeal and thus the way they apprehend is incorporeal: "An angel can . . . have a more exalted apprehension about God through its nature than a human being, because of the perfection of its intellect. And such apprehension about God remains also in devils."[40] Regarding the second form of cognition, a purely theoretical cognition achieved through grace, a devil, just like an angel, has access to certain revealed truths which a human cannot have. As Aquinas writes: "all angels from the beginning apprehended in some manner the mystery of the reign of God, which was fulfilled through Christ."[41] Although the access to the revealed truths was diminished by the devils' fall, it was not totally lost; the devils still received communications from the blessed angels after the fall.[42] Consequently, because the angels have cognitive abilities superior to humans', and because they have access to certain revealed truths which humans do not have, they can, through the evidence of signs, be intellectually convinced of certain truths in a way in which humans cannot be. This is why devils do not need a good will in order to come to faith, and hence why their faith is not laudable: "the faith of devils is forced by the evidence of the signs. And therefore it does not accrue to praise of the will of those who believe."[43] The NI, then, is correct with regard to the faith of devils: their assent does arise from a consideration of the credibility evidence in the light of their UNO-natural intellect. As such, their faith is "forced from them by the evidence of the signs". But Aquinas indicates clearly in article eight that this is *not* the way human beings can or do come to faith, for their faith is of a fundamentally different nature. As Aquinas says in the *De veritate*: "*to believe (credere)* is said equivocally of the human faithful and devils, and faith is not in [devils] from some infused light of grace, as it is in the [human] faithful."[44] *Summa theologiae* II–II.5.2, therefore, does not commit Aquinas to the naturalist position. On the contrary, it commits him to the view that human faith does not arise from an impartial consideration of the credibility evidence with UNO-natural intellectual faculties; it requires some infusion of grace.[45]

Alvin Plantinga cites *Summa contra gentiles* 1.6 in support of his reading of Aquinas. In this passage Aquinas presents arguments from credibility evidence to show that the assent of faith is not foolish ("Assentire his quae sunt fidei non est levitatis quamvis supra rationem sint"). About this passage Plantinga writes:

What [Aquinas] means to say, I think, is that to believe in the mysteries of faith is not foolish or to believe with undue levity, because we have *evidence for* the conclusion that God has proposed them for our belief. The evidence consists in the fulfillment of prophecy and in the signs and wonders accompanying these mysteries . . . I think he means to suggest, furthermore, that if we did *not* have this evidence, or some other evidence, we would be foolish or irrational to believe. It is just because we have evidence for these things that we are not irrational in accepting them.[46]

As I said above, we are taking Plantinga to be saying that the evidence to which he refers appeals to the UNO-natural intellect, and he seems to be saying here that such evidence is necessary and sufficient for the assent of faith to be rational. Let us look more closely at the passage on which Plantinga bases his interpretation, which is the following:

To such truth "of which human reason does not provide a test," those having faith do not believe lightly as if they are ignorant people "following fables" (2 Peter 1:16). For the Divine Wisdom itself, which knows all things most fully, deigned to reveal to humans these divine "secrets of wisdom"; and He shows by fitting arguments His presence and the truth of doctrine and inspiration, while to confirm these things which exceed natural cognition He shows visible works which surpass the power of the whole of nature – namely, wondrous healing of the sick, raising of the dead, alteration of moveable celestial bodies, and, what is more wondrous, the inspiration of human minds so that even the uneducated and simple-minded, filled with the Gift of the Holy Spirit, in an instant attain the highest wisdom and eloquence. Having considered these things, through the efficacy of the previously mentioned proofs – not by violence of arms, nor the promise of sensual delights, and, what is most wondrous, amid the tyranny of persecutions – a countless crowd not only of the simple, but even of the wisest of humans, flocked to Christian Faith, in which things surpassing the human intellect are preached, the delights of the flesh are curbed and contempt for all worldly things is taught. That the souls of mortals assent to these things is the greatest of miracles, and it is manifestly a work of divine inspiration that, while having contempt for visible things, people desire invisible things. And that this has come to be neither spontaneously nor by chance, but from divine disposition, is evident from the fact that God predicted that it would occur in many oracles of the prophets, whose books we hold in veneration as bearing witness to the testimony of faith [SCG 1.6].

It seems strange that Plantinga should support his naturalistic interpretation with this passage. For, first, in it Aquinas says the greatest of miracles (*maximum miraculorum*) is that the minds of mortal men assent to what is presented for faith. But if the credibility evidence is sufficient to convince the UNO-natural intellect, it is very hard to see why Aquinas calls the assent of faith the greatest of miracles. Secondly, Aquinas makes a point of mentioning the assent of the uneducated and simple-minded (*idiotae et simplices*). But this does not favor Aquinas's case as Plantinga presents it, for it would seem that they are the worst judges of whether there is sufficient evidence for the assent of faith. Thirdly, Aquinas criticizes Islam and contrasts it with Christianity on the grounds that the former's proofs are too readily understandable and persuasive: "[Mohammed] brought forward only the proof of truth which can easily be apprehended by any moderately wise person by means of his natural ingenuity."[47] But if Plantinga is right about the passage in question, Aquinas seems to be doing the same thing for which he criticizes the Muslims.

Plantinga, I think, has misread this passage. In it Aquinas is citing credibility evidence because, as I suggest below, these are "fitting arguments" (*convenientia argumentiva*, as Aquinas calls them in this passage) for disposing one to listen to what is proposed for faith. However, he places most emphasis on the miraculous character of the assent of many through the ages. In fact he says that the clearest evidence that the signs of the past were genuine is that so many came to believe because of them. As he writes, "such a wondrous conversion of the world to the Christian Faith is the most certain test of the previously mentioned signs; so it is not necessary to repeat them, since they are most evident in their result."[48] What is Aquinas's point here? We must remember that *miracle* (*miraculum*) was a technical or quasi-technical term for Aquinas. As he says elsewhere in the *Summa Contra gentiles*, "Those things . . . which are properly called miracles are those which divinely come to be outside the commonly observed order of things."[49] Thus, when he speaks of the miraculous character of the assent of so many, he is drawing attention to the fact that their assent does *not* arise from the appeal of arguments to the UNO-natural intellect, but from the appeal of God's revelation to an intellect supernaturally illumined by grace. It is because he thinks faith arises from this supernatural illumination and *not* from the acumen of the natural intellect that Aquinas mentions the assent of the uneducated and simple-minded, who assent "filled with the Gift of the Holy Spirit."[50] Just how this assent comes about will be discussed in section 6.4 below. With regard to the present point, I conclude that this passage does not support Plantinga's naturalist view that the assent of faith arises from the appeal of evidence to the UNO-natural intellect. Rather, it supports the denial of this claim.

The NI, I conclude, is untenable. I have spent a good deal of time refuting it, but not because the evidence in its favor is so strong. Rather, I have done so, first, because I believe it is a prevalent view among many contemporary philosophers, whether or not they have defended it in print, and it is useful to disabuse them of this view. For if contemporary philosophers do generally accept the NI, it is perhaps no wonder that Aquinas receives little serious attention from them: they would naturally be reluctant to pay much attention to a thinker as given to confusion and self-contradiction as the naturalist interpreters suggest Aquinas was. A second reason for the lengthy discussion is that the inadequacies of the NI will help point us to a more adequate interpretation to be presented in section 6.4. Before that, however, we will consider what is, I contend, another unsatisfactory interpretation of Aquinas.

6.3 THE VOLUNTARIST INTERPRETATION

James Ross and Eleonore Stump, rejecting the naturalist view that the assent of faith is motivated solely by an impartial consideration of credibility evidence, have emphasized the role of the will in commanding assent.[51] In cases of *scientia*, according to Aquinas, the intellect is compelled to assent. But in cases of assent which fall short of perfect *scientia*, as we find in faith, assent is not compelled, but requires a command of the will. What moves one to command assent? How does assent so commanded have warrant? How is assent so commanded justified? In his article "Aquinas on Belief and Knowledge" Ross suggests that what brings about this assent is a form of "wishful thinking." Ross calls our attention to passages in which Aquinas seems to say that it is the desire for a certain end which causes assent. In the *De veritate* discussion of faith, Aquinas says of voluntary assent:

And the disposition of the believer is like that of someone believing the words of some human because it seems fitting or useful to do so. And so also we are moved to believe the words of God insofar as the reward of eternal life is promised to us if we have believed; and this reward moves the will to assent to what is said even though the intellect is not moved by anything which has been understood. Therefore Augustine says . . . "an unwilling person is capable of other things, but one can only believe willingly."[52]

This passage on its own seems to suggest that it is primarily or even exclusively the anticipation of the reward of eternal life which moves the will to command assent. In article two of the same question this reading is further supported, for there Aquinas speaks of only two principles of faith:

Since the disposition of the one believing . . . is such that the intellect is determined to something through the will, but [since] the will does nothing except insofar as it is moved through its object, which is the desirable good and end, two principles are required for the end: one is the good moving the will, and the second is that to which the intellect assents with the will acting.[53]

If these are the *only* principles, then it seems that what moves one to assent to the articles of the Creed is simply the end (the reward of eternal life). These articles claim that such eternal life is in fact a possibility, and the Church claims that by believing these articles and living a Christian life one can attain eternal life. Thus, assent seems to be motivated by a wish that the articles were true and a means to eternal life. But how is such wishful thinking psychologically possible? And, if possible, how can beliefs so formed be justified, or have any positive epistemic status at all?

Regarding the first question, Ross says that "coming to believe willingly does not require the ability to elect to believe just any-thing."[54] But Ross's Aquinas thinks that our cognitive and volitional makeup is such that in certain circumstances the will's desire for an end can move it to command the intellect to assent to certain propositions. Regarding the second question, Ross suggests that Aquinas was a reliabilist in epistemic matters. He does not discuss in detail the character of the reliabilism he attributes to Aquinas, and there are some unclarities in his interpretation, but I think it is best understood as an epistemically externalist account of the positive epistemic status of faith; it is an account, that is, of the *warrant* for faith. Reliabilism claims, roughly, that S's belief that p has the positive epistemic status of knowledge or, in this case, faith for S, if and only if S's belief was produced and is causally sustained by a reliable cognitive belief-forming process; and a belief-forming process is reliable if, given a certain kinds of input, it tends to produce true rather than false beliefs with sufficiently high frequency. As an *externalist* account, the reliable character of S's belief-forming process is not something which must be known by S in order for S's belief to have positive epistemic status.

Ross claims, then, that we often do believe because we want certain things to be true – we do engage in wishful thinking – and that certain sorts of wishful thinking constitute a reliable cognitive belief-forming process. He writes:

> Suppose the human being as a "cognition device" is constructed (or has evolved) successfully. Suppose (by adaption, of course) humans "fit" the earth so well that . . . the benefits from *believing* certain things (for instance, coherence, consistency, simplicity, elegance, pleasure, survival, dominance and various rewards promised, like life in the company of God) *are* really obtainable and *are* got by so believing; *then* the device is *not* unreliable.[55]

In the case of such "wishful thinking" or voluntary assent, it is not, as with *scientia*, the "manifest vision of truth" which moves one to assent, but the strength of the desire for the reward of believing. As Ross paraphrases Aquinas:

> In a word, in the absence of the "plain sight of truth," when "the perceived reward from commitment or reliance on a source of what is so gets great enough, the will presses the BELIEVE-button" (to use a contemporary metaphor), and cognition, *ceteris paribus*, results.[56]

In the case of voluntary assent there is a reliance on certain putative sources of truth, and because this reliance is motivated by some anticipated reward, Ross says the assent is motivated by "satisfaction-in-reliance." But this does not constitute further evidence, though of a different kind: "Satisfaction-in-reliance . . . is what *fills the gap in evidence* [my italics]. (Yet do not think it is *more* evidence; not at all; it fills the gap in evidence with something else that is reality-based, namely, SATISFACTION.)"[57] Let us say that insofar as a person is moved to assent to a proposition, p, by the expectation of some desired reward from believing (aside from that of believing the truth regarding p), he is moved by *utilitarian considerations*; insofar as he is moved by considerations which favor p being true but are not utilitarian considerations, he is moved by *strictly epistemic considerations*. Ross is claiming that, for Aquinas, we humans "fit" the environment so that some beliefs motivated by utilitarian considerations do in fact advance us toward the end we seek.

There are two points about the voluntarist position which need to be clarified. First, many passages in Ross's article are ambiguous with regard to just what benefits are to be gained by believing because of the will's command. A person can attain significant benefits in certain circumstances by acquiring false beliefs. Jones, for example, may attain the benefit of peace of mind by coming to believe the airplane he is on is perfectly safe, even though it is replete with structural and electronic faults. Thus, Ross may be saying that (A) our fit with the environment is such that benefits are attained by believing what we are inclined to choose to believe for the sake of these benefits, whether or not these beliefs are true. Each of the passages quoted above could be read as making this claim. Alternatively, Ross could be claiming (B) our fit with the environment is such that benefits are attained by believing what we are inclined to choose to believe for these benefits, and if we believed these beliefs would be true. It seems Ross intends to make the stronger claim (B), for he is concerned to show that on Aquinas's view a voluntary belief is not "cut loose from the 'reality-base' that *makes it true* [my italics]."[58] In what follows we will take him as claiming (B).

The second clarificatory point concerns the distinction we made in chapter four between justification and warrant for a belief. There we said that a person's justification for a belief is the reasons or grounds he has for holding that belief, while the warrant is the collection of conditions which give that belief the positive epistemic status of knowledge. In both Ross's and Stump's articles, as in many discussions of reliabilism, we do not find a clear distinction between what we are calling justification and warrant. This seems to be due at least in part to the fact that in Alvin Goldman's classical exposition of reliabilism, "What Is Justified Belief?", he seems to use *justification* as we are using *warrant* and does not give much attention to what we are calling justification.[59] Subsequent discussions have tended to follow Goldman in this. Still, although Ross and Stump do not use our terminology, the distinction between warrant and justification is implicit in what they say and we can state their views in our own vocabulary.

For both Ross and Stump the reliable character of the belief-forming process which leads to the assent of faith is part of its warrant – part of what is required for it to have the positive epistemic status of faith. However, S's justification (as we are using this term) need not include any proof that this cognitive process is reliable. Ross's claim that "satisfaction-in-reliance . . . fills the gap in the evidence" suggests the following picture about the justification for the assent of faith. A subject S has some reason to believe the articles of faith are true, but this is insufficient to bring about assent, or at least is insufficient to bring about the firm assent which faith requires. (Hence, there is a *gap in the evidence*.) However, the anticipation of a reward or, in other words, the satisfaction one has by relying on the evidence is sufficient to bring about assent, or perhaps to move weak assent to firm assent. Thus, S's justification for firm assent to p would be S's evidence for p along with the satisfaction-in-reliance S feels when he assents. More precisely, justification would consist of the set of propositions which make up the evidence along with the condition that S considers this evidence with the anticipation of obtaining satisfaction through assenting. Stump's view of justification seems close to this, for she uses the example of an experiment in which assent is influenced by the "desire to have results turn out a particular way."[60] In such an experiment, the researcher would have some reason to believe a certain conclusion, but the desire for a particular result is what brings about assent.

I want to argue in what follows that the voluntarist interpretation is implausible as an interpretation of Aquinas. First, both Ross and Stump seem to take Aquinas as saying that the will commands assent to a proposition only when evidence for assent to that proposition is lacking.[61] The role of the will in assent is complex, and we will discuss it more fully below, but it suffices to say here that Aquinas says that only in cases of *scientia*, in the full apprehension of first principles or the conclusions deduced from these, in cases in which there is a "manifest vision of the truth," is assent spontaneous and not voluntary.[62] However, it is possible and even common for one to have ample evidence for assenting to a proposition even though one lacks *scientia* of the proposition, and hence assent to it is voluntary. Suppose a student has a teacher who has consistently proven to be trustworthy and competent, and that teacher tells the student that Gödel's theorem is true. It would certainly seem this student then has sufficient evidence to believe Gödel's theorem is true, even though he does not have *scientia* until he has worked through and fully grasped the proof.[63] Thus, though both Ross and Stump suppose that the will has a role in assent only when evidence is insufficient, this does not appear to be Aquinas's view.

Let us grant, however, that the evidence for assent to the propositions of faith is insufficient, and consider in greater detail how the wishful thinking of voluntary assent is supposed to come about. Since such assent is a fully voluntary act, on Aquinas's account it includes the exercise of various powers which go to make up such an act.[64] Aquinas's most mature and elaborate account of a fully voluntary human act is found in the *prima–secundae* of the *Summa theologiae*. However, since Ross's discussion focuses on the *Quaestiones disputatae de veritate*, and since the essentials of Aquinas's *Summa* view are present in this earlier work, I will include citations of the *De veritate* in the following summary.

According to Aquinas, a simple act of will consists in the willing of an end understood by the subject's intellect as good.[65] For example, I may, after several hours of hard work, decide it is time to find some nourishment. Were I marooned on a desert island and unable to obtain food and water, this good or end would be the object of a mere wish. Since I am at home and there are several courses of action I could take to nourish myself, this end is the object of an intention.[66] The means or way to attain this end are discovered through deliberation (*consilium*):[67] I realize, after a moment's reflection, that I could fix something in the kitchen or go to the Chinese restaurant that is open down the street. When I settle on going Chinese, I choose this means, and this means can become the object of an intention as well.[68] Following choice, I exercise a command of will by which I move my other faculties to get myself out of my chair and down the street to a plate of chow mein.[69]

Choice and a command of will, then, occur only when it is thought that a prospective end is attainable by some course of action. The possible means to the end are discovered through deliberation, and one such means (if there are two or more) is settled upon by choice. The end of faith is eternal life and, as Ross would have it, firm belief is commanded because it is thought to be a means to this end: "when the perceived reward from commitment or reliance on a source of what is so gets great enough, the will pushes the BELIEVE-button,"[70] as he says. What Ross does not discuss is any process of deliberation by which the subject discovers that firm belief in the articles of the Christian Creed as revealed by God is a means to the reward of eternal life, and indeed the best means. As Aquinas says, "to command is an act of reason, although one presupposing an act of will; in the power of this [act of will], reason moves one to act through its command."[71] That is, although it is by one's will that something is commanded, it is one's reason which intimates what is to be commanded.[72] Thus, if the will is to command, there must be some act of reason by which the content of the command is intimated. But one's reason must intimate not only an end to be pursued (e.g. eternal life), but also the action or actions which are the preferred means to this end (e.g. assenting firmly to the articles of the Christian Creed). Ross, however, does not discuss how reason is to arrive at this determination of the means.

The difficulty here is that it seems one could only arrive at this determination of means if one had access to sufficient evidence (or, at least, what one took to be evidence) that the articles of the Creed were true. For Ross's Aquinas, however, this is precisely what is lacking, for he thinks there is a *gap* in the evidence which only the will can traverse. Still, it seems there must be *some* evidence that beliefs in the Creed are true and that holding them is a means to eternal life, otherwise there would be no more reason to choose to believe the articles of the Creed as a means to eternal life than to choose to stand on one's head and whistle *The Battle Hymn of the Republic*.

Perhaps the best construal of Ross's interpretation is the following. One strongly desires eternal life, and it is claimed (by the Church, or perhaps by Scripture itself) that believing the Creed is a means to this end. This claim is at least slight evidence that believing is in fact a means. And, indeed, believing is the *only candidate* as a means to the desired end. The situation is perhaps like that of a mountain climber with a ferocious and hungry grizzly bear in front of him and a long and very deep crevasse behind him. He thinks there is only a slight chance that he can leap across the crevasse to safety, but he also believes that this is the *only chance* of surviving. So he jumps. Similarly, in the case of faith, it may be that (1) there is slight evidence that the articles of the Creed are true and believing them is a way to eternal life, and (2) this is the only candidate as a means which is even slightly plausible. So a person commands firm belief.

Although Ross does not explicitly claim the above, it is difficult to make sense of his suggestion that one believes as a means to eternal life in any other way; for, if this is not what he is saying, it is hard to see why standing on one's head and whistling is not as plausible a means to eternal life as believing the articles of the Christian Creed.

And whether or not it is actually Ross's position, it is worth considering. I want to raise a question about whether the process of belief-formation it suggests is reliable, and about whether Aquinas considered it such.

A belief-formation process is reliable, as was said above, only if it tends to produce beliefs with sufficiently high frequency. The belief-formation process in question is the one in which a person desires a certain end, eternal life. Although there is not sufficient evidence to assent firmly to the articles of the Creed, assenting firmly to these articles is the only plausible means to attain eternal life. Thus the will commands firm assent to the articles of the Creed.

Consider, though, two people. Mohammed is born into the Muslim world in the thirteenth century, he has a pious love of God, and deeply desires eternal life with God; Peter is born into the Christian world at the same time, he also has a pious love of God and deeply desires eternal life with Him. Both are, of course, told that eternal life can be obtained by, *inter alia*, believing the tenets of the religion which dominates their respective cultures. Thus, Mohammed has at least slight evidence that the tenets of Islam are true, and that his believing them, *inter alia*, will enable him to attain eternal life, and Peter has parallel evidence for the truth of the Christian Creed and the consequences of believing in it. Given Ross's account, Mohammed would command belief in Islam and Peter in Christianity. But since at least some of the central tenets of Islam contradict those of Christianity, either Mohammed or Peter will form false beliefs by the "cognition device." And, indeed, since the known world for Aquinas was more or less evenly divided between Christian and Muslim at that time, about half the human race would have been led to form false beliefs by this process. Although it is hard to say precisely what frequency of forming true as opposed to false beliefs would be required for a process to be reliable, it seems clear that this is insufficient. In any case, Aquinas would not have thought it reliable. If he did, he would have to admit that Mohammed's beliefs were reasonable and well-formed, which he certainly denies.[73]

Ross may respond to this objection by specifying the cognition device involved in the assent of faith more precisely so that Christian beliefs are formed by this device and non-Christian beliefs are not. There is room for further clarification in Ross's account. The above objection is against the understanding of Ross's interpretation that we have been able to develop above.

Eleonore Stump also argues for a voluntarist interpretation which is quite similar to Ross's, but she offers a more explicit account of why assent issuing from a command of the will is reliable.[74] The good will is drawn to its ultimate end, union with God, and the propositions of faith describe this end and present it as available to the believer. These propositions, together with whatever else is known or believed by the intellect, are insufficient to move the intellect to assent. "But," writes Stump, "the will is drawn to the great good presented in the propositions of faith, and it influences the intellect to assent, in the sort of way familiar to us from science, where the design of experiments is often tailored to rule out just this kind of influence of will on intellect."[75] In double-blind experiments, Stump explains, "experimenters frequently must design their experiments to take account of the fact that, as Aquinas would put it, their wills may bring about the intellectual assent largely in consequence of their desire to have results turn out a particular way."[76]

Given that assent moved by the will in this way is clearly unacceptable in the empirical sciences, why does Aquinas think it is acceptable in the case of faith? When one believes in this way one believes because one desires something to be true, but how can such a belief be warranted? "The easiest way to answer this question," writes Stump, "will be to focus on one particular proposition appropriately held in faith, namely, the proposition that God exists."[77] According to Aquinas, being and goodness are convertible, so what is perfectly good necessarily exists. If the will hungers for something of limited goodness, and the will moves the intellect to assent because of its hungering for that thing, then the resulting belief will be unwarranted. A limited good need not include actual existence, and so if the will commands the belief that a limited good exists because of the desire for such a good, this belief-forming process would not reliably produce true beliefs. Stump writes:

On the other hand, if the will hungers for goodness that is perfect and unlimited, and if the intellect is moved to assent to the proposition that what is hungered for exists or obtains largely because of that hunger on the part of the will, the resulting belief will not similarly be unjustified [i.e. unwarranted, in our terminology], for there is perfect goodness, there is perfect being; and perfect being necessarily exists.[78]

Stump concludes, "it is not too hard to see how to extend this account to deal with other beliefs of faith."[79]

There are, however, some serious problems with Stump's

interpretation. First, it is not clear that beliefs produced in the way Stump describes would be believed as genuine faith requires. According to Aquinas, the formal object of faith is God, and this means that "the faith about which we speak does not assent to anything except on the grounds that it has been revealed by God; hence it relies on the Divine Truth as its proof."[80] If a subject, S, is to have faith in a proposition, p, then, it is not enough that S firmly believes p; S must believe that p is true *because* it has been revealed by God; S must believe *God* that p is true. Since this is so, Aquinas's claim that the proposition that God exists can be believed in faith is problematic for any interpreter. It is hard to see how S can believe God that God exists, since believing that God exists seems to be a presupposition of believing God. I will attempt to resolve this below. Stump, however, does not address this issue, and takes the belief that God exists as paradigmatic in her discussion of faith. As we are understanding her account of a subject's reasons or justification (in our sense of this word) for believing that perfect goodness exists, a subject has some evidence supporting the proposition that God exists, and this presumably consists of a cluster of natural theological arguments. However, this evidence is not sufficient to bring about assent. S only assents because of his desire for union with the highest good, God. But S would not assent because God revealed the proposition in question; he would believe on the basis of natural theological arguments, along with the command of the will which issues from desire for union with God. And although Stump does not discuss extensively the assent to other propositions of faith, a similar problem would arise for them.

Moreover, in spite of what Stump claims, it is far from easy to see how this account could be extended to belief in other propositions of faith. Consider, for example, the proposition that God became incarnate. Regarding another proposition of faith, Stump writes:

we would have to add [to our account of the warrant of the belief that God exists] some considerations either of other metaphysical attributes of God and their relation to the divine goodness or of the perfectly good will of God, and these additional considerations will be the basis of a metaphysical strand . . . of a theory of the justification [i.e. warrant] of this belief.[81]

This metaphysical strand of a theory of warrant would provide "an account of the nature of human knowing or of the world and our epistemic relation to it, or something of this sort, which explains the fact that [the belief in question] is justified [i.e. warranted]."[82] Regarding S's belief that God became incarnate, it would seem that such an account would have to show, minimally, that given that S came to believe this proposition in the way Stump describes, it is likely that the belief is true. But for this to be so, it seems there must be either a necessary or a probabilistic connection between God's goodness, which makes Him the object of S's desire, and the occurrence of the incarnation. But it is difficult to see how the needed connection could be established by Stump's metaphysical account. God wills by absolute necessity only His own goodness, and He wills other things as ordered to this end. Whatever He wills regarding other things, however, is not willed because necessary to God's own goodness, but in a wholly gratuitous fashion. As Aquinas writes about created goods and their order to the divine good:

For the divine goodness is not the sort of end which is produced by the things which are ordered to the end; but is more that by which things ordered to it are produced and perfected. Hence Avicenna says . . . that the action of God alone is purely free and generous (*liberalis*) because nothing is added to Him from the things which He wills and does concerning His creatures.[83]

Hence, though God is perfectly good and wills His own goodness by absolute necessity, that He wills to save – and even to create – human beings is wholly gratuitous and not necessary. There is no metaphysical argument, then, which could establish a connection between God's goodness, making Him the object of S's desire, and the truth of the proposition that God became incarnate. Indeed, if there were such an argument, then this proposition would not be an *article* of faith, as Aquinas clearly says it is,[84] but a preamble, for the articles of faith are those propositions which we cannot establish by a metaphysical argument – i.e. one which does not appeal to Divine revelation.[85] Thus, though one's will may hunger for perfect goodness, and his will may move the intellect to assent to the belief that perfect goodness exists, the further belief that the human race will be or was saved by an incarnate God would be unreliably formed and unwarranted.

6.4 A SUPERNATURAL EXTERNALIST INTERPRETATION

In section 6.2 I argued that, although the credibility arguments play some role in bringing one to the assent of faith, they are insufficient on their own to move one to assent to the articles of faith, and these arguments do not constitute the justification for the assent of faith. In section 6.3 I argued that, though it is clear that the assent of faith is voluntary and it requires a good will, utilitarian considerations are not what make up any putative "gap in the evidence" in the justification of the assent of faith; that believing by way of such a volitional leap was not in fact a reliable process of belief-formation; and that Aquinas did not think that warrant for faith (i.e. whatever conditions are required in order for an assent to have the positive epistemic status of faith) included the conditions that this process operated and that it was reliable. The results of these arguments, however, are not entirely negative, for they point us toward three desiderata for an interpretation of Aquinas on the assent of faith: (1) assent is not based solely upon the credibility arguments; (2) it is voluntary; (3) it requires a good will; (4) it is not motivated by utilitarian considerations in such a way that these "make up a gap in the evidence." In the remainder of this chapter I will try to present an interpretation which achieves these desiderata, which is in accord with the findings of previous chapters of this work, and which is supported by what Aquinas says on faith.

I will argue that Aquinas's view of the warrant for faith is epistemically externalist and parallels his view of the assent to principles in merely human *scientiae*, discussed in chapter four above. Unlike the UNO-natural apprehension of principles, however, the cognitive faculties involved in the assent of faith are due to the supernatural gifts or graces from God. For a convenient label, I will call my reading the *supernatural externalist* interpretation.

We must first consider the dates of composition of Aquinas's various treatments of faith. There is a tendency in much of the literature on Aquinas to ignore the dates of composition of his various works and the possibility of any development of his views. But, although Aquinas's thinking on this issue seems not to have undergone any fundamental shift, we must be alert to the possibility of some development over time. Among the discursive works in Aquinas's corpus intended for academic audiences, there are three major, extended treatments of faith: the *Scriptum super libros sentientium magistri Petri Lombardi* dis. 23 & 24, the *Quaestiones disputatae de veritate* q. 14 and the *Summa theologiae* qq. 1–16. Although our primary concern is with the most mature work, the *Summa*, I will briefly consider the earlier works on faith as well.

Aquinas's *Scriptum* on the sentences of Peter Lombard was a work he did as a *bacalaureus sententiarius* in Paris between 1252 and 1256. This exercise was a part of the academic training of that time. Both I. T. Eschmann[86] and James A. Weisheipl[87] put the work's completion roughly around 1256, and Aquinas's earliest biographer, William of Tocco, reports that he had not finished writing the work when he was incepted as a Master, *Magister sacrae paginae*, in the Spring of 1256. His first period as a Master at the University of Paris was September of 1256 to July of 1259, and in this office he was required to hold disputations a number of times during the year. Aquinas's disputations during this period constitute the *De veritate*. There is general agreement that qq. 1–8 were disputed during Aquinas's first year as Master (1256–57), qq. 8–20 during the second (1257–58), and qq. 21–29 during the third (1258–59).[88] Hence, a little more than a year elapsed between Aquinas's final editing of his *Scriptum* on the sentences of Peter Lombard and his disputation of q. 14 of the *De veritate*. We would not expect much of a change in his views during such a short period, and indeed, an initial look at the text confirms this expectation. In fact, much of the *De veritate* discussion reads like a second draft of that in the *Scriptum*.

The treatise on faith in the *Summa* is at the beginning of the *secunda–secundae*, and relies much on the *prima–secundae*. The *prima–secundae* was written approximately between 1268–70 and the *secunda–secundae* between 1270–72.[89] Thus over ten years elapsed between the *De veritate* treatment of faith and that of the *Summa*. Furthermore, the period before and during the composition of the *Summa* was one of prodigious scholarly output: Aquinas commented on most of Aristotle's work and on Scripture, including the letters of Paul, which are so important for the Christian view of grace and faith.

I will argue that, although in essentials Aquinas's views remained constant, the *Summa* is a much more detailed and elaborate account, and it brings in elements, such as the Gifts of the Holy Spirit, which are not prominent in the earlier accounts. In developing my interpretation, I will first look briefly at the two earlier works together and then consider the *Summa* at somewhat greater length.

As I said in chapter five, the doctrine of the *prima–secundae* of the *Summa* is that the theological virtues are not themselves steady dispositions for a certain sorts of action; they are merely *principia*, rudimentary inclinations for the virtuous action. Just as the natural fellow-feeling human beings naturally feel is not yet the virtue of generosity, but only an inclination toward it, so the theological virtues are inclinations toward their actions, but not yet steady dispositions or habits. For this steady disposition the prompting of the Holy Spirit is required, along with the Gifts of the Holy Spirit, which are dispositions to respond to such promptings. Thus a theological virtue is complemented by its corresponding Gifts so that a steady disposition to the corresponding act results.

The relationship of the doctrine of the Gifts in the *Scriptum* to that in the *Summa* is disputed. Some have argued that the same view is expressed in both works, while others have claimed that, although there is a certain continuity, there are important differences.[90] Although I will not argue for a position on the general question, I will maintain that there is at least one very important difference between the earlier and later doctrines: namely, whereas in the *Summa* the Gifts are complementary to the theological virtues, in the *Scriptum* they do not play this complementary role. For, first of all, when we compare the *Scriptum* discussion of the relationship of the Gifts to the theological virtues (*SSS* III. ds. 34 q. I art. I, "Whether the Gifts are virtues") with the parallel passage in the *Summa* (*Summa theologiae* I–II.68.I, "Whether the Gifts differ from the virtues") we find crucial discrepancies. Whereas in the *Summa* the inadequacy of the theological virtues to bring about their corresponding action is central, in the *Scriptum* this is not mentioned. Furthermore, in this article in the *Scriptum* he distinguishes the Gifts from the virtues as follows: "And accordingly I say that the Gifts are distinguished from the virtues in that virtues perfect action in the human manner, but Gifts perfect it beyond the human manner."[91] When discussing the Gift of chaste fear (*timor castus*), he explains that the mode is derived from the measure or rule (*mensura*) of an act, and the measure of a Gift is God.[92] However, this seems clearly at odds with the *Summa*, where he says the measure or rule of the Gifts is the theological virtues.[93]

What these differences suggest is that in the *Summa* the Gifts complement the theological virtues so as to give the individual a steady disposition for the corresponding action, and in this sense the theological virtues measure or rule the Gifts. In the *Scriptum*, however, the Gifts are dispositions for a higher, though closely related, action, and thus they have God, and not the virtues, for their measure and rule. This interpretation is borne out, I believe, when we look at the theological virtue of faith and its corresponding Gifts. In the *Summa*, the *donum intellectus*, or Gift of Understanding, allows one to grasp clearly what is to be believed and understand that nothing contradicts this, though the Gift does not give any deeper understanding into the mysteries of faith.[94] In the *Scriptum*, faith enables us to understand in the connatural mode according to which the matters having to do with God are apprehended through mundane forms, but, Aquinas writes, "the Gift of Understanding . . . illumines the mind about things heard, so that a human can even in this life receive a foretaste of the manifestation to come."[95] Also the other Gift which is relevant to faith in the *Summa*, *donum scientiae* or the Gift of *scientia*, seems in the *Scriptum* to have do only with moral decision.[96]

Although a fully adequate, detailed comparison of the early and later works cannot be made here, the observations made so far suggest that in the *Scriptum*, but not in the *Summa*, the theological virtues of themselves constitute steady dispositions for their respective actions. In the *Scriptum*, the Gifts are not required to complement the theological virtues so that one has a steady disposition to, for instance, the assent of faith. Rather, the Gifts enable one to perform related actions: for example, the Gift of Understanding enables one to have some foretaste of perfect beatitude beyond what is had by faith alone. I think this is also the view of the *De veritate*, for when Aquinas discusses faith in question 14, he does not even mention the Gifts. And so, when I discuss the view of these earlier works on the assent of faith, I will assume this is the correct understanding and focus only on the infused, theological virtue, setting aside the corresponding Gifts, for on this assumption the assent of faith arises from the virtue alone.[97]

We turn, then, to the *Scriptum* account of the assent of faith. First of all, regarding the credibility arguments, in the *Scriptum* Aquinas says that arguments which do not produce *scientia* may nevertheless lead one to faith by *disposing the will* to command assent. He writes: "An argument which is adduced in accord with faith does not make seen what is believed; and hence the difficulty of the work, as it is in itself, is not diminished. But with respect to [the work] in itself, [the argument] makes the will more prompt to believe."[98] The credibility arguments are arguments which help bring one to faith without producing *scientia* of the articles of faith. Aquinas's point here, it seems, is that the credibility arguments play a role in disposing the will to prompt assent, but they are not sufficient to bring about this assent. What, then, does bring it about?

In the *De veritate* Aquinas says faith is "from infused light."[99] In the *Scriptum* we find the same claim with a suggestion of how the infused light brings one to faith: "Faith can be called an argument insofar as the infused light, which is the habit of faith, makes manifest the articles [of faith], just as the intellectual light makes manifest principles naturally known."[100] An infused light, then, plays a role in the assent of faith similar to that which the natural light of the intellect plays in assent to principles. This natural light was extensively discussed in chapter four. In the first operation of the intellect, one grasps the quiddity of something in *phantasmata* by virtue of a first operation of the natural light, as when, for example, the *ratio hominis*, the idea of man, is apprehended. From this one comes spontaneously to the second operation of the intellect, a judgment, which one makes by virtue of a second operation of the natural light. In this second operation one comes spontaneously to an (existential) judgment, such as "Man is a rational animal," which is a principle naturally known. As argued in chapter four, as to the justification of this judgment, it is believed as basic. As to its warrant for *scientia*, included are the conditions that the judgment arose from the proper operation of a cognitive process which was designed to attain the truth in the sphere in question.

In the assent to the articles of the Creed, there is no full understanding of that to which one assents; there is no grasp of the quiddity of that about which one knows. Thus, the assent of faith does not begin with a grasp of the divine essence, as the principle "Man is a rational animal" begins with a grasp of the essence of man. But if the light of faith acts as the natural light does, what is grasped in a first operation of the intellect? As Aquinas understands it, the *ratio* or idea under which the articles of faith are grasped is that of *being divinely revealed*. He writes: "Insofar as an idea [*ratio*] inclines the will to the act of faith it is *believing God*, for the idea in accord with which the will is inclined to assent to things which one does not see is that God says these things."[101] The *ratio* which is immediately grasped by the infused light of faith is that of *being divinely revealed*. In a second operation and in virtue of a second use of the light, one assents firmly to these articles as divinely revealed. This assent, unlike the assent to principles naturally known, is voluntary and requires a command of the will. The belief which results is basic, and it has warrant for faith in part because it was arrived at by the proper operation of a cognitive process which, though infused and not UNO-natural, was nevertheless designed to attain the truth in this sphere.

In the *De veritate* Aquinas speaks generally about the infused light of faith and is much less explicit about its role, but it seems most plausible to take his silence there to be concurrence with the *Scriptum* view.[102] Admittedly, this is an elaborate interpretation of those two works on the basis of just a few lines, although those few lines do, I think, strongly support it. The difficulty is that Aquinas does not say much more about the motive of the assent of faith, its justification and its warrant in these early works. More is said in the *Summa*, to which I now turn. A good deal more support of the general view outlined above is found there, or so I will argue.

In the *Scriptum super libros sententiarum*, then, we found a strong though undeveloped suggestion that the process which issues in the assent of faith is analogous to the process of UNO-natural cognition which issues in judgments about principles. The latter process begins from sense perception, moves to the first operation of the intellect, the grasp of quiddities, and terminates with an act of the second operation of the intellect, the judgment of principles. In the *Summa* discussion, I believe, we find analogues of each of these three elements in the process leading to the assent of faith.

The first stage is sense perception. According to Aquinas, all human thought on this earth, whether of material or immaterial beings, must turn to *phantasmata* or sense images, for it is only in *phantasmata* that abstract ideas can be first apprehended and then deployed in thought. Faith also begins from a certain sort of sense perception: "Faith is 'from hearing', as is said in Romans 10:17. Hence it must be that some things proposed to a human person for belief are not [proposed] as seen, but as heard, to which he assents through faith."[103] Faith, then, begins from a certain sort of sense perception, the hearing of the proclamation of the articles of faith (or, perhaps, reading such a proclamation). As the UNO-natural cognitive process leading to judgments of principles naturally known begins from sense perception and its *phantasmata*, so the process leading to the assent of faith begins from a certain sort of sense perception. Of course, my hearing the Gospel message proclaimed is a very different sort of sense perception from my seeing, say, a herd of cattle before I have acquired the concept of a cow or made any judgments about them. Aquinas's point is that these two processes are *analogous*, not *identical*. And he is saying that as the UNO-natural process begins with a certain sort of sense perception, so the process leading to faith begins with a certain sort of sense perception, namely, hearing a proclamation of the Creed, the articles of faith, presumably uttered and described as a report of God's word to the prospective believer.

Mere sense perception in UNO-natural cognition does not require the natural light of the intellect; the mere grasp of *phantasmata*, before these *phantasmata* are illumined, does not involve the intellect at all. Similarly, merely hearing the Gospel proclaimed does not involve the infused light of grace; believers and infidels alike can at least listen to a preacher and hear what he says. Understanding and judgment, however, of either UNO-natural cognition or of the cognition leading to faith do require respectively the natural and infused light. And as the natural light illumines *phantasmata* so that intelligible forms can be grasped, so the infused light illumines the Gospel proclamation which has been heard. In a passage which echoes the *Scriptum super libros sententiarum*, Aquinas writes:

As a human person through the natural light of the intellect assents to principles, so the virtuous person through the virtuous habit has correct judgment about the things which concern that virtue. And in this way through the light of faith divinely infused a person also assents to these things which belong to faith, but not to their contraries. And therefore there is "no" danger nor "condemnation in those who are in Christ Jesus" (Romans 8:1), by whom we have been illumined through faith.[104]

But just what sort of understanding is attained through the infused light of faith? Before attempting an answer to that question we must consider the role of the Gifts in faith.

In the *Summa*, as we have said, the infused, theological virtues are rudimentary inclinations to virtuous actions. For a steady habit, the prompting of the Holy Spirit is required along with the Gifts which dispose one to obey these promptings. Thus, for firm assent to the articles of faith the corresponding Gifts are required to complement the theological virtues. They are the *donum intellectus* (the Gift of Understanding) and the *donum scientiae* (the Gift of *Scientia*). The names for these Gifts can be somewhat confusing, for Aquinas is clear that one with faith does not have understanding or *intellectus* of the quiddities of the terms of the propositions of faith, nor does one have *scientia* of these propositions. As will become clear, however, Aquinas uses these terms in senses analogous to those in which they are used with respect to the merely human *scientiae*.

As understanding precedes judgment, so the Gift of Understanding proceeds that of *Scientia*, which concerns judgment. Faith, as was said, begins with hearing the Gospel proclaimed. In the normal case, once an utterance is heard, understanding it would consist in grasping the quiddities of things signified by the words heard. And one might initially think that the role of the intellect, strengthened by the infused light of faith and the Gift of Understanding, is to grasp the quiddities of those things signified by the words in the proclamation of faith. Some of what Aquinas says might be taken to suggest this.[105] But it is clear from a consideration of Aquinas's texts that even a believer whose cognition is strengthened by the grace of faith cannot in this life grasp the divine essence, which is spoken of in the articles of faith. To have such a grasp of God's essence would be to enjoy the state of beatitude, a state in which one does not have faith.[106] In this life we grow in our understanding of God insofar as we better understand that God surpasses whatever we can comprehend intellectually.[107]

Just what is understood by the light of faith and the Gift of Understanding is made clear in several passages. In *Summa theologiae* II–II.8.4 we find an objection which claims that not all who have faith have the Gift of Understanding, for, as Augustine says, "he who believes must pray that he may understand" (*De Trin.* L.xv.). Aquinas responds: "although not all having faith fully understand the things which are proposed to be believed, they nevertheless understand that these things are to be believed and that one ought not deviate from them for any reason."[108] The Gift of Understanding, which all the faithful enjoy, does not give any positive understanding of God's essence or of other things or events mentioned in the Creed. Rather, the faithful understand that these propositions are *to be believed* and that for no reason is one to deviate from adherence to them.

Further support for this reading is found in another passage, *Summa theologiae* II–II.8.2. There Aquinas asks whether the Gift of Understanding can co-exist with faith. It could not, he admits, if the understanding in question is taken as complete understanding (*intelligere perfecte*), in which the very essence of God is grasped, for this would be to enjoy the state of perfect beatitude in which faith is no longer necessary. The understanding which springs from grace and which co-exists with faith is incomplete understanding (*intelligere imperfecte*):

In another way something can be understood imperfectly: this occurs when one does not apprehend the essence of a thing or the truth of a proposition, as to "what it is" or "how it is," but nevertheless one does apprehend that external appearances do not contradict the truth; that is, insofar as a person understands that because of these external appearances one ought not draw back from the things which belong to faith.[109]

What the believer understands through the Gift of Understanding, then, is not the nature of the Triune God or of the Incarnate Christ. What he understands is that the articles are to be adhered to on divine authority even in the face of considerations which seem to render them implausible (e.g. a being cannot be both three and one, or God cannot or would not become incarnate in His creation). This is understood in a non-discursive intuition in the first operation of the intellect in the process leading to the assent of faith.

Having grasped that the propositions of faith are to be believed, the prospective believer subsequently judges them to be true. Since the prospective believer lacks the understanding which comes with perfect *scientia*, the assent requires a deliberate act of will; and this act of will in turn requires a distinct gift or grace from God. This is the "Gift of *Scientia*":

And therefore two things are required for the human intellect to assent perfectly to the truth of faith. The first of these is that one soundly grasps the things which are proposed; and this pertains to the Gift of Understanding, as has been said. But the other is that one has certain and correct judgment about these matters, distinguishing what is to be believed from what is not to be believed; and for this the Gift of *Scientia* is necessary.[110]

In the first objection of the article just quoted, the objector argues that *scientia* cannot be a Gift of the Holy Spirit, for such a Gift would exceed natural faculties; but *scientia* is a result of the UNO-natural process of syllogistic reasoning. Aquinas responds that assent to these propositions is not the result of any discursive, syllogistic reasoning (as the NI suggests), but is immediate and intuitive:

The certitude of cognition in diverse natures is found to exist in diverse ways, according to the diverse conditions of each nature. A human being attains certain judgment about truth through discursive reason: and therefore human *scientia* is acquired through demonstrative reasoning. But in God there is certain judgment of truth without any discursive reasoning *through simple intuition* [my italics], as said in the First Part: and therefore divine *scientia* is not discursive nor ratiocinative but absolute and simple. Similar to this is the *scientia* which is affirmed as a Gift of the Holy Spirit: since it is a certain participatory similitude of this [divine *scientia*].[111]

Thus, having understood what is proposed for faith through the Gift of Understanding, one firmly assents, through a non-discursive apprehension, to those propositions as divinely revealed.

As for the credibility arguments, in the *Summa* Aquinas clearly implies these arguments have a role in bringing an individual to the assent of faith.[112] In *Summa theologiae* II–II.6.1.ad 1 Aquinas meets the objection that the credibility arguments and the intuitive certainty due to grace cannot *both* play a role in bringing one to faith. As Augustine writes, "*Scientia* engenders, nourishes, protects and strengthens faith in us." But, the objector contends, "what is produced in us through *scientia* seems to be more acquired than infused. Therefore faith does not seem to be in us from divine infusion."[113] Aquinas responds: "Through *scientia* faith also is nourished in the manner of external persuasion, which comes to be from a certain sort of *scientia*. But the principle and proper cause of faith is that which moves internally to assent."[114] That which moves internally is the infused, theological virtue and the promptings of the Holy Spirit moving someone with the Gifts; this is, Aquinas says, the principle and proper cause of faith. But what role do the credibility arguments have, moving *per modum exterioris persuasionis*? Although Aquinas is not entirely clear on this point in the *Summa*, the most natural interpretation is to understand it in accord with the *Scriptum* view discussed above. That is, the credibility arguments serve to dispose one's will to prompt assent to the articles in light of the interior cause of faith. For, although the interior cause is primary in bringing one to assent, it does not compel it; a person who is resistant, although he may hear the Gospel proclaimed, may believe only reluctantly, or even refuse assent. The credibility arguments dispose a person to be moved by the primary, interior cause of faith.

Perhaps the role of the credibility arguments can be made clear by the following analogy. Suppose Jones is very impressed by the phenomena of out-of-body experiences of those near death, and he is trying to convince his skeptical friend Smith that she should take them seriously. A speaker is coming to deliver a lecture on such phenomena, and though Jones urges Smith to go, she does not think the topic is serious enough that she should attend a lecture on it. Jones, however, tells Smith about the speaker's renown as a serious scientist and of his substantial accomplishments in research. Smith is sufficiently impressed, and agrees to attend the lecture. Because of her newly acquired respect for the speaker, she listens carefully, considers the evidence adduced judiciously, and by the end is convinced that such phenomena are important and should be taken seriously.

The credibility arguments with regard to faith, I would suggest, play a role similar to Jones's presentation in the story above of the speaker's scientific reputation and accomplishments. They do not convince Smith that what the speaker says should be accepted; rather, they dispose her to take the speaker's lecture seriously and consider carefully the arguments and evidence he presents. When she is convinced of the speaker's claims, it is his arguments and evidence which convince her, not Jones's claims about the speaker's reputation and past accomplishments. However, Jones's arguments are important for disposing Smith to go to the lecture, and consider seriously the arguments and evidence which eventually convince her. Similarly, the credibility arguments are important in bringing one to attend to and take seriously what is put forward for belief in the proclamation of the Gospel. However, it is the interior movement of grace and the Holy Spirit which is primary in bringing one to see that these truths have been divinely revealed and are to be believed.

In summary, then, my interpretation of the more mature, *Summa* treatise is the following. Faith must begin with a hearing of the Gospel, the essentials of which are contained in the Creed, which is proclaimed as divinely revealed. This requires no infused light. Subsequently, by virtue of the infused light of faith and with the theological virtue along with the Gift of Understanding, the prospective believer, by a non-discursive intuition, understands the articles of faith as propositions to be believed on divine authority and to which he should adhere in spite of considerations to the contrary. Finally, through a second operation of the infused light and with the theological virtue along with the Gift of *Scientia*, one immediately (i.e. not as the result of discursive reasoning) assents to the articles as divinely revealed. Unlike assent to principles naturally known, this assent requires a deliberate act of the will co-operating with grace, and so it is voluntary and meritorious.

According to this interpretation, the assent of faith, like assent to principles in the merely human *scientiae*, is justified as basic. The credibility arguments may play an important role in disposing one to attend to a proclamation of the Gospel in a favorable frame of mind, but assent to the propositions of faith is not inferred from such arguments; rather, one apprehends that the propositions have been divinely revealed, and assents immediately.

The assent of faith is warranted, at least in part, because (A) the individual's cognitive faculties have been heightened so that they have acquired a design with which he can discover the truth about putative divine revelations (i.e. as to whether or not they are genuine) and because (B) the individual's assent to the articles was produced and is sustained by such heightened cognitive faculties when operating properly. This interpretation is *externalist*, for the individual has no privileged access to whether his cognitive faculties have the appropriate design and were operating properly in producing his assent. It is also *supernaturalist*, for the cognitive abilities in question are not part of his UNO nature, but are divinely given graces over and above his UNO nature.

6.5 FURTHER QUESTIONS

The above, then, is the gist of my interpretation of Aquinas on faith's justification and warrant. We will now consider in turn three questions about this interpretation: (1) How can one come to assent as part of faith to the proposition *God exists*? (2) What, more precisely, is the nature of the non-discursive understanding and judgment involved in the assent of faith? (3) Though the credibility arguments are not sufficient for the assent of faith, are they necessary? Considering these questions will allow us to clarify and elaborate the account of Aquinas's view of faith given above. However, Aquinas's own explicit remarks on these issues are few, terse and difficult. The answers we will give can only be somewhat speculative descriptions of what was probably his view, given what he did say.

Our first question, then, concerns how one comes to believe *God exists*. One cannot have perfect *scientia* of this proposition, for that would require that he grasp the divine essence, which is not possible for humans in this life. However, a person can have a demonstration *quia*, a demonstration of the fact that God exists, which moves from certain effects to the assertion of the existence of their cause.[115] One who has grasped such a demonstration has imperfect *scientia* of this proposition.

Others who do not have this demonstration, Aquinas says, can believe this proposition "per modum fidei" – "in the manner of faith."[116] But it is difficult to see how this could be so, for believing a

proposition in the manner of faith requires that one believe *God* that
the proposition is true; but one cannot believe God that God exists.
Aquinas himself states the problem very clearly in objection nine of
De veritate 14.9, where he writes, "We cannot believe this by the fact
that it is acceptable to God [*eo quod sit Deo acceptum*], because no one
can think something to be acceptable to God unless he first thinks
that there exists a God who finds it acceptable."[117] He responds to
this objection as follows:

> Someone can begin to believe firmly (*credere*) that which he earlier did not
> firmly believe but tentatively conjectured; hence it is possible that before
> someone firmly believes that God exists, he conjectured that God is, and
> that it would be pleasing to [God] if one firmly believes that He is. And in
> this way someone can firmly believe that God is, by the fact that it is
> pleasing to God [*eo quod sit placitum Deo*], although this also is not an article,
> but it is antecedent to the articles because it is proved demonstratively.[118]

What can Aquinas's point be here? He is clearly speaking about
the person who does not have a scientific demonstration that God
exists, but assents to this proposition "in the manner of faith." His
point seems to be that before such a person comes to an assent of
faith he has an a tentative conjecture (*existimatio debilis*) that God
exists. This seems to be an opinion (*opinio*),[119] which is based on
considerations which favor the truth of the proposition *God exists*,
though these considerations do not constitute a rigorous scientific
demonstration. Aquinas does not say what motivates this *existimatio*,
but perhaps it is the sort of broad, non-rigorous considerations an
ordinary, man-in-the-street theist would offer in support of his
theism: e.g. the world must have a creator or designer, or someone
must have brought about all this natural beauty in the world.
Although they are not scientific demonstrations which engender
scientia, they could bring about an opinion.

The person having an opinion that God exists, Aquinas says, can
subsequently come to assent to this proposition in the manner of
faith. One reading of this passage is to take Aquinas as saying that
one believes firmly that God exists because he thinks God will be
pleased by his so believing and he wants to please God ("sic potest
aliquis credere Deum esse, eo quod sit placitum Deo"). But it seems
absurd to say that, though I have only a weak opinion that God
exists, I could bring myself to firm conviction that He does exist
because, if He exists, He would be pleased and I want to please Him.
First, this view presupposes an extreme voluntarism about belief

which is implausible both in itself and as an interpretation of Aquinas. Secondly, it is hard to see why God would want a person to believe something for which he lacked evidence. Thirdly, even if we accept this voluntarism and that God could want me to believe with insufficient evidence, it is hard to see why a person would be moved to form a firm conviction on the basis of only weak opinions that God exists and wants me to believe firmly. Since there is doubt about these opinions, then how could such unsure opinions move even the person wanting to please God to form a firm conviction?

Perhaps a more plausible suggestion is that one who first opines that God exists on the basis of broad non-rigorous consideration subsequently, after the supernatural illumination of the light of faith, comes to a firm conviction that God has revealed certain truths to him and, along with this, to the firm conviction that God exists. This is similar to the case in which a person, George, say, who first has a suspicion that he has a long-lost relative, Uncle Harry, subsequently comes to the firm conviction that such an Uncle Harry exists when he receives a letter from him. George does not, of course, believe Uncle Harry that he exists, but he does come to the firm conviction that Uncle Harry exists because he has taken the communication as genuine. My suggestion is that in a similar fashion one comes to a firm conviction that God exists because one believes that he has received a genuine revelation from God.

But what of Aquinas's statement that one can firmly assent to the proposition that God exists "eo quod sit placitum Deo"? To avoid attributing to Aquinas an absurd view, I think the ablative "eo quod . . ." should not be taken as an ablative of cause, but of manner. What Aquinas is concerned with here is to say that one who lacks *scientia* that God exists can assent to this proposition "per modum fidei". The difficulty is that, as Aquinas understands it, faith requires not only that assent be firm, but that it be in some way a *credere Deo*, a believing while trusting in or clinging to God. He seems to be saying here that although one cannot believe God that God exists, (A) one can come to believe that God exists in the way described in the previous paragraph, (B) one can also believe that it would be pleasing to God that he firmly assent to His existence and (C) one can want to please God by so believing. If (A)–(C) were fulfilled, then although one would not be believing God, one would be believing while wanting to please God, rather than believing with reluctance. And this could be described as a sort of *credere Deo*, assenting while clinging to God. Thus Aquinas could claim, as he wants to claim, that one could assent to this preamble of faith "per modum fidei" – in the manner of faith.

A second question concerns the non-discursive nature of the assent of faith. As I read Aquinas, the illumination from the light of faith and the prompting of the Holy Spirit are such that one immediately and non-discursively understands that the articles are genuine revelations of God and he then arrives at knowledge which is similar to divine knowledge in that it is "certain judgment of truth without any discursive thought through simple intuition."[120] Since his belief is not the result of discursive demonstration, it seems that, with regard to justification, what is believed in faith is *basic* in the sense that the propositions are believed, but are not believed on the basis of any other beliefs. However, it cannot be that the articles are believed as basic, for then one would not believe them on *divine* authority, as genuine faith requires. How then are we to understand the assent of faith?

As G. E. M. Anscombe has argued,[121] when an individual, A, believes another individual, B, that certain propositions are true, A "relies on B that p," and for this to be true several conditions are necessary. First, it is not enough that A believes B when B tells A that p, for A might already have believed p. Furthermore, even if A believes p upon hearing it from B, this would not be a case of believing B if A, upon hearing it from B, formed his own judgment regarding p. And moreover, if A is to believe B that p, then he must hold certain other beliefs. A must believe:

(1) B himself believes what he is saying.
(2) Something (which A takes to be a communication) is a communication from B.
(3) By this communication B means to be telling him *this* (what A takes him to mean).
(4) B's communication is addressed to A.

In the case of faith, "A" would be the prospective believer, "B" would be God, and the communication referred to would be the content of the Creed. Let us refer to the propositions which result from making these alterations (1)–(4) as (1')–(4'). What are we to say about these beliefs? It seems most plausible to say that the non-discursive, immediate assent of faith is such that the supernaturally illumined prospective believer firmly believes (1')–(4') as epistemically basic. This is not an unlikely reading, for, I think, in ordinary human-to-human communication we, upon receiving what is apparently a verbal or written message, believe (1)–(4) as epistemically basic unless there are special circumstances which call them into question. Similarly, upon hearing a proclamation of the Creed and when enjoying the infused light of faith, a person believes (1′)–(4′) as epistemically basic and so firmly assents to the articles on divine authority.

It may be argued, though, that assent to the various articles of faith ought to be understood as a series of *inferences* from (1′)–(4′), and not as epistemically basic, as I have claimed above. When Aquinas speaks of assent to the articles of faith, however, he does not say that they are inferred from (1′)–(4′) or from propositions like them, but that one assents to the articles under the *ratio* of their being divinely revealed. How are we to understand Aquinas on this point?

Let us return for illumination to an example considered in chapter five. When Smith walks outside she forms the belief that it is chilly as epistemically basic. It seems implausible to say that she has inferred this from other beliefs, for it simply seems obvious to her that it is chilly. It is nevertheless true that this belief would not be justified as basic for Smith unless she had good reason to believe other propositions at the time – e.g. she is not presently chilled with a fever, and she is being attentive to the temperature. Hence, that Smith holds these other beliefs is a condition for her belief that it is chilly being epistemically basic for her, but her belief is not inferred from these other beliefs. Similarly, I want to suggest that Aquinas is best understood as claiming that believing (1′)–(4′) is a *condition* for assenting to the articles of faith as epistemically basic, but assent to the articles is not *inferred* from (1′)–(4′). In this way one assents to the articles of faith under the *ratio* of their being divinely revealed, but does not infer the articles from other beliefs.

A third question concerns the necessity of the credibility arguments. I have argued that in both the early and later works these arguments dispose the will to an assent whose primary cause is the infused light and the Holy Spirit. But are they necessary for a justified assent of faith? In response to this question let us first distinguish between two sorts of considerations which may be called credibility arguments. So far we have been taking them as rigorous metaphysical and historical arguments. The metaphysical arguments which establish that God exists are not, of course, *propter quid* demonstrations, for they do not move from full apprehension of the cause to the effect; but they are rigorous demonstrations *quia*, which move from effects to the existence of their cause. In addition there are rigorous historical arguments establishing the genuineness of alleged miracles in Biblical times and in the history of the Church, and arguing from these to the conclusion that what has been claimed in the Bible and by the Church to be divinely revealed is in fact such. However, in addition to these rigorous arguments, there are also considerations of a less rigorous sort which favor the claim that God exists and revealed the articles of faith. These less strict credibility arguments may include, first, the ordinary considerations, spoken of above, which the man in-the-street theist offers in support of his theism – e.g. there must be a cause of the world, there must be a cause of the beauty we find around us. In addition, there may be similar broad considerations for the divinity of Christ and the authority of the Christian Church – e.g. general testimony that Jesus worked miracles and that miracles have occurred throughout the history of the Church, though no critical historical inquiry into these events has been undertaken.

If we take the credibility arguments in the former, stricter sense, I know of no passages in Aquinas suggesting that such rigorous arguments are necessary for a justified assent of faith, whether one constructs these for oneself or believes 'experts' that there are such. And, indeed, if the primary causes of faith are the infused light and the Holy Spirit, there is no reason to suppose such rigorous arguments are necessary, for the infused light of faith seems sufficient. Regarding the latter, less rigorous form of credibility arguments, the situation is not so clear. We have seen that Aquinas thinks one may first opine on the basis of a non-rigorous argument that God exists, and subsequently come to believe this more firmly. Yet it is not clear whether he thinks such weaker considerations to be necessary for justified faith, or just the usual way one comes to the assent of faith. Perhaps the only conclusion to be drawn is that though the weaker sort of credibility arguments may commonly or even universally dispose people to assent, Aquinas nowhere clearly indicates whether or not he thinks these necessary for justified assent.

6.6 THE WILL AND THE ASSENT OF FAITH

We turn now to the question of the role of the will in the assent of faith. According to the interpretation presented above, one who enjoys the infused light and has the theological virtue along with the Gifts of Understanding and *Scientia* voluntarily assents to the articles of faith as divinely revealed. But if, by the infused virtue and the Gifts, one grasps the articles of faith as divinely revealed, what role can the will have in assent? If it is clear that God revealed something and that God does not lie, why would a good will be necessary for one to assent to that truth? It seems that even a selfish or malevolent interest in knowing the truth would be sufficient for assent.

Let us begin by considering more fully a point which was made in our discussion of voluntarism in section 6.3 above, and let us do this by recalling some terms we introduced there. Recall that we distinguished two sorts of considerations which might move a subject, S, to assent to a proposition, p. *Utilitarian considerations* concerned some desired reward from believing p (aside from that of believing the truth about p), while *strictly epistemic considerations* were those which constituted support for p being true but were not utilitarian considerations. In chapter four we said that a belief that p or assent to p is *justified* just if its justification is unimpeachable according to some specified standards of justification. In the following discussion, let us use the term in such a way that an assent is justified only if it is justified on the basis of strictly epistemic considerations.

Penelhum, Ross and Stump all seem to agree that if the assent of faith is voluntary then it must be unjustified. That is, they hold that a condition of the voluntary character of a subject S's assent to the propositions of faith is that, from the perspective of a judicious, unbiased observer – one who is unaffected by utilitarian considerations for or against assenting to p – strictly epistemic considerations supporting the propositions of faith are insufficient for S's assent. Thus Penelhum claims, "Thomas asserts a necessary connection between freedom of assent and the inconclusiveness of the reasons available in support of the propositions to which assent is given."[122] Ross says that in the firm, voluntary assent which Aquinas calls *credere* the will is moved to rely on a putative source of information because it seeks satisfaction, and he says that "satisfaction . . . is what fills the evidential gap to cause assent."[123] And Stump writes that in the case of faith the will moves one to assent "in the sort of way familiar to us from science, where the design of experiments is often tailored to rule out just this kind of influence of will on intellect."[124] Since experimental design is intended to rule out assent which is not in accord with an objective consideration of the weight of the evidence, Stump implies that the assent of faith is unjustified by strictly epistemic considerations.[125]

Attributing this view to Aquinas, however, would imply that the vast majority of beliefs we hold are unjustified by strictly epistemic considerations. For Aquinas claims that whenever one falls short of "the manifest vision of truth" which is had in the perfect *scientia* of principles or of the conclusions deduced from these, then assent is voluntary. As we saw in chapter one, perfect *scientia* is only of general and necessary truths, and it is attained only after long inquiry and an extended process of intellectual habituation. Yet there is a vast array of other beliefs we hold. First, as we saw in chapter one, before we fully apprehend the principles in a field we can and must know a great deal about the subject matter, and so have many beliefs which are not instances of perfect *scientia*. Moreover, day-to-day life involves innumerable beliefs which are not perfect *scientia*. There is no reason to suppose that Aquinas thought all these beliefs were unjustified. Consider, for example, all that we believe on the basis of testimony, which certainly does not constitute the manifest vision of truth. It simply seems absurd to say that, for example, my belief that Australia (which I have never visited) exists is unjustified by strictly epistemic considerations.

In what sense, though, is the assent of faith voluntary, and why is a *good* will required? If strictly epistemic considerations are sufficient to justify assent, why should not a person with strictly selfish interests be moved to assent as well as one of good will? Although the selfish person may try to use the knowledge for evil purposes, it doesn't seem that his evil will should prevent him from assenting. In order to avoid attributing to Aquinas a belief in widespread unjustified assent, we must offer an account according to which assent is justified and yet the subject's will plays a role. As a start in developing such an account, let us consider his views on the voluntary generally.

In *Summa theologiae* I–II.13.6 ("Whether a human being chooses from necessity, or freely") Aquinas says that human choices are free because they are undetermined. That is, it is possible for a person to choose or not to choose something, and this is so in two senses. First, a person may choose to act or choose not to act, or, secondly, having chosen to act, a person may choose this or that. The reason for these alternative possibilities is that one's intellect is capable of considering a prospective end in more than one way. Aquinas writes:

The will can tend toward whatever reason can understand as good. But reason can understand as good not only this, viz. *to will* or *to do*; but also this, viz. *not to will* and *not to do*. And again in all practical goods reason can consider the *ratio* of some good and the defect of some good, which has the *ratio* of evil. And in this way one can apprehend any one of these goods as something to be chosen or something to be avoided.[126]

Consider the example of a student deliberating about how to spend a Saturday evening. He may consider an evening in the library working on a philosophy paper a good thing insofar as it will deepen his understanding of the material and will help him fulfill what he is obligated to do for his course of studies. Alternatively, he can consider it an evil in that it will be demanding and difficult, and will take him from the good of conviviality with his friends at the party to which he has been invited. Because he can consider both an evening in the library and an evening at the party as good in some way, each is a possible object of choice for him.

An important basis for freedom of choice for Aquinas, then, is the possibility of various considerations of a prospective end or means to an end by the intellect.[127] Regarding the formal object of this will, which is the abstract consideration under which anything is willed, the simple act of will is not free, for one always wills beatitude or human fulfillment. Regarding its material object, the actual concrete ends which are willed, the will necessarily wills that object which perfectly realizes its formality, and this is perfect beatitude, the apprehension of the divine essence. Since an intellectual apprehension of God's essence is beyond us in this life, however, the will is not determined to will perfect beatitude. And regarding any other end which it can will as partially realizing this beatitude, such an end does not perfectly fulfill the formality under which it wills. That is, although a prospective end may be, all things considered, partially constitutive of beatitude, it can also be considered as defective in some way; although an evening working on the paper will increase a student's understanding, it will take him away from conviviality with friends. Thus, one can consider it as something either to be willed or not. Moreover, given an end or ends, a certain means to it may be chosen or avoided, depending on how that means is considered by the intellect.

Human choices are free, then, insofar as a subject can consider a prospective end or means as good or as bad. A rather widely held presupposition of contemporary discussions of human freedom is that whether a subject, S, freely performs an action, A, depends only upon what is true of S at the moment of choice, t. It may be said, for instance, that S voluntarily chooses A only if S could have done otherwise at t. We can label this sort of view a *synchronic* view of free, voluntary choice, for it considers only what is true of the subject at the moment of choice. On such a synchronic view, Aquinas's subject is free only if he can, at the moment of choice, consider some possible end or means as either good or bad.

Aquinas's view, however, was not a synchronic one. His was close to Aristotle's, who wrote:

> Someone may say that all men desire the apparent good, but have no control over the appearance, but the end appears to each man in a form answering to his character. We reply that if each man is somehow the cause of his habits, he will also be himself somehow the cause of the appearance.[128]

That is, whether a prospective end appears good to a person depends upon his character, which consists of his habits. But since this character has been produced by his past free actions, whatever appears good to him because of his character is also voluntary, even though he may not, at the moment of choice, have any control over this character and how things appear to him. Thus, if our student is a slothful or intemperate person, he may, when he receives an invitation to a party, immediately decide to go, without serious consideration to the good of an evening of scholarly work in the library. This Aristotelian view of free will is *diachronic*, for whether or not a choice is free depends not only on what is true of the subject at the moment of choice, but also on what was true in the past; it depends upon his past actions, which brought about his dispositions, which in turn brought about his present choice.[129]

Although Aquinas's account of human action and choice differed in significant respects from Aristotle's, Aquinas accepted this diachronic view of the voluntary. As he writes:

> For if one wills some cause from which he knows such and such an effect results, it follows that he wills that effect. . . . Yet it is evident that unjust people in acting do injustices. . . . But it is evident that if one who is not ignorant does voluntarily those things from which it results that he is unjust, he will be voluntarily unjust.[130]

Moreover, because he is the free, voluntary cause of his habits, "it follows that he is also the cause of the appearances which result from such a habit (i.e. of the appearance according to which it seems that this is good in itself)."[131] And, finally, he is the free, voluntary cause of choices which result from what appears good to him.

Of course one is not always completely determined to act in accord with character; if this were so, all actions would be determined. One can, through conscious effort, have some immediate control over what appears good and thus act against one's character. This seems to be possible, according to Aquinas, through exercising some control over the *phantasmata* with which the intellect is presented.[132] But, though this may be achieved on occasion, nevertheless, when unforeseen temptations present themselves, one slips back into acting in accord with character.[133] It is only by continued diligent choices that character can be changed, and this requires a sustained effort and exertion.[134]

The brief discussion of will and choice above allows us to see how the assent of faith is free and voluntary and why a good will is needed. As I have argued, through the theological virtue of faith and Gift of Understanding one is moved to grasp the articles of faith as divinely revealed and to be believed. If one is of a bad character, however, this understanding may be obscured or repressed. If one is, for instance, proud, assent to the articles may appear bad to one, for faith requires that one's intellect be subject to God's teaching. Thus Aquinas says that infidelity in the face of the proclamation of the Gospel arises from pride: "Insofar as it is sinful, infidelity arises from pride, because of which the person does not want to subject his intellect to the rule of faith and to the sound understanding of the Fathers."[135] And the heretic is one who "though he intends to assent to Christ, yet goes wrong in choosing the things whereby he assents to Christ; because he does not choose the things which have truly been handed on by Christ, but the things which his own mind suggests to him."[136] This arises "from pride or concupiscence."[137] In these cases, then, a bad will and the vices to which such a will gives rise obscured the understanding of the propositions of faith as divinely revealed, and causes one to consider assent to them as something to be avoided. Presumably, in these cases some degree of self-deception is involved. Just as the greedy person does not say that he refuses to give more to the needy because of his greed, so the proud person does not say that he refuses assent to the propositions of faith because of his pride. Rather, a person's greed influences his consideration of whether to give to the needy by causing him to focus

on the ways in which giving can be considered bad – e.g. the poor
deserve their lot because of laziness, hand-outs undermine initiative
and self-reliance, I may need the money for unforeseen contingen-
cies. Similarly, a person's pride leads him to focus on apparent
implausibilities of the claims of faith – e.g. God could not be three
persons and yet one, God would not become incarnate in His
creation, a person could not rise from the dead. In the voluntary
assent of faith, then, a bad will and bad habits obscure and bias one's
evaluation of the evidence.

Thus Aquinas's view is not, as Penelhum, Ross and Stump would
have it, that the will plays a role in the assent of faith (as in other
volitional assents) only because it enables one to ignore, repress or in
some other way traverse a gap in the evidence. Rather, the will plays
a role because in most cases it, and our habits and character which
are shaped by it, influence the way we evaluate the evidence. A bad
will, and the bad character to which it leads, bias our evaluation, and
cause us to believe, contrary to the weight of the evidence, what will
serve our pride, give license to our sensual desires or demand least of
us. (Hence, it is only a bad will and bad character which bias our
consideration and cause us to override a gap in the evidence.) A
good will, on the other hand, does not impede an impartial evaluation of what has been proposed. And in the case of faith, a good will
is not needed to make up any putative deficiency in the evidence; on
the contrary, it permits us to see clearly and impartially that truths
which are beyond our understanding, and which may demand much
of us, nevertheless have been revealed by God and are to be believed.
And when we have apprehended the articles of faith in this way, the
will commands firm assent.

An analogy may be helpful here. For approximately fifty years
evidence has been mounting that smoking is harmful to a person's
health. The evidence is merely probabilistic, and is not sufficient for
scientia, so on Aquinas's view a command of will is required for
making a judgment about the proposition, *Smoking is harmful to a
person's health*. But consider Winston, who is inordinately attached to
the pleasures of smoking. He is deeply reluctant to kick the habit,
and when evidence is presented to him about the harmful effects of
smoking, he is skeptical: he points out problems with the studies, and
emphasizes the incompleteness of the research. In this case, Winston's attachment to the pleasures of smoking does not lead him to
ignore the evidence, but it biases his evaluation of a body of evidence

which can be viewed in more than one way: it leads him to emphasize the problems and weak points of the research, and thus be agnostic about its conclusions. Another person who is not attached to the pleasures of smoking, though he may acknowledge some weaknesses in the research, concludes that the weight of the evidence clearly shows that smoking is harmful to health.

It is in a similar way that a bad character influences the way the articles of faith appear to one, and it can impede assent. And since a person in some sense freely chooses his character through having freely chosen his past actions, the failure to assent is free and voluntary. Of course, as mentioned above, it is possible for a person to choose against the inclination of his character, but this assent would be unstable, for in weaker or unguarded moments one's character would influence the intellect. Since faith is for Aquinas a habit, a steady disposition, this unstable assent would not yet be faith. Alternatively, a good will does make the assent of faith possible. Someone who is steadily disposed to desire eternal life with God and who does not suffer from pride or concupiscence will understand the articles of faith, through the theological virtue and Gifts, as divinely revealed and to be believed. And when the articles of faith are understood in this way, the will commands firm assent.[138]

An interesting view of the epistemic evaluation of the assent of faith, or of any voluntary assent, seems implicit in Aquinas's account. He seems to imply that moral virtues and vices, which enable us to act well or poorly in non-epistemic matters, also enable one to act well or poorly in attaining the epistemic goal of believing truths and disbelieving falsehoods. In other words, for Aquinas the *moral* virtues and vices are at the same time *epistemic* virtues and vices. Consequently, as with moral evaluation, the epistemic evaluation of a belief depends upon whether one has the appropriate virtues.

In recent philosophical literature we can find discussion of a similar view. Hilary Kornblith, without reference to Aquinas, has invited us to consider the following situation:

Consider the case of Jones. Jones is a headstrong young physicist, eager to hear the praise of his colleagues. After Jones reads a paper, a senior colleague presents an objection. Expecting praise and unable to tolerate criticism, Jones pays no attention to the objection: while the criticism is devastating, it fails to make any impact on Jones's beliefs because Jones has not even heard it.[139]

Kornblith believes that Jones's behavior is epistemically objectionable because it proceeds from a certain epistemic vice (which is also a moral vice). And in order to see this, we must take a diachronic view of the person's behavior and take into account his habits. Kornblith continues:

> In determining whether a belief is justified, we must look at the processes responsible for the presence of that belief. This involves . . . looking at the state of the believer, not merely at the instance at which his belief is justified, but over some period of time.[140]

We have argued that Aquinas also takes a diachronic view of the epistemic evaluation of voluntary assent, and he too holds that at least some moral virtues and vices are also epistemic virtues and vices. And because one's will is the cause of one's virtues and vices, it plays a role in the assent to or rejection of the propositions of faith.

6.7 CONCLUSION

I claimed in chapter three that the *Summa theologiae* was intended as a work of second-level pedagogy in the *scientia* of sacred doctrine. As such, it was written for extremely well-prepared students, those who had already grasped the fundamental concepts of sacred doctrine and were familiar with its claims, and it was meant to instill in them intellectual habits so that the principles of sacred doctrine become the foundation for their thinking in this area. For this to be possible, their assent to the principles of this *scientia* must not be inferred from its conclusions. Although these principles, the articles of faith, can only remain mysteries which we cannot understand in this life, we must be able to apprehend them non-inferentially – as principles.

In this chapter I have argued that by the infused virtue of faith and the Gifts of Understanding and *Scientia* we can assent to the articles of faith immediately and without inferring them from any claim which is a conclusion of this *scientia*. We understand these propositions of faith as revealed by God and can immediately assent to them. These articles of faith, then, can serve as the principles of a *scientia* for us. In the present life, however, this *scientia* must remain imperfect in us.

Conclusion: pedagogy in the Divine 'scientia'

CHAPTER SEVEN

The 'scientia' of sacred doctrine

In the Spring of 1256, in the midst of a fierce controversy at the University of Paris, Thomas Aquinas delivered his inaugural lecture as a theological Master. The Dominican Order and Aquinas's own appointment to a chair of theology were at the center of the conflict, and the Order's opponents tried to prevent people from attending the inaugural lecture, but in his text Aquinas does not allude to this trouble. Rather, Aquinas – as legend has it, acting on the advice of a venerable friar who came to him in a dream or vision – chose to deliver a characteristically clear and succinct lecture about the calling of a Christian teacher, and based it on a verse from Psalm 103: "Watering the earth from his things above, the earth will be filled from the fruit of your works" (Ps. 103:13; 104:13 in modern Bibles).[1]

Water from the heavens falls first on the mountains, producing rivers, and the rivers in turn flow to the earth making it fertile. Similarly, Aquinas explains, the highest teaching is from God, and human teachers, enlightened by God's teaching, serve as ministers of divine instruction to enlighten others. Some awareness of God's existence is implanted in everyone by nature, and the wise through the exercise of their reason can know higher things; but "the highest things, in which wisdom is said to dwell" transcend human reason and are passed on to us in Sacred Scripture. Human teachers of this highest wisdom, sacred doctrine, pass on to their students what comes from God and is contained in Scripture, and the goal of this instruction is to bring them to eternal life with God. For their high calling these human teachers must be people of highest moral quality whose hearts are set on heaven and not on the things of this world; they must be enlightened; and they must be capable of defending the truths of faith. Their students must have humility to receive the teaching, sound judgment to assess it correctly, and fertile minds to apply and develop it. No one is capable of the high calling of a Christian teacher on his own, Aquinas concludes; he must hope that God will make him adequate for the task.

When Aquinas began work on the *Summa theologiae* ten years later it was a continuation of his work as a Christian teacher, the calling to which he had given his life. Aquinas recognized, of course, that preaching a sermon or writing a catechism for ordinary Christians were forms of Christian teaching. But the *Summa theologiae*, as I argued in chapter three, was not intended for ordinary Christians. It was for very well-prepared and gifted students, and was meant to be the culmination of their instruction, of their pursuit of the *scientia* of sacred doctrine. This work was intended to teach those who were themselves preparing to become Christian teachers, whether as priests or bishops who instructed or preached to the faithful as part of their pastoral duties, or as Masters in a theological faculty. While ordinary Christians receive instruction from human preachers and ministers and need only an adequate share in the teaching, as Aquinas stated in his inaugural lecture, teachers must share "abundantly" in it. Thus the *Summa theologiae* is a specialized sort of Christian teaching, the highest form of teaching for the most able and best prepared, so that they themselves may become effective preachers and teachers of divine wisdom. It is meant to instill in students the highest form of divine *scientia* of which humans are capable in this life.

At the end of chapter three several objections were raised about understanding the *Summa theologiae* as an attempt to instill the *scientia* of sacred doctrine. In chapters four to six we discussed the first two of these, and in this chapter we will briefly consider the remaining two objections. First, Aquinas clearly states that we cannot have *scientia* of the articles of faith, the principles of sacred doctrine, because we cannot apprehend the mysteries of faith in this life. Because Aquinas's students could not have *scientia* of the principles of sacred doctrine, it does not seem they could have *scientia* of the conclusions, and thus could not in this life possess the *scientia* of sacred doctrine. Second, if the *Summa theologiae* is second-level pedagogy as I have claimed, the presentation should move from the first cause, God, to effects in creation. Although this may explain the general structure of the *prima pars*, it is more difficult to see how other parts of the *Summa theologiae* fit into this structure.

We cannot have *scientia* of the principles of sacred doctrine in this life, Aquinas clearly states, because we are not capable of a full vision of their truth.[2] Such a full vision of the truth of these principles would require that we fully grasp the terms of these assertions through apprehending the intelligible forms they signify, and thus understand that the predications are – as principles of a *PA scientia* must be – true and necessary, and that they identify the causes of conclusions within the field. In this life, however, we cannot apprehend the Divine essence nor many of the forms signified in the articles of faith, and so we cannot have a full vision of the truth of these propositions; they must remain mysteries for us. Nevertheless, although he holds that we cannot have *scientia* of these principles, Aquinas is just as clear that the sacred doctrine is a *scientia*, albeit a subaltern *scientia*, and that the *Summa theologiae* is a work which is intended to instruct people in this *scientia*.[3] How, then, can we fail to have *scientia* of the principles of sacred doctrine and yet to some degree acquire the intellectual virtue of the *scientia* of sacred doctrine?

On some readings of Aquinas and the *PA* it is difficult to see how one could fail to have *scientia* of the principles of sacred doctrine, and yet in some sense have *scientia* of sacred doctrine. At the end of chapter one we mentioned one understanding of the *PA* according to which it puts forth a foundationalism which is, at least in large part, driven by a concern to respond to certain skeptical objections. Scott MacDonald has recently argued for what seems to be a version of this kind of interpretation. It will be helpful here to set forth MacDonald's reading in some detail, and then to see how the interpretation developed in the preceding chapters of this work differs from it.

According to MacDonald's Aquinas, *scientia* is "certain and complete cognition," and it is the paradigm of cognition, for such "cognition of the truth of a given proposition constitutes impeccable justification – a kind and degree of justification that guarantees the proposition's truth."[4] In chapter three and the corresponding *lectiones* of the *PA* we find an argument that there are indemonstrable foundations of scientific demonstration. The first part of Aquinas's argument establishes that circular demonstration is incoherent, so that if there is demonstrative *scientia* we must have knowledge of indemonstrable principles. When faced with skeptical objections that we do not know indemonstrable principles and hence do not have *scientia*, Aquinas concedes that the skeptical objection is coherent, but simply asserts that we can know indemonstrable principles. But this assertion "[leaves] open the skeptical possibility that there is not inferential justification" (166). A second argument is needed, therefore, and, MacDonald claims, "Aquinas's positive characterization of the nature of non-inferential justification constitutes his second sort of defense of foundationalism" (166). Aquinas's second defense of his foundationalism, then, is to show, against skeptical objections, that we do have non-inferential *scientia* of principles, and we have inferential *scientia* of the conclusions we deduce from them. Aquinas's account of the paradigm case of *scientia*, MacDonald suggests, is constructed to respond to skeptical objections that we do not have *scientia* at all.

The immediate propositions identified in the *PA* can serve as indemonstrable principles because, MacDonald contends, "the facts expressed by immediate principles are such that when we are acquainted with them, we cannot fail to see their necessity" (171). Thus, when one grasps such a truth "one cannot doubt its truth (since one cannot conceive of it being false) or be mistaken in holding it" (ibid.). If we had such an indubitable apprehension of a truth, it would, of course, be immune to skeptical doubts and objections. And indeed, MacDonald writes, "Aquinas seems to suppose that we have phenomenological evidence for the existence of non-inferential justification of this sort" (172). This implicit phenomenological appeal, MacDonald contends, is the heart of Aquinas's response to the skeptical objections of chapter three of Book 1 of the *Posterior Analytics*.

However, only a limited number of truths could be known with the certainty of perfect *scientia*. In fact, MacDonald writes, "only *a priori* truths of axiomatic systems such as logic and mathematics could satisfy its strict conditions" (174). Aquinas's strategy, MacDonald contends, is to take these cases in which all conditions of *scientia* are fully satisfied as paradigmatic, but allow that other cases which fall short of the paradigm can nevertheless be called *scientia* in a qualified sense. Propositions about particular sensible objects, for example, can be better known to us and "can constitute immediate propositions *for us* and function as epistemically first principles grounding what is *for us* (though not unqualifiedly) *scientia*" (175). Moreover, we can have non-paradigmatic *scientia* of truths which are not absolutely necessary. We can, for instance, have *scientia* of the proposition that the moon is eclipsed, which, though it does not express an absolutely universal and necessary truth, is nevertheless always true whenever the cause is present. We can also have *scientia* of propositions which are true "for the most part" (176).

At the end of his article MacDonald comments, "for the modern reader, it is a striking feature of Aquinas's various epistemological discussions that he seldom explicitly addresses skeptical worries" (185). This is somewhat confusing, for MacDonald has suggested that Aquinas's account of paradigmatic *scientia* is a "second sort of defense of foundationalism" which would respond to skeptical objections. But, as MacDonald notes, paradigmatic *scientia* is limited: "only *a priori* truths of axiomatic systems such as logic and mathematics could satisfy its strict conditions" (174). MacDonald seems to be asking here why Aquinas did not explicitly address skeptical worries about non-paradigmatic *scientia* and other sorts of apprehension.

MacDonald explicitly rejects and argues against the position I have argued for in previous chapters and elsewhere, that Aquinas was an externalist and that his epistemological writings were not driven by a concern to respond to skeptical worries. MacDonald's Aquinas feels he needs a response to the skeptic, but has confidence in a Cartesian argument. MacDonald writes:

It seems to me clear that Aquinas's own grounds for thinking our faculties reliable are similar to Descartes's. If asked what justifies him in thinking our faculties reliable, he would surely reply . . . by pointing us to his philosophical theology and its foundationalist arguments for the existence of a good creator of human cognizers and by appealing to cases in which we have certain and infallible cognition of truth (187).

Aquinas did not develop this argument explicitly, MacDonald concedes, but he perhaps felt he did not need to do so. For his account of paradigmatic *scientia* had shown that we have some certain *scientia*, and thus that global skepticism – the thesis that we have no knowledge at all – is false. And "the direct guarantee we do have for some [of our cognitive faculties] gives us good reason to trust others" (ibid.).

MacDonald's Aquinas is a Cartesian, then, although some of his arguments were not explicitly developed. A major problem for MacDonald's understanding of Aquinas's account of *scientia*, however, is that it is hard to see how it can make sense of the field of inquiry which was Aquinas's central concern throughout his life – sacred doctrine. MacDonald does not and, it seems, cannot admit as *scientia* any cognition which essentially relies on authority or instruction. To the extent a person relies on another's authority, he does not see the truth for himself, and does not have *scientia*, even of a non-paradigmatic sort. On MacDonald's reading, because the central concern is with the refutation of skepticism, the acquisition of *scientia* becomes a process of intellectual bootstrapping in which one relies only on what one can apprehend for oneself in moving from ignorance to *scientia*. Hence, because sacred doctrine essentially relies on authority, MacDonald thinks, it cannot be a *scientia* for us (180). Although it has some positive epistemic status for us, it is not even non-paradigmatic *scientia* (174–80). But if MacDonald is right, then Aquinas's answer to "Whether sacred doctrine is a *scientia*?" in *Summa theologiae* 1.1.2 should be "No." But, in fact, Aquinas there affirms that sacred doctrine is a *scientia* in which we rely on God's authority.[5]

On the reading argued for in previous chapters of this work, however, we can make better sense of what Aquinas says about whether sacred doctrine is a *scientia*. According to that reading Aquinas is not primarily concerned with skeptical worries and the intellectual bootstrapping needed to overcome them. Certainly *scientia* is perfect apprehension of truth within a field and one feature of such apprehension is certainty, but Aquinas is not concerned to attain the indubitable certainty which would satisfy the skeptic. On my reading of Aquinas, central to his understanding of the acquisition of *scientia* is not intellectual bootstrapping but intellectual apprenticeship. Although principles are most knowable in themselves, they are frequently least knowable to us, at least initially. To acquire perfect apprehension of a *scientia* one must submit oneself to training and instruction by the masters within the field. In a first stage of pedagogy, through both experience and instruction, one acquires the concepts and learns key truths within the field. In a second stage, one moves toward full apprehension of principles, so that one becomes fully familiar with them, and one can come to believe the conclusions in the *scientia* on the basis of the principles.

Given the centrality of the notion of apprenticeship in the understanding of a *PA scientia*, we can see how a person can fail to apprehend fully the truth of principles and yet still make significant progress in the acquisition of a *scientia*. Relying on one's teacher for the truth of principles, and under his guidance, a person can come to believe the fundamental truths of the system and its demonstrative structure. Although he falls short of a fully adequate grasp of the principles of the *scientia*, and falls short of the certainty which a reply to the skeptic requires, he still can make real progress in understanding the *scientia* and could be said to have acquired the *scientia*, albeit imperfectly.

According to our understanding of the *PA*, then, one who falls well short of perfect apprehension of the principles of any *scientia* can nevertheless be said to have acquired *scientia* of the field imperfectly. But this is particularly so in the case of sacred doctrine. For although its principles are most knowable in themselves, they are least knowable to us. Unlike other *scientiae*, then, one must rely on the guidance and instruction of a teacher for the principles. In this case the teacher is God, and through believing the articles of faith as revealed by God, and through guidance by the Holy Spirit, one relies on God as a master in the acquisition of this *scientia*.

It is in this way, then, that we can fail to have full *scientia* of principles and yet nevertheless acquire *scientia* of sacred doctrine. In this life we cannot, given our cognitive structure, fully apprehend the principles of sacred doctrine. For this we rely on Divine revelation. Yet we can make progress in our grasp of the demonstrable structure of this *scientia*, and though many people share faith, some can understand more clearly and fully the conclusions which flow from this *scientia*.[6] It is progress in this sort of imperfect apprehension which Aquinas is trying to instill through *Summa theologiae*.

The imperfect acquisition of the *scientia* of sacred doctrine in this life is, of course, directed to the perfect acquisition of sacred doctrine in heaven. When we are transformed and enjoy the vision of God's essence in heaven, we will adequately apprehend the principles of sacred doctrine and will fully attain this wisdom. The mastery of sacred doctrine in this life must remain imperfect, even though it is an inchoate present of the vision we will enjoy in heaven.[7] In this life we are, as Aquinas says, *in via* – on the way – to this perfect *scientia*.

7.2 THE STRUCTURE OF THE *SUMMA THEOLOGIAE*

The second issue to be considered in this chapter concerns the structure of the *Summa theologiae*, and whether the work as a whole actually has the structure which second-level pedagogy requires.

Within a broad concern about structure we can distinguish two different objections to the claim that the *Summa theologiae* is a work of second-level pedagogy. First, an objector may argue, although the *prima pars* moves from God as the first cause to God's effects in creation, it is not immediately clear how the other parts of the *Summa theologiae* fit into this structure. The *prima–secundae* begins with the final end of human life; the *secunda–secundae* treats various virtues and vices individually; and the *tertia pars* concerns the incarnation and sacraments. It is not immediately apparent how these disparate elements fit into the exposition moving from cause to effect which we find in the *prima pars*. A second objection argues that, though it may be granted that the general structure of the *Summa theologiae* accords with second-level pedagogy, nevertheless some parts within that structure seem to contain reasoning *to* first principles, which is part of first-level pedagogy, and not *from* first principles, which is appropriate to second-level pedagogy. For example, the second question of the *Summa theologiae* contains arguments that God, the subject of sacred doctrine, exists. But the *PA* tells us that in second-level pedagogy the existence of the subject of a *scientia* must already be known or assumed, but is not proven.[8]

In order to respond to the first objection let us recall, first of all, what was said in chapter two about the mixed character of the *scientia* of sacred doctrine. Through faith humans, who are the lowest intellectual beings, participate in the *scientia* of the highest intellect, God. For this the believer must accept on God's authority that the articles of faith, the principles of sacred doctrine, are true. Thus he relies on God's authority for *what* he believes. But this is not all. Aquinas makes it clear that propositions have their place in sacred doctrine not according to the way humans conceive and understand them, but according to the way God has *scientia* of them. The structure and unity of sacred doctrine, then, are determined by divine and not human understanding. Thus the believer relies on God not only for what he believes, but also, in some sense, for the *manner* or *mode* in which these propositions are known. In this life, of course, the human believer does not share fully in God's understanding, but still the unity and order of sacred doctrine are determined by divine understanding.

Aquinas appeals to this point to explain how both speculative and practical truths, which fall in distinct merely human *scientiae*, are nevertheless both included in sacred doctrine. Sacred doctrine, he writes, considers things pertaining to diverse (merely human) *scientiae* "because of the formal *ratio* which it considers in diverse things – viz. as they are apprehensible by the divine light."[9] Thus, while other *scientiae* are divided into speculative and practical, "sacred doctrine includes both under itself; as God by the same *scientia* apprehends both Himself and the things He made."[10] This explains, then, why the apparently disparate material of the *prima pars*, on the one hand, and that of the *prima* and *secunda–secundae*, on the other, are joined in the *scientia* of sacred doctrine. And because, as we saw in chapter two, God's own *scientia* moves from cause to effect, the *Summa theologiae* moves from cause to effect, as second-level pedagogy requires.

There is, however, one significant qualification which must be made regarding the second-level pedagogy of the *Summa theologiae*. In the merely human *scientiae*, the process of second-level pedagogy brings about the full virtue of *scientia* immediately. If a student has successfully completed second-level pedagogy in geometry, for example, he will fully possess the intellectual virtue of the *scientia* of geometry. But this is not the case in sacred doctrine. A human can fully possess the *scientia* of sacred doctrine only when he is separated from his earthly body and he is free from the cognitive structure according to which he must abstract intelligible forms from *phantasmata*. In heaven, a person receives intelligible forms directly from God, and in this state, with this cognitive structure, he will fully possess the *scientia* of sacred doctrine. However, although one may study and make great progress in the *scientia* of sacred doctrine, he can only possess it imperfectly. The pedagogy of the *Summa theologiae*, then, can only imperfectly attain its goal in this life.

The pedagogy of the *Summa theologiae*, then, must be adapted to the limitations of the human intellect in this life. For example, although God's own understanding of the truths of sacred doctrine is utterly simple, the presentation of these truths in the *Summa theologiae* must be according to the complexity of composing and dividing in judgments.[11] Consequently, though the order and unity of the *scientia* of sacred doctrine is determined by God's understanding, its presentation in the *Summa theologiae* is of course adapted to human understanding. God knows the speculative and practical in His simple act of understanding, but in humans these must be understood by discrete acts of understanding. Consequently in the *prima–secundae* the *Summa theologiae* treats in a general way the end, nature and principles of human action, but in the *secunda–secundae* it discusses particular virtues and vices, for in practical matters it is the particular which is significant. Thus, although the order and unity of sacred doctrine are determined by God's understanding, the presentation of the *scientia* in the *Summa theologiae* is adapted to human understanding. This accounts for some of the complexity in the *Summa theologiae*.

One further point about the pedagogy of the *Summa theologiae* is needed here. The movement from the imperfect possession of sacred doctrine in this life to its perfect possession in heaven is not achieved simply through further intellectual perfection. Perfection is attained only when we are separated from our bodies by death, and God grants us the vision of the divine essence. For this a good will is required.[12] Although God can make a person's will good immediately by His power, He has ordained that rectitude of the will should be attained through good works, and through the salvific power of Christ.[13] The second and third parts of the *Summa theologiae* fit into the second-level presentation which moves from cause to effects. These parts are lengthy and detailed, however, because they are of particular importance to humans who are striving to attain perfection in this *scientia*. The discussion of good and bad action in the *prima* and *secunda–secundae*, and the discussion of Christ and the sacraments in the *tertia pars*, instruct us how to attain the virtue and holiness needed to enjoy the vision of God in heaven, in which the perfection of sacred doctrine consists.

Taking note of these points we can, I believe, understand the *Summa theologiae* as a work of second-level pedagogy, albeit one geared to the Christians in this life who are on the way to the perfection of this *scientia*, the vision of God in heaven. The *prima pars*, after an introductory question about sacred doctrine itself, considers in turn God, creation, the distinctions among creatures, angels and humans and the conservation and governance of creatures. The movement here is clearly from cause to effect, as we would expect in second-level pedagogy.

The second part of the *Summa theologiae* concerns the actions of a particular species within the created order, human beings. It concerns the ultimate end of human life and the ways in which a person can attain or deviate from this end. An extended treatment of these issues is necessary, for the perfection of this *scientia* requires rectitude of the will which is attained by performing good actions. And although in speculative *scientiae* the subject is treated in its generality and principles are universals, in practical *scientiae* discussion must deal with particulars, for "universal moral discussions are less useful, since actions are performed in particular circumstances."[14] Hence, the second part of the *Summa theologiae* moves from a discussion of the general components and principles of action in the *prima–secundae* to a consideration of particular virtues and vices in the *secunda–secundae*. As Aquinas writes: "because operations and actions concern individual things, every practical *scientia* is completed by a consideration of particulars. Hence the consideration of morality, since it is about human actions, must first be propounded universally, and then in its particulars."[15]

The treatment of practical matters in the second part begins with the final cause, for, as Aristotle wrote, "in actions that for the sake of which [i.e. the final cause] is the first principle."[16] Whereas a principle stating the quiddity of something is the first principle in speculative *scientiae*, in practical or moral *scientiae* it is the final end.[17] Thus the treatment of morality begins with the first cause, the ultimate end of human life, or beatitude. It then treats human action, by which the properly human end is attained, and the components of action. It distinguishes good and bad actions, and discusses the consequences of such actions. It then takes up the passions of the soul, which are not proper to humans but common to all animals. Next it discusses the principles of action, and first considers the intrinsic principles, which are the potencies and habits of the agent. And finally it treats extrinsic principles, and primarily the principle of good actions, God, who instructs us through the law and aids us through grace.

In the *secunda–secundae*, as we mentioned earlier, Aquinas takes up particular virtues, vices, gifts and beatitudes. He first treats those common to all people, and arranges this discussion around the three theological virtues (faith, hope and charity) and the four cardinal virtues (prudence, justice, fortitude and temperance). He then treats virtues proper to particular states and callings in life.

In the *tertia pars* of the *Summa theologiae* Aquinas turns to Jesus Christ. As he writes, "in order to complete this theological work, it is necessary that, after the consideration of human life's ultimate end, of virtue and of vice, there follow our treatment of the Savior of all and of his surpassing benefits for the human race."[18] Thus in this third part he treats first the mystery of the incarnation of Christ and what Christ did and suffered. He then discusses the sacraments, which have effect from Christ. And although Aquinas died before he could complete the *tertia pars*, he intended to discuss immortal life to which all are called in Christ.

The *Summa theologiae* is a work of second-level pedagogy, albeit one with some structural peculiarities. These peculiarities are due first to the fact that God's understanding determines the order and structure of this *scientia*, and secondly to the need for instruction in this *scientia* to instill moral and spiritual as well as intellectual perfection. Moreover, the *scientia* of the *Summa theologiae* is such that it can only be imperfectly instilled by its human teachers, for it must wait for God's action to perfect it through the beatific vision. Still, the *Summa theologiae* offers second-level pedagogy which attempts to inculcate in its students the most perfect possession of sacred doctrine possible in this life.

We turn now to the second objection regarding the structure of the *Summa theologiae*. This objection concedes that the general structure of the *Summa theologiae* moves from cause to effect, but points out that parts of it seems to argue *to* and *not from* first principles. For example, at the start of the *prima pars* Aquinas considers the question "Whether God exists?", and argues in his famous five ways for an affirmative answer. But God is the subject of the *scientia* of sacred doctrine, and according to the *PA*, in second-level inquiry one must already know that the subject of the *scientia* exists. Moreover, the first five questions of the *prima–secundae* seem to mirror the *Nicomachean Ethics* in arguing to perfect beatitude as the ultimate end for human beings. But in practical matters the final end is the first principles, and so these are arguments to a principle of this *scientia*. Hence, the objection concludes, contrary to what we expect in second-level pedagogy, parts of the *Summa theologiae* reason to and not from principles.

Even when one apprehends principles within a *scientia*, however, one's reasoning to such principles is not to be entirely set aside, for it shapes one's understanding of those principles. In *Posterior Analytics* 1.33 Aristotle says that although two people may have *scientia* and opinion about the same thing, their apprehension differs in manner.[19] One person apprehends a truth by one description, under one *ratio*, and the other person under another.[20] If one is to have *scientia*, it is not enough that one have true opinions about principles, but one must apprehend them under the proper description or *ratio*, and this requires reasoning to them in the right way.[21] If this is so, then one's reasoning to principles is important even in second-level pedagogy, for such reasoning determines one's understanding of the principles. Hence, there is good reason to include a recapitulation of the reasoning to principles in second-level pedagogy, for it illustrates the proper understanding of the principles.

The inclusion of reasoning to principles is particularly significant in the *scientia* of sacred doctrine. In this *scientia*, even at the second level we are considering, the student does not fully grasp the principles; he cannot apprehend God's essence, nor can he fully understand the good which consists in the vision of the divine essence. According to Aquinas, in this life we understand God negatively, by understanding what He is not, and by analogy with creatures. Thus the arguments for God's existence in *Summa theologiae* 1.2.3, and the reasoning toward the ultimate end of human life in the first five questions of the *prima–secundae*, are included in the *Summa theologiae* not to establish the conclusion, but to clarify the student's understanding of these notions. Although the student would have already been familiar with these sorts of arguments, they are recapitulated here so that the principles will be correctly understood.[22]

It seems something like this *must* be the case for many of the arguments of the *Summa theologiae*. Consider the "five ways" in *Summa theologiae* 1.2.3. In question 1, article 8 of the *prima pars* we are told that we cannot, within this *scientia*, argue about the truths of the principles of the science, the articles of faith; but in question 2, article 3 of the *prima pars*, we are asking whether God exists. That God exists is not a principle of this *scientia*, but it is certainly presupposed by the principles. Indeed in *Summa theologiae* 1.2.3 itself, the *Sed contra* passage quotes the Book of Exodus, where God says "I am who am." One who comes to the *Summa theologiae* is supposed to accept Sacred Scripture, for the principles of sacred doctrine are a summary of its revelation. But how can one accept this Exodus passage and still raise the question, "Does God exist?" It seems clear that in the *Summa* these arguments are not attempts to establish a conclusion which is in doubt in the context of the work, but ways to help us understand and speak adequately (or less inadequately) about God, to understand God according to the proper, or least improper, description or *ratio*.[23]

7.3 CONCLUSION

A concern with skepticism in modern Western philosophy has led us to take as first principles of our knowledge what is better known to us and to see the account (λόγος) or justification necessary for knowledge to be linked with skeptical challenges. Consequently the thought that the causal principles (in Aristotle's sense of αἰτία, or Aquinas's sense of *causa*) of a science should or even could also be the principles of our apprehension of truths of that science, and that this apprehension might be expressed in an account which is a demonstration from such causes, seems passing strange to us. Thus Burnyeat writes, "it may be counted a permanent victory of skepticism that . . . it has made Aristotle's *Posterior Analytics* remarkably hard for us to read."[24] I have argued that the epistemological notion which shapes Aquinas's *Summa theologiae* was Aristotle's concept of ἐπιστήμη, which Aquinas developed into his concept of *scientia*. I believe, furthermore, that the concerns of modern philosophy to which Burnyeat alludes have made Aquinas's *Summa theologiae* remarkably hard for us to read as well. In this work I have tried to gain a clearer picture of Aquinas's concept of *scientia* and of his project in the *Summa theologiae*, so that we may become better readers of this great work and benefit more fully from its pedagogy.

Notes

INTRODUCTION

1   The end of the Second Vatican Council in 1965 is a somewhat arbitrary date to pick as a watershed for attitudes toward Aquinas. But at that time great Neo-Scholastic Thomists, such as Etienne Gilson and Jacques Maritain, had published their major works, and the writings of others, such as Bernard Lonergan and Karl Rahner, were no longer focused on Aquinas. At the same time, there arose a greater interest in the thought of Aquinas by those outside the traditional Neo-Scholastic circles.

2   Anthony Kenny, "Introduction" in *Aquinas: A Collection of Critical Essays*, ed. Anthony Kenny (Notre Dame: University of Notre Dame Press, 1969), 1.

3   Although not numerous, there were important exceptions to this. They include some of the writings of G. E. M. Anscombe, F. C. Copleston, P. T. Geach and Anthony Kenny.

4   Joseph Maréchal, SJ, *The Starting Point of Metaphysics: Lessons on the Historical and Theoretical Development of the Problem of Knowledge, Cahier One: From Antiquity to the End of the Middle Ages: The Critique of Knowledge*, trans. Joseph Donceel, SJ in *A Maréchal Reader* (New York: Herder and Herder, 1970), 3.

5   Bernard Lonergan, SJ, *Verbum: Word and Idea in Aquinas*, ed. David Burrell, CSC (Notre Dame: Notre Dame Press, 1967).

6   Karl Rahner, SJ, *Spirit in the World*, trans. by William Dych (New York: Herder and Herder, 1968). Maréchal was clear that the transcendental critique is not found in Aquinas's own writings, but that he arrived at his Transcendental Thomism by developing Aquinas's views in light of Kant's critique. But passages in Rahner and Lonergan suggest that the Kantian critique is in fact found in some form in Aquinas's own writings.

7   E.g., L. Noël, *Le Réalisme immédiat* (Louvain, 1938).

8   Etienne Gilson, *Thomist Realism and the Critique of Knowledge*, trans. by Mark A. Wauck (San Francisco: Ignatius Press, 1986), 149.

9   Jacques Maritain, *Distinguish to Unite, or The Degrees of Knowledge*, trans. by

228 *Notes to pages 6–12*

Gerald B. Phelan (New York: Charles Scribner's Sons, 1959), especially chs. ii–v; *Essence and the Existent*, trans. by Lewis Galantiere and Gerald B. Phelan (New York: Pantheon, 1948), especially ch. 1.

10 Henry Frankfurt, "Presidential Address of the Eastern Division of the American Philosophical Association," in *Proceedings and Addresses of the American Philosophical Association* (November, 1992), vol. 66, no. 3, 8.

11 Gilson argued against this second sort of distortion in several works. See, for example, his introduction to *The Christian Philosophy of St. Thomas Aquinas*, trans. by L. K. Shook, CSB (New York: Random House, 1956), 3–25.

12 Among the major figures in more recent scholarship on Aquinas and in a Thomistic vein are the contributors to *The Cambridge History of Later Medieval Philosophy*, eds. Norman Kretzmann, Anthony Kenny & Jan Pinborg (Cambridge University Press, 1982), and the contributors to *The Cambridge Companion to Aquinas*, eds. Norman Kretzmann & Eleonore Stump (Cambridge University Press, 1993). See also the forthcoming edition on Analytical Thomism in *The Monist* 8:2 (April, 1998); and the forthcoming *Analytical Thomism*, Oxford Companion to Philosophy Series (Oxford: Oxford University Press).

13 See *Whose Justice? Which Rationality?* (Notre Dame: Notre Dame Press, 1988).

1. *SCIENTIA* IN THE *POSTERIOR ANALYTICS*

1 Aristotle, *Posterior Analytics*, 1.2, 71b 10–11. Translations of the *Posterior Analytics* are mine, though I often (as in this case) follow closely that of Jonathan Barnes in *Aristotle's Posterior Analytics*, trans. by Jonathan Barnes 2nd edn. (New York: Oxford University Press, 1992). When the difference between the translation of Aquinas's Latin text and that of Aristotle's Greek text is significant, I follow the Latin text.

2 There is an enormous amount of work on Aristotle's *Posterior Analytics*. My interpretation has been influenced by Richard McKirahan's *Posterior Analytics, Principles and Proofs: Aristotle's Theory of Demonstrative Science* (Princeton University Press, 1992) and M. F. Burnyeat's "Aristotle on Understanding Knowledge" in *Aristotle on Science: The Posterior Analytics. Proceedings of the Eighth Symposium Aristotelicum*, ed. E. Berti (New York: Editrice Antenore, 1981), 97–139. Other important recent works on Aristotle's *Posterior Analytics* are: Jonathan Barnes, "Aristotle's Theory of Demonstration," in *Articles on Aristotle: 1., Science*, eds. Jonathan Barnes, Malcolm Schofield & Richard Sorabji (London: Duckworth, 1975), 65–87, and "Proof and the Syllogism," in *Aristotle on Science: The Posterior Analytics Proceedings of the Eighth Symposicum Aristotelicum*; *Posterior Analytics*, trans. Barnes; Michael Ferejohn, *The Origins of Aristotelian Science* (New Haven: Yale University Press, 1991); R. J. Hankinson, "Philosophy of Science," in *The Cambridge Companion to Aristotle*, ed. Jonathan Barnes,

(Cambridge University Press, 1995), 109–139; T. H. Irwin, *Aristotle's First Principles* (Oxford University Press, 1988); C. C. W. Taylor, "Aristotle's Epistemology," in *Epistemology*. ed. S. Everson (Cambridge University Press, 1990), 116–142.

These works are of great help in understanding Aristotle, but a careful discussion of this literature would require more space than is available in this work. Moreover, such a discussion would take us too far afield, for, as was said above, our primary interest is not in Aristotle's *Posterior Analytics*, but in Aquinas's understanding and reception of this work.

Literature on Aquinas's commentary on the *Posterior Analytics* is much more limited, though there is an important recent article by Scott MacDonald ("Theory of Knowledge," in *The Cambridge Companion to Aquinas*, eds. Kretzmann & Stump, 160–95). The approaches of MacDonald and myself differ in certain fundamental ways, and my intention in this work is to develop, present and argue for my own interpretation. In chapter seven I will discuss some fundamental differences between MacDonald's approach and my own with respect to the *scientia* of sacred doctrine. However, a thorough discussion of my differences with MacDonald will have to wait until another occasion.

3 This subject genus is primarily a common nature, but Aristotle and Aquinas at times speak of it as the collection of individuals sharing this common nature, and at times as including the attributes which belong to them by virtue of this common nature.

4 This summary as well as subsequent discussion in this chapter draw a great deal from McKirahan's thorough and extremely illuminating study of Aristotle's understanding of science in the *Posterior Analytics*, *Principles and Proofs: Aristotle's Theory of Demonstrative Science*.

5 The principles of a science also include those common to several sciences, such as the principle of non-contradiction. These are discussed below, and are not mentioned here for the sake of simplicity.

6 Burnyeat, "Aristotle on Understanding Knowledge." The influence of Burnyeat's article on the present chapter is pervasive, as will be apparent to anyone familiar with it.

7 See *Posterior Analytics* II.16 & 17.

8 "For having broad leaves is a cause of the leaves of a tree falling" (*In Post. anal.* II.18.567).

9 See *In Post. anal.* II.18.574; II.18.578.

10 Perhaps more precisely, one must come to believe that vines are sap-congealers at the leaf stalk because one believes they are broad-leaved; and then one comes to believe they are deciduous because one believes they are sap-congealers at the leaf stalk.

11 For an excellent discussion of translation problems regarding Aristotle's *Posterior Analytics*, see Burnyeat, "Aristotle on Understanding Knowledge." See also Eleonore Stump, "Aquinas on the Foundations of

Knowledge," in *Aristotle and His Medieval Interpreters*, eds. Richard Bosley & Martin Tweedale, *Canadian Journal of Philosophy*, Supp. vol. 7, 125–58. Stump's discussion of *cognitio* and *scientia* in Aquinas is very helpful, though our respective understandings of Aquinas's notion of *scientia* differ.

12 *In Post. anal.* 1.1 (*proemium*) 6.

13 Ibid.

14 *In Post. anal.* 1.iv.29.

15 *Posterior Analytics* 1.1, 71a 1–2.

16 *In Post. anal.* 1.1.9.

17 *In Post. anal.* 1.ii.14.

18 The status of the other middle term, *being a sap-congealer in the leaf stalk*, will be discussed in section 1.3 below.

19 *In Post. anal.* 1.iv.28.

20 As Aristotle writes, this is the accepted view "for both those who do not have *scientia* and those who do – the former think they are themselves in such a state, while the latter actually have *scientia*" (*Posterior Analytics* 1.2, 71b 13–15).

21 *In Post. anal.* 1.iv.32.

22 Ibid.

23 Aquinas writes: "one having *scientia* in an unqualified sense must also apprehend the application of cause to effect" (*In Post. anal.* 1.iv.32).

24 *In Post. anal.* 1.iv.32.

25 Later Aquinas writes: "Although any necessary truth can be syllogized from contingent premises, nevertheless *scientia* of a necessary truth cannot be had through a contingent middle . . . And because not only is the conclusion of a demonstration necessary, but also one has *scientia* through the demonstration, as has been said, it follows that a demonstrative syllogism is from necessary premises" (*In Post. anal.* 1.ix.77; see also *In Post. anal.* 1.xiii.116). The requirement that the premises be necessary only makes sense here if "having *scientia* through demonstration" means "having *scientia* of the conclusion as necessary through demonstration."

26 *In Post. anal.* 1.iv.36.

27 *In Post. anal.* 1.iv.37.

28 See *Posterior Analytics* 1.2, 70b 9 and *In Post anal.* 1.iv.32.

29 *In Post. anal.* 1.ix.78.

30 Ibid.

31 Aquinas adds that in dialectic the 'is said of all' may cover only a particular time or period of time, whereas in demonstration it is taken to cover all times (*In Post. anal.* 1.x.79).

32 *In Post. anal.* 1.x.83.

33 *In Post. anal.* 1.x.84.

34 Ibid.

35 Ibid.

36 *In Post. anal.* I.x.85.

37 *In Post. anal.* I.x.88.

38 As we will see in section 1.4 below, the *PA* uses *necessity* in a somewhat loose sense.

39 Accidents which are *per se* in the fourth mode are also called proper accidents, and are distinguished from accidents due to extraneous causes. See *In Meta.* v.xxii.1139–43.

40 *In Post. anal.* I.ix.78.

41 *In Post. anal.* I.xi.97.

42 As Aquinas writes, "if it be asked what it is to have leaves fall off, we will say that it is nothing more than 'the seminal sap congealing at the point of contact,' – i.e. of the leaf with the branch" (*In Post. anal.* II.xix.579).

43 McKirahan's solution to this problem with regard to the *Posterior Analytics* is to introduce what he calls a "fat definition" which includes all such immediate, indemonstrable attributes. On this reading, *Broad-leaved plants are sap-congealers at the leaf stalk* would be a *per se* predication in the first mode. But McKirahan admits that the notion of a fat definition is not found in the *Posterior Analytics*, and he introduces it as a development of Aristotle's doctrine. See McKirahan, *Posterior Analytics*, chapter ix.

44 *In Post. anal.* II.xvii.561.

45 For a discussion of application syllogisms in Aristotle's *Posterior Analytics*, see McKirahan, chapter xiv.

46 *In Post. anal.* I.xv.127.

47 *Posterior Analytics* 1.7, 75b 10–13. The translation is my translation of Aquinas's Latin text. For Aquinas's summary of the main argument, see *In Post. anal.* I.xiv.132.

48 *In Post. anal.* I.xx.167.

49 *In Post. anal.* I.xx.168.

50 *In Post. anal.* I.xx.169.

51 *In Post. anal.* I.xviii.156.

52 *In Post. anal.* I.xv.131.

53 Ibid.

54 *In Post. anal.* I.xvii.145.

55 *In Post. anal.* I.xx.171.

56 *In Post. anal.* I.xvii.146.

57 *In Post. anal.* I.xx.171.

58 *Posterior Analytics* 1.6, 74b 5–12.

59 *Posterior Analytics* 1.8, 75b 21–5.

60 "A potency of the soul flows from its essence, not through a transformation, but as a certain natural result, and it is simultaneous with the soul" (*ST* I.77.7.ad 1).

61 *ST* I.78.3.

62 *ST* I–II.85.2.3; *De pot.* 6.1.

63 It also seems to be possible for a predicate P to belong without exception to a subject S, and yet for P not to belong necessarily to S. In his commentary on the *Physics* II.1, where Aristotle discusses what belongs to a nature, Aquinas writes: "[Aristotle] adds 'primitive' [to his definition of nature] because nature, although it is a principle of the *motio* of composites, is nevertheless not primitive. Hence that animal is moved downward is not due to the nature of animal as animal, but to the nature of the dominant element" (*In Physica* II.i.145). Thus *moves downward* does not belong to *animal* qua animal, but belongs to the dominant element – presumably, earth – in the bodies of animals. Thus this predicate, although it belongs without exception to animal, does not belong *per se*, and hence does not belong necessarily. Thus we have a predicate which belongs without exception to a subject, and yet does not belong necessarily (in the sense in which the *PA* uses this term).

64 *In Post. anal.* I.xlii.374.

65 Ibid.

66 Although I have used *certitude* and *certain*, *certitudo*, *certus* and their cognates are difficult to translate. In classical usage these terms had not only the subjective sense of being beyond doubt or sure, but also the objective sense of being settled, fixed or established. (See Charlton T. Lewis & Charles Short, *A Latin Dictionary*, [1879], s.v. *certus, a, um.*) In the *PA* the terms have both the subjective and objective connotations. Thus the fact that the physical sciences deal with objects which are subject to chance changes due to their matter make them less *certae*, even though one may be more subjectively sure about conclusions in physics than in mathematics.

67 *In Post. anal.* I.xli.358.

68 *In Post. anal.* I.xvi.142.

69 MacDonald, "Theory of Knowledge," 174.

70 *In Post. anal.* v.xiii.936.

71 Aristotle's favorite examples of demonstrative syllogisms in the *PA* are geometrical. In all such demonstrations there is no priority with respect to place, time, motion or discrete things, and so it cannot be priority in any of these senses which is required for demonstration.

72 See, for example, *In Post. anal.* I.viii.71 and I.xvii.147.

73 See the discussion of the 'better known' condition below.

74 *In Meta.* v.xiii.950.

75 Aristotle, *Categories* 12, 14a 30–5.

76 E.g. *In Post. anal.* I.ix.78.

77 *In Meta.* v.xiii.951.

78 Ibid.

79 Priority in this sense seems to amount to the condition that demonstration proceeds from definitional truths, which are *per se* in the first or second mode, to demonstrating proper or *per se* accidents, which are *per se* in the fourth mode.

80 *In Post. anal.* 1.iv.42.
81 Aristotle, *Categories* 12, 14a 11–14.
82 *In Meta.* v.xiii.952.
83 *In Post. anal.* 1.v.45.
84 *In Post. anal.* 1.xviii.197.
85 This example may be over-simplified, for, although alkane hydrocarbons are particularly combustible, other compounds are combustible under certain conditions. Combustibility, then, would not seem to be exclusively an attribute of alkane hydrocarbons.

One might argue, however, that because alkane hydrocarbons share a similar chemical structure, the cause of their combustibility would be the same. The cause of the combustibility of other compounds would be different, and thus they would require a different explanation and a different demonstrative syllogism. As Aristotle writes about another case: "it is possible for there to be several explanations of the same feature – but not for items of the same form. E.g. the explanation for longevity in quadrupeds is their not having bile, while for birds it is their being dry (or something else)" (*Posterior Analytics* II.17, 99b 4–7).

86 *In Post. anal.* 1.ii.14.
87 Aristotle and Aquinas add here that this prior knowledge may be prior either in time or, though apprehended simultaneously, may be prior only in nature but not in time. This distinction is illustrated by the following syllogism:

(1) All triangles have three angles equal to two right angles.
(2) The figure described in this semicircle is a triangle.

---

(3) This figure has three angles equal to two right angles.

Normally, the apprehension of proposition (1) is temporally prior to the apprehension of (2). However, for one who already knows (1), once proposition (2) is apprehended, (3) is apprehended immediately. Still, although the apprehension of (2) and (3) may be simultaneous, the apprehension of (2) is naturally prior to that of (3), for the apprehension of the former is what brings about the apprehension of the latter.

88 For those who have read Aquinas along the lines of a skepticism-driven foundationalism, see Peter Hoenen, SJ, *Reality and Judgement According to St. Thomas*, trans. by Henry F. Tiblier, SJ (Chicago: Henry Regenery, 1952), esp. Part Two; Scott MacDonald, "Theory of Knowledge," 160–95; and Jonathan Dancy and Ernest Sosa, eds. *A Companion to Epistemology* (Oxford: Blackwell, 1993), s.v. "Aquinas, Thomas" by Scott MacDonald. Marie-Dominique Chenu, OP in *La théologie comme science au XIIIe siècle* (2nd edn. 1943), a work we will discuss extensively in chapter two, also adopts this view of the *PA*.
89 *Posterior Analytics* 1.9, 76a 26.
90 *In Post. anal.* 1.xviii.149.

91 *In Post. anal.* 1.xiii.119.
92 Burnyeat in "Aristotle on Understanding Knowledge" discusses in an illuminating way the differences between Aristotle's foundationalism and that of those concerned with skeptical doubts. See esp. pp. 137–38.
93 *In Post. anal.* 1.iv.42.
94 Ibid.
95 See *Posterior Analytics* 11.19, 100a 4–14; and *In Post. anal.* 11.xx.592–5.
96 The *PA* gives several examples of a faltering approach to a grasp of the universal, which is expressed in the middle terms of a demonstrative syllogism. See Aristotle's discussion of and Aquinas's commentaries on the non-twinkling planets (1.10), an eclipse of the sun (11.1 & 2) and thunder (1.10).
97 *Posterior Analytics* 1.1, 71a 1–2.
98 "Ad ostendendum igitur necessitatem demonstrativi syllogismi, praemittit Aristoteles quod cognitio in nobis acquiritur ex aliqua cognitione praeexistenti" (*In Post. anal.* 1.i.9).
99 *In Post. anal.* 1.ii.14.
100 *In Post. anal.* 1.iii.22.
101 *In Post. anal.* 1.vi.54.
102 Ibid.
103 Ibid.
104 *In Post. anal.* 11.i.416.
105 *In Post. anal.* 1.ii.14.
106 Ibid.
107 *In Post. anal.* 1.iv.43bis.
108 "Per effectum notiorem causa potest fieri demonstratio non faciens scire propter quid, sed tantum quia" (*In Post. anal.* 1.xxiii.195).
109 *In Post. anal.* 1.xxiii.197.
110 "There is such a thing as intellectual habituation as well as moral habituation, and in Aristotle's view both take us beyond mere knowing to types of contemplative and practical activity which are possible only when something is so internalized as to have become one's second nature" (Burnyeat, "Aristotle on Understanding Knowledge," 130).
111 *Metaphysics* 1.2, 983a14–21. My translation is based on William of Moerbeke's Latin translation of Aristotle and I have added the phrases in brackets to elucidate Aquinas's understanding of this compressed and difficult text. Aristotle's phrase τῶν θαυμάτων ταὐτόματα is translated "automatic marionettes" in W.D. Ross's translation (*The Complete Works of Aristotle*, ed. Jonathan Barnes [Princeton University Press, 1985], vol. 2, 1555). Moerbeke translates it *mirabilium automata*, and Aquinas understands Aristotle to be speaking of events which seem (at least to those ignorant of a cause) to happen without cause and of themselves, and thus to be wondrous. Thus I have rendered the Latin phrase "automatism of marvelous occurrences."

112 *Nicomachean Ethics* 1.4, 1095a31–b1.

113 Jonathan Barnes, "Aristotle's Theory of Demonstration," in *Articles on Aristotle: 1. Science*, 77.

114 Alasdair MacIntyre, *Three Rival Versions of Moral Enquiry: Encyclopaedia, Genealogy, and Tradition* (Notre Dame: University of Notre Dame Press, 1990), 63–8.

2. *SCIENTIA* AND SACRED DOCTRINE

1 M.-D. Chenu, OP, *La Théologie comme science au XIIIe siècle*, 2nd edn. (1943). The first edition appeared as an essay in *Archives d'Histoire Doctrinale et Littéraire du Moyen Age*, 2 (1927), 31–71.

2 *ST*1–11.57.5.ad 3; 11–11.4.8.

3 *ST*1.12.7; 1.14.3; 1.117.1; 111.9.3.obj 2 & ad 2.

4 *ST*1.2.2; 11–11.174.3.*sed contra*.

5 *ST*1.1.3; 1–11.54.2.ad 2; 111.11.6.

6 *ST*1.1.2.

7 *ST*1.12.13.ad 3; 1–11.51.2.*corpus* & ad 3.

8 The example of harmonics and arithmetic which Aquinas discusses in 1.1.2 is found in *Posterior Analytics* 1.9, 76a 10–11; the example of geometry and optics, or perspective, is found in 1.9, 78a 24; the example of the angles of a triangle equaling two right angles which is discussed in *ST*1.12.7 is found throughout the *Posterior Analytics*, e.g., 1.1, 71a 19–20; 1.4, 73b 25ff.; 1.5, 74a 25ff.; 1.24, 85a27 & b 5.

9 Chenu, 73. All translations of Chenu's work are mine.

10 Ibid.

11 *ST*1.1.8.

12 *ST*1.12.13.ad 3; 11–11.2.1.1–3.

13 *ST*1.12.11.

14 For a much more extensive description of Aquinas's very complex account of the distinction between natural potencies and virtues, on one hand, and those due to a further grace or gift of God, on the other, see chapters five and six below.

15 *ST*1.1.7.

16 *ST*1.1.2.

17 Ibid.

18 Chenu, 87.

19 Ibid., 88.

20 SSS 1 *prologus*, quaest. 1, art. 3, quaestincula 3, sol. 2. This passage is not included in Busa's more recent edition of the *Scriptum* on the *Sentences*, but is found in the earlier Mandonnet edition. See *Scriptum super libros Sententiarum Magister Petri Lombardi Episcopi Parisiensis*, ed R. P. Mandonnet, OP (Paris: Lathielleux, 1929).

21 Chenu, 90.

22 Ibid., 92.

23 Ibid., 73.
24 *ST*1.14.2.
25 *ST*1.22.4.
26 *ST*1.23.5.ad 3; 1.47.2; *SCG* II.45.
27 *ST*1.47.2.
28 *ST*1.14.1.
29 *ST*1.85.1.
30 See chapter four below for a more detailed discussion of human cognition.
31 Aquinas's central arguments for these claims can be found in *ST* 1.3. For a very helpful summary and discussion of Aquinas's views on divine simplicity and divine *scientia*, see Brian Davies's *The Thought of Thomas Aquinas* (Oxford University Press, 1992), especially chs. 3 & 7.
32 *ST*1.14.4.
33 *ST*1.14.2 & 3.
34 *ST*1.14.5.
35 *ST*1.14.8.ad 3.
36 *ST*1.14.11.
37 *ST*1.14.11.ad 1.
38 *ST*1.14.13.
39 *ST*1.14.15.
40 *ST*1.54.1,2 & 3; 1.55.1.
41 *ST*1.50.1, 2 & 4; 1.55.3.
42 *ST*1.55.2.
43 *ST*1.58.1.
44 *ST*1.55.3.
45 ST 1.57.2.ad 3.
46 *ST*1.57.3.
47 *ST*1.57.1.
48 *ST*1.85.1.
49 *ST*1.89.1.
50 *ST*1.13.5.
51 *ST*1.13.3.
52 *ST*1.13.1; 1.13.2; 1.13.3.*corpus* & ad 2; 1.13.8.ad 2.
53 *ST* 1.13.5. For a fuller discussion of Aquinas's complex and very significant doctrines about and uses of analogy, see Ralph McInerny, *Studies in Analogy* (The Hague: Marinus Nijhoff, 1968); David Burrell, CSC, *Analogy and Philosophical Language* (New Haven: Yale University Press, 1973), esp. chs. 6 & 7; and Davies, *The Thought of Thomas Aquinas*, ch. 4. For an illuminating contemporary account of analogy, see J. F. Ross, *Portraying Analogy* (Cambridge University Press, 1981).
54 *ST*1.14.1.ad 1.
55 Although the differences between angels and humans are not as great as between God and humans, Aquinas's remarks about the differences between angels and humans and about our inability to understand

angels imply that predications of each group are analogous (see *ST* 1.88.2), though he does not discuss analogy in this context.

56   *Posterior Analytics* 1.2, 71b 9–12. My translation.
57   *In Post. anal.* 1.iv.32.
58   *Posterior Analytics* 1.2 71b 17
59   *In Post. anal.* 1.iv.35.
60   *ST* 1.14.5.
61   *ST* 1.14.8.
62   *ST* 1.14.7. *corpus*, ad 2 & 3.
63   *In Post. anal.* 1.iv.32.
64   *ST* 1.86.1.
65   *ST* 1.14.11.
66   *ST* 1.14.13.
67   Aristotle, *De Interpetratione* 9, 19a 23–24.
68   See *In Periherm.* 1.xv.
69   *ST* 1.14.13.ad 2.
70   Someone may object here that human cognizers can have exactly the same sort of necessary and certain knowledge of singular, contingent events which are present to them through sense perception. If I am watching Fred do pushups, it would seem the proposition *Fred is doing pushups* is just as present to my intellect, and so is just as necessary, by necessity of supposition, for me as it is for God.

Several points are worth noting in response to this objection. First, God knows all events at all times, while humans are aware of only the individuals and events they apprehend through sense perception. Secondly, as I have said, for Aquinas the human intellect cannot apprehend individuals as such, but is only aware of them indirectly.

Still, it certainly is the case that humans apprehend individuals in some way, for they know that propositions about individuals, such as *Fred is doing pushups*, are true. Do they not then know such propositions as necessary by necessity of supposition, just as God does? Here I think the objector's point must be granted: we can know such propositions as necessary in this sense (though I know of no text in which Aquinas explicitly asserts this). But we cannot have *scientia* of them, for we cannot grasp their causes, which are in the matter, which the human intellect cannot grasp. But since God knows all things through Himself, who is "the principle of all principles which enter into the composition of something, whether . . . of the species or the individual" (*ST* 1.14.11.ad 1), He can have *scientia* of individuals as individuals through their causes.

71   *ST* 1.57.1.
72   See e.g. *ST* 1.14.7.obj. 1 & ad 1; 1.14.11.obj. 1 & ad 1; 1.14.13.obj. 1 & ad 1, obj 2 & ad 2, obj. 3 & ad 3; 1.52.2.obj. 1 & ad 1.
73   *Metaphysics* 1.2 983a 9–10; 12.7 1072b 14–30; 12.9 1074b 15–34.

74 For a fuller discussion of the ways in which Aquinas thought he could remain true to Aristotle's doctrine while going beyond Aristotle's explicit claims, see my "Expositions of the Text: Aquinas's Aristotelian Commentaries," *Medieval Philosophy and Theology* 5 (1996), 39–62.

75 As Aquinas makes clear in *ST* 1.1.1, God reveals some truths which could be discovered by unaided human reason. They are revealed because they are necessary for salvation, and if left for humans to discover, they "would only be known by a few, and that after a long time, and with the admixture of many errors." But the proper principles of sacred doctrine are the articles of faith (*ST* 1.1.8), and these cannot be proven by unaided, natural human reason (*ST* 1.2.2.ad 1).

76 *In De Trin.* 2.2.

77 *ST* 1.1.3.ad 2.

78 *ST* 1.75.5. See also 1.57.1 and 1.89.4.

79 Ibid., 73.

80 *ST* II–II.2.3.

81 *SSS* 1, quaest. 1. art. 3, quaestincula 3, sol. 2 (Mandonnet edition). Chenu discusses this on pp. 89–92.

82 See *Oxford Latin Dictionary*, ed. P. G. W. Glare (Oxford: Clarendon Press, 1982), s.v. "quasi." The word clearly has this sense in many passages in Aquinas. See e.g. *ST* 1.7.1; 1.12.2; 1.13.2; 1.23.7; 1.36.1.ad 2; 1.41.3.obj. 2; II–II.1.10.ad 3; II–II.3.1.ad 2; II–II.8.1.ad 2; *In De Trin.* 2.2.ad 4; 5.1.ad 2; 4.1.

83 *In De Trin.* 2.2.ad 4.

84 "Incertitudo causatur propter transmutabilitatem materiae sensibilis; unde quanto magis acceditur ad eam, tanto scientia est minus certa" (*In Post. anal.* 1.xli.358).

85 *In Post. anal.* 1.xlii.376.

86 *ST* 1.1.2.obj. 2.

87 *ST* 1.1.2.ad 2.

88 ST II–II.1.6.ad 1.

89 *ST* 1.1.7.

90 *ST* 1.1.1; 1.2.2. obj. 1 & ad 1.

91 *ST* 1.46.2.

92 Ibid.

93 *ST* 1.19.3.

94 Ibid.

95 Ibid.

96 Of course, Aquinas believes that we can give a *quia* demonstration that, given the existence of the world, God created it.

97 *ST* 1.1.3.ad 2.

98 *ST* 1.1.4.

99 See the discussion of divine *scientia* in section 2.2 above.

3. *SCENTIA* AND THE *SUMMA THEOLOGIAE*

1 The purpose of the Aristotelian commentaries is somewhat controversial. See note 40 below.

2 *ST* 1, *prologus.*

3 For a helpful discussion of the centrality of Aquinas's role as a teacher of Christian theology, see Etienne Gilson, *The Christian Philosophy of St. Thomas Aquinas*, 3–25; and for an excellent discussion of his vocation as a member of the Dominicans, the Order of Preachers, see Josef Pieper, *Guide to Thomas Aquinas*, trans. by Richard & Clara Winston (Notre Dame: University of Notre Dame Press, 1962), chs. 2 & 3.

4 *ST* 1, *prologus.*

5 Marie-Dominique Chenu, OP, *Towards Understanding Saint Thomas*, trans. by A. M. Landry & D. Hughes (Chicago: Regnery, 1964), 297–98.

6 James A. Weisheipl, OP, *Friar Thomas D'Aquino: His Life, Thought, and Work* (New York: Doubleday, 1974), 222.

7 Leonard E. Boyle, OP, *The Setting of the Summa theologiae of Saint Thomas*, The Etienne Gilson Series 5 (Toronto: Pontifical Institute of Mediaeval Studies, 1982), 7.

8 Weisheipl, 223.

9 Boyle, 17.

10 Chenu, 298.

11 Weisheipl, 222–3.

12 Some details of the procedures for disputation at Paris are unclear. I have here followed Weisheipl's description, 124ff..

13 *ST* 1.*prologus.*

14 *De ver.* 10.6.

15 *ST* 1.*prologus.*

16 *ST* 1.2.2.

17 *In Physica*, 1.i.7. Since this principle is repeated in Aquinas's own works, we can suppose that Aquinas embraced what he here attributes to Aristotle.

18 "Sed quia de Deo scire non possumus quid sit, sed quid non sit, non possumus considerare de Deo quomodo sit, sed potius quomodo non sit" (*ST* 1.3.*prologus*).

19 "Deus . . . maxime cognoscibilis est" (*ST* 1.12.1).

20 We find a different procedure in Aquinas's *De ente et essentia*. There Aquinas first treats (in chapter two) essence as found in composite, material substances – which are better known to us but less well known by nature. He only then considers (in chapter four) simple substances – which are better known by nature but less well known to us. This order of treatment follows more closely Aquinas's pedagogical principle for initial instruction in a field, and is not the one we find in the *Summa theologiae*.

21   Chenu, 303.

22   Ibid., 306.

23   Boyle, *The Setting of the Summa theologiae of Saint Thomas.*

24   Since before 1228, each Dominican province had been permitted to send three friars for study to Paris, which was then the only *studium generale*. After the foundation in 1248 of *studia generalia* at the Universities of Cologne, Oxford, Montpellier and Bologna, each Dominican province was also entitled to send two students to each of these general *studia*.

25   William Hinnebusch writes (*The History of the Dominican Order*, vol. 2 [New York: Alba, 1973]) that a consequence of the opening of further *studia generalia* in 1248 was that "by gathering advanced students preparing for the professorship into selected houses of studies, the Order distinguished between advanced theological work and theological preparation for the ministry" (39).

26   Boyle, 7.

27   Ibid., 16.

28   Ibid., 1.

29   Ibid., 14.

30   Ibid., 17.

31   Ibid., 19.

32   Ibid., 17.

33   Ibid., 17. My emphasis.

34   I owe the following point to conversations with my colleague Joseph Wawrykow. But, of course, the claims I make are not necessarily to be attributed to him.

35   *Acta capitulorum provincialium provinciae Romae*, ed T. Kaeppeli, OP, Monumenta Ordinis Fratrum Praedictorum Historica, xx (Rome: Institutum Historicum Fratrum Praedictorum, 1941), 39. See also Weisheipl, 294–6.

36   There would have been reason to continue to teach the *Sentences* to those students destined for university study, for this was still the standard university text. However, for the *fratres communes* in the priories, who were not destined for the universities, there would have been no reason not to substitute the *Summa* as the standard theological text – if, in fact, it was intended for this group.

37   Tolomeo of Lucca, *Historia ecclesiastica*, lib. 23, c. 15, in L. A. Muratori, *Rerum italicarum scriptores*, xi, (Milan: 1724), 1172–73.

38   *ST* 1.*prologus.*

39   *Chartularium universitatis Parisiensis*, ed. Henricus Denifle, OP (Paris: 1889) 1, 277–79. For the best discussion of the course of studies in the arts at Paris and Oxford see Gordon Leff's *Paris and Oxford Universities in the Thirteenth and Fourteenth Centuries* (New York: John Wiley & Sons, 1968), esp. 137–60; and his "The *Trivium* and the Three Philosophies" in *Universities in the Middle Ages*, ed. Hilde de Ridder-Symoens (Cam-

bridge University Press, 1992), vol. 1, of *A History of the University in Europe*, ed. Walter Rüegg, 307–336.

40 See James A. Weisheipl, OP, *Friar Thomas D'Aquino: His Life, Thought, and Work* (Garden City: Doubleday, 1974), 272–85. Weisheipl believes that Aquinas was combating the rise of the heterodox Aristotelianism of the Averroists, and that he undertook the Aristotelian commentaries as "an academic apostolate demanding his best efforts" (284), an apostolate which was to provide "an exegetical guide [to young masters] in order to understand and teach the Aristotelian books accurately without being led into heresy "(284–5).

This view has been challenged, however, by René-A. Gauthier, OP in *Preface to the Sentencia libri De anima* in the Leonine edition of Thomas's *Opera omnia* (Rome: 1882–), 45: 283*-294*. According to Gauthier, Aquinas was not combating Averroists in the Aristotelian commentaries, but had a positive theological and philosophical project. He was trying to extract (*dégager*) from Aristotle's texts a philosophical account of the soul which was valid not just for the ancient Greeks, but for all times, and which could give the Christian a better understanding of the human being as revealed by the Word of God (293*).

41 At Oxford, it seems to have been seven or eight years. See Leff, *Paris and Oxford* 157–8; "The *Trivium*" 328.

42 A cursory lecture was one which sought simply to instill familiarity with a text by reviewing its content and structure with students, but it did not attempt to deal with any philosophical or theological problems arising from the text. These problems were treated in the Master's lecture.

43 See Paris statutes of 1215 in *Chartularium universitatis Parisiensis*, 1, 78–9.

44 At Paris, members of the mendicant orders were permitted to begin theology studies without a university arts degree. At Oxford a 1253 decree made the status of Master of Arts a prerequisite for becoming a Master of Theology. Until 1303, however, dispensations from this requirement were liberally granted. See Hinnebusch OP, *The History of the Dominican Order*, vol. 2, 78.

45 *Chartularium universitatis Parisiensis* 1, 385–86. See also Hinnebusch, 7–8, 27.

46 Leff, *Paris and Oxford*, 165.

47 Ibid., 166.

48 Hinnebusch, 59.

49 The *Sentences* of Peter Lombard were glosses on the sayings of Church Fathers, which theology students first studied and then lectured and commented upon. I do not want to claim that Aquinas expected the *Summa theologiae* to replace the *Sentences* entirely, nor that students were to comment on the *Summa* as they had on the *Sentences*. My claim is only that Aquinas intended the *Summa* to serve as the basis for a final, comprehensive course for theology students, as the Lombard's *Sentences*

had been doing. He may have nevertheless envisioned that study of and commenting on the *Sentences* would still be done to some extent and in some manner.

50 Monika Asztalos, "The Faculty of Theology," in de Ridder-Symoens ed., *Universities in the Middle Ages*, 417.

51 See my "Exposition of the Text: Aquinas's Aristotelian Commentaries," 39–62.

52 Of course, it is not twentieth-century biology and physics one should have in mind here, but the inquiries of the sort we find in Aristotle's works, such as *De partibus animalium* and *De generatione et corruptione*, which served as the basis for speculations about nature in thirteenth-century Europe.

53 This account of Aquinas's view of the epistemic justification of the assent of faith is what I call the "naturalistic interpretation," and it is discussed in chapter six below.

54 *ST* II–II.2.1.

55 *ST* I.12.11.

56 *In Post. anal.* 1.ii.15.

4. THE NATURAL LIGHT OF THE INTELLECT

1   Portions of the chapter were previously published as "Aquinas on the Veracity of the Intellect," in *The Journal of Philosophy*, 88, no. 11 (Nov. 1991), 623–32.

2   *ST* I.1.7. See also *ST* II–II.3.6; *ST* II–II.4.1; and *In ethica* I.xi.138.

3   We saw in chapter one that propositions in which an immediate, indemonstrable *per se* attribute is predicated of a subject can be principles (e.g. *Broad-leaved plants are sap-congealers at the leaf stalk*). Presumably, these sorts of attributes are immediately known once the essence of the subject is fully known.

4   *ST* I.17.3.2.

5   *De ver.* 1.12.

6   This claim is most extensively discussed in Aquinas's *In De anima* III.xi and in *ST* I.85.6. Among the other places one finds it are: *ST* I.17.3 and 1.58.5; *SCG* 1.59 and III.108; *De ver.* 1.12; *In Periherm.* 1.iii; and *In Meta.* VI.iv.

7   E. Gilson, *Thomist Realism and the Critique of Knowledge*, trans. M. A. Wauck (San Francisco: Ignatius Press, 1986), especially 199–203.

8   Lonergan, *Verbum: Word and Idea in Aquinas*, especially ch. II.

9   Alasdair MacIntyre, *First Principles, Final Ends and Contemporary Philosophical Issues* (Milwaukee: Marquette University Press, 1990), 46–7.

10 Among the places in which the respective senses of these and other terms to be discussed are revealed are: *De ente et essentia*, chaps. 2, 3 & 5; *ST* I.85.1.ad 2; *In Meta.* v.ii.764 & VII.xi.153.

11 *In Periherm.* 1.i.1 (*proemium*). (Ironically, although we generally use the

Latin title *De Interpretatione* to refer to this work of Aristotle, Aquinas used a transliterated version of the Greek title, *Perihermineias*. Thus I refer to Aristotle's work with its Latin title, but cite Aquinas's commentary by the title he gave it.) The distinction drawn in this passage is described most clearly in this Aristotelian commentary, but it is present in many passages in Aquinas's own works. See e.g. *ST* 1.85.6; *De ver.* 1.12; *SCG* 1.59 and III.108.

12 Lonergan distinguishes these two stages, calling them respectively "insight into phantasm" and "eminatio intelligibilis," in *Verbum*, 25–46. Although I disagree with other aspects of Lonergan's interpretation of Aquinas, in this respect his discussion is accurate and extremely helpful.

13 *In Periherm.* 1.iii.26.

14 Kenny, *Action, Emotion and Will*, 225–27.

15 *De ver.* 1.12.

16 *ST* 1.85.6.

17 *De ver.* 1.12.

18 *In De anima* III.xi.760.

19 Aquinas makes it clear that definitions formed by the apprehension of quiddities in the first operation of the intellect are neither true nor false, and must be distinguished from a universal assertion, such as "Homo est rationale animal mortal," for (Aquinas believes) the latter involves an existential claim. In his commentary on the *Posterior Analytics*, Aquinas says that definitions are to be distinguished from hypotheses (*suppositiones*) and postulates (*petitiones*) for two reasons: "(1) Every postulate, or hypothesis, says that something is or is not; terms (i.e. definitions) do not say that something is . . . or is not. . . . (2) Every hypothesis or postulate is in whole or in part (i.e. it is a universal or particular proposition); but definitions are neither of these, because in them nothing is posited or predicated, either universally or particularly" (*In Post. anal.* 1.xix.163 & 165). For Aquinas, then, both universal and particular assertions make existential claims, whereas definitions do not.

20 Some scholars caution against attributing to Aquinas views expressed in his commentaries on Aristotle, for these "are so many expositions of the doctrine of Aristotle, not of what might be called his own philosophy" (E. Gilson, *History of Christian Philosophy in the Middle Ages* [London: Sheed & Ward, 1955], 376). My own position is that what Aquinas attributes to Aristotle in the commentaries is close to his own view. (See my "Expositions of the Text: Aquinas's Aristotelian Commentaries.") In any case, whatever one's general understanding of the commentaries, one can take Aristotle's views of the indefectibility of the intellect in Book III of the *De anima* – as Aquinas understands them, of course – to be Aquinas's own; for Aquinas, when writing not exegetically but on his own, regularly refers us to this part of the Aristotelian corpus. (See *ST* 1.58.5 & I.5.6, *SCG* 1.59, *De ver.* 1.12.)

21   *In De anima* III.xi.746.

22   *In De anima* III.xi.761.

23   "Intellectus . . . secundum quod intelligit quid est res, verus est semper
     . . ." (ibid.).

24   Lonergan, 66.

25   Lonergan, 65.

26   Lonergan, 82.

27   One difficulty in reading Lonergan is that it is often not clear whether
     the view being put forward is what Lonergan thinks Aquinas actually
     believed, or whether he is presenting it as an interesting reconstruction
     or development of Aquinas's views. Lonergan's method in this work
     seems to be to seek an interpretation of Aquinas which would save him
     from the charge of "naive realism." "Is one to say that Aquinas was
     innocent of modern, critical complication?"(74), he asks. Lonergan
     thinks one can and should save Aquinas from this charge of naivety by
     finding, at least in certain passages, some version of what Lonergan
     calls a "program of critical thought." This program arises from the
     realization that "to know the truth we have to know ourselves and the
     nature of our knowledge, and the method to be employed is reflection"
     (75). Through this reflection "we come to grasp just how it is that our
     minds are proportionate to knowledge of reality" (85). This program of
     critical thought, Lonergan concedes, if it is in Aquinas, is found only in
     an underdeveloped form. And so, with regard to crucial questions of
     just how reflective understanding is to verify (or reject) the apprehen-
     sion of direct understanding, Lonergan admits that Aquinas did not
     specify this, "so it is only by piecing together scattered materials that
     one can arrive at an epistemological position that may be termed
     Thomistic but hardly Thomist" (ibid.). Insofar as Lonergan is merely
     using Aquinas's texts as a springboard for his own metaphysical and
     epistemological reflection, I have no argument with him. However,
     although he admits to filling in lacunae and developing underdeve-
     loped parts, he indicates that, in its fundamental outline, the view he
     presents is, in fact, Aquinas's. The work on Aquinas's theory of
     cognition is meant as an introduction to a discussion of Aquinas's view
     of the Divine Trinity, and so we certainly should expect that the
     former is, in fact, Aquinas's own view. Thus we are justified, I believe,
     in taking Lonergan's view as a rendering of what Aquinas actually
     held.

28   Lonergan, 8.

29   Ibid.

30   *In De anima* III.xi.747.

31   Ibid.

32   *In De anima* III.xi.755.

33   An example of this is found in *ST* 1.29.1 ad. 3. This and other passages
     are discussed more fully below.

34 R. Chisholm, *Theory of Knowledge*, ed. Elizabeth & Monroe Beardsly (Englewood Cliffs: Prentice-Hall, 1966), 34.

35 *ST*1.85.6.

36 Ibid.

37 Ibid.

38 *In De anima* III.xi.760.

39 Ibid.

40 Lonergan, *Verbum*, 23.

41 *In De anima* III.xi.761.

42 *ST*1.16.2.

43 Thomas Aquinas, *In symbolum apostolorum, prologus* 864, in *Opuscula theologica*, vol. II.

44 Ibid.

45 *ST*1.29.1.ad 3.

46 *ST*1.77.1.ad. 7.

47 Thomas Aquinas, *Lectura super Johannem* 1.i.

48 *ST*1.85.3.

49 Ibid.

50 Ibid.

51 *In Post. anal.* II.vii.475.

52 Ibid., 475.

53 Ibid.

54 *ST*1.29.1ad. 3.

55 A good example of a recent exposition of this sort of externalism can be found in C. McGinn, "The Structure of Content," in *Thought and Object*, ed. A. Woodfield (Oxford: Clarendon Press, 1982), 207–58.

56 Norman Kretzmann has developed a similar account of the veracity of the first operation of the intellect in "Infallibility, Error, and Ignorance," in *Aristotle and His Medieval Interpreters*, eds. Richard Bosley & Martin Tweedale, *Canadian Journal of Philosophy*, Sup. Vol. 17 (1991), 159–94. My interpretation, which was developed independently of and nearly simultaneously with Kretzmann's, appeared as "Aquinas on the Veracity of the Intellect," *The Journal of Philosophy* 88 (November 1991), 623–32.

57 *De ver.* 1.9.

58 An excellent discussion of the concept of justification in contemporary and historical works can be found in chapter one of Alvin Plantinga's *Warrant: The Current Debate* (New York: Oxford University Press, 1993), 3–29. Plantinga offers a brief synopsis of the "welter of views as to the nature of justification" in the current debate, and attempts to introduce some order into the chaos by trying to show how contemporary views arose from the deontological epistemology of Descartes and Locke. My own use of *justification* and *warrant* in the following discussion is very close to Plantinga's.

59 There is a tradition that this belief and others like it are not properly

basic, but are, or should be, inferred from beliefs about sense data, such as Smith's belief that she now feels chilly. Obviously, however, this is not the sort of justification people actually offer and accept for this sort of belief in ordinary contexts, and that is what I am concerned with here.

60 Edmund Gettier, "Is Justified True Belief Knowledge?" in *Analysis* 23 (1963), 121–23.

61 *Knowledge*, ed. G. S. Pappas (Dordrecht: D. Reidel, 1979), 10.

62 R. Nozik, *Philosophical Explanations* (Oxford: Clarendon Press, 1981), 178.

63 F. I. Dretske in *Knowledge and the Flow of Information* (Oxford: Basil Blackwell, 1981), 84.

64 Plantinga, *Warrant: The Current Debate*, 214.

65 Lonergan, 65.

66 The passages Lonergan offers in support of this aspect of his interpretation do not strongly support it. As we said above, Lonergan seems to recognize that his interpretation goes beyond Aquinas's texts in significant ways.

67 Aquinas distinguishes these two forms of *scientia* when he writes: "it is possible to have *scientia* 'through the effect' (*per effectum*) . . . [and] one is also said in some way to have *scientia* of the indemonstrable principles" (*In Post. anal.* i.iv.33). Aquinas believes that Aristotle is primarily concerned with *scientia* of conclusions in Book i of the *Posterior Analytics*, and with *scientia* of indemonstrable principles in Book ii. (See *In Post. anal.* ii.i.407.)

68 *Cognitio* is also used of cognitive states which are in some sense false, and lack the positive epistemic status that the apprehension of imperfect principles has. And using *scientia* for imperfect *scientia* might lead to confusing it with perfect *scientia*.

69 Eleonore Stump, "Aquinas on the Foundations of Knowledge," in *Aristotle and His Medieval Interpreters*, 148. Regarding warrant for *notitia*, Stump and I seem to be in general agreement that Aquinas held a "theological externalism" (158). But we differ, I believe, on Aquinas's views on the nature of and warrant for *scientia*.

70 As Stump has pointed out, this view of warrant bears strong similarities to Plantinga's account of warrant in *Warrant and Proper Function* (New York: Oxford University Press, 1993).

71 *Posterior Analytics* i.1, 71a 1–2.

72 *Posterior Analytics* i.2, 71b 16–17; *In Post. anal.* i.iv.35.

73 *In Post. anal.* ii.xx.582.

74 Ibid., 585.

75 Ibid., 588.

76 Ibid., 592.

77 Ibid.

78 Ibid., 596.

79 Ibid.

80 *In De anima* III.xvii.859.

81 *In Physica* I.ix.65.

82 See Keith Hutchison, "What Happened to Occult Qualities in the Scientific Revolution?," in *Isis* 73 (1982), 233–53.

5. GRACES, THEOLOGICAL VIRTUES AND GIFTS

1 *ST* I–II.62.1.

2 See also *ST* I.29.1.ad 4.

3 *ST* III.2.1.

4 *In Physica* II.i.141–48.

5 *In Post. anal.* I.x.83.

6 *In Physica* II.i.145.

7 *In De anima* II.vii.323.

8 *ST* I.77.1.

9 *De pot.* 3.7.

10 Ibid.

11 *ST* I.103.1.ad 1; cf. *ST* I–II.1.2.

12 Although I think it is clear that Aquinas adopted the Aristotelian account of the motion of simple bodies found in *De generatione et corruptione*, nothing essential to my argument hangs on whether he did. My concern is to note several key distinctions Aquinas makes regarding what is natural to non-cognizant entities and to elucidate his views on divine action in entities of this sort. The reader can view the Aristotelian account as simply a vehicle for illustrating some of Aquinas's views on the actions of non-cognizant entities, even if he does not accept this particular account of the action of this sort of non-cognizant things.

13 *De pot.* 6.1.ad 1.

14 As Aquinas puts it, some thing is moved violently by another whenever "that which is directed to an end is propelled and moved solely by the one directing, without acquiring from the one directing some form in virtue of which such direction or inclination is fitting to that thing" (*De ver.* 22.1).

15 *De pot.* 6.1.ad 1.

16 *ST* I.70.3; *SCG* III.23 & 24.

17 *ST* I–II.1.2.

18 We are ignoring the case of brute animals, who, Aquinas holds, are directed toward an end, although they do have an imperfect apprehension of it. This is not particularly relevant to our purposes.

19 *ST* I–II.8.1.

20 *ST* I–II.8.2.

21 We find, therefore, a certain asymmetry between the hierarchy of corporeal bodies and that of intellectual substances. As we have seen, lower corporeal bodies (e.g. water) have a natural passive potency to be moved directly by higher corporeal bodies (e.g. celestial bodies).

Among intellectual substances there is a hierarchy which descends from God, through the various orders of angels, to human beings, the lowest intellectual substance (*SCG* III.80). However, the angels cannot directly move either the human intellect or will. The human intellect can be directly moved by God alone.

22 *ST* I–II.9.6.
23 SCG III.17.1992.
24 Regarding Aquinas's view of the intrinsic goodness of basic goods, see my "Good and the Object of Natural Inclination in St. Thomas Aquinas," in *The Journal of Medieval Philosophy and Theology* 3 (1993), 62–96.
25 *ST* I.105.5.
26 *ST* I.6.4.
27 Ibid.
28 *SCG* III.17.1990.
29 *De ver.* 22.2.
30 *ST* I.105.5.
31 *De ver.* 22.2.ad 3.
32 *SCG* I.14; III.17.
33 *SCG* III.17.2003.
34 *SCG* III.18.2003.
35 *De pot.* 3.7.
36 *ST* I.105.5.
37 *ST* I.77.6.
38 This is somewhat over simplified. The RSV version says, "Then Moses stretched out his hand over the Sea; and the Lord drove the sea back by a strong east wind all night, and made the sea dry land, and the waters were divided" (Ex. 14:12). It is unclear whether the miraculous effect was the strong wind, of which the sea's parting was a natural effect; also unclear is whether Moses was an intermediary cause. These complications do not affect the point of my discussion, so I will speak of the parting of the water as a direct, miraculous effect of the divine power.
39 *De pot.* 6.1.ad 1.
40 *ST* I.105.6.
41 *De pot.* 6.1.ad 18.
42 Thomas Aquinas, *De virtutibus in communi* 1.10.ad 13 in *Quaestiones disputatae*, vol. II (Rome: Marietti, 1965).
43 Josh. 3:13–17.
44 *De ver.* 8.4.ad 13.
45 Some of the works in which Aquinas's views on the human good are discussed and some controversies taken up are the following: G. Grisez, "The First Principle of Practical Reason: A Commentary on the *Summa Theologiae*, 1–2, Question 94, Article 2," in *Natural Law Forum* 10 (1965), 168–201, hereafter cited as *FPPR*; J. Finnis, *Natural Law and Natural*

Rights (Oxford University Press, 1980), hereafter cited as *NLNR*; R. McInerny, *Ethica Thomistica* (Washington: Catholic University of America Press, 1982) and "Ethics" in *The Cambridge Companion to Aquinas*, eds. Kretzmann & Stump, 196–216; G. Grisez & J. Finnis, "The Basic Principles of Natural Law: A Reply to Ralph McInerny," in *The American Journal of Jurisprudence*, 26 (1981), 21–31, hereafter cited as *BPNL*; Alasdair MacIntyre, *Whose Justice? Which Rationality?* (Notre Dame: University of Notre Dame Press, 1988), 183–208; Jean Porter, *The Recovery of Virtue: The Relevance of Aquinas for Christian Ethics* (Louisville: Westminister/John Knox Press, 1990). I discuss and attempt to resolve some of the controversies between Grisez and Finnis, on the one hand, and McInerny, on the other, in "Good and the Object of Natural Inclination in St. Thomas Aquinas."

46 *FPPR*, 175.
47 *ST*I–II.62.1.
48 Grisez and Finnis contend "that there is no objective hierarchy (i.e. none which would imply commensurability of value) among the basic forms of human good" (*BPNL*, 28). However, Aquinas says, "Secundum igitur ordinem inclinationum naturalium, est ordo praeceptorum legis naturae" (I–II.94.2). Finnis suggests that speculative considerations are intruding into practical principles which are independent of the speculative. Hence, "In ethical reflection the three fold order should be set aside as an irrelevant schematization" (*NLNR*, 95). I find McInerny's claim that the natural good is an "ordered set of goods" (29) a more natural interpretation of what Aquinas very straightforwardly says.
49 McInerny, 32.
50 *ST*I–II.62.1.
51 *ST*I–II.110.1.
52 Left out of this consideration is God's efficient causality. Since we are speaking about rational, human actions, divine efficient causality is not involved.
53 *ST*I–II.113.1.
54 *ST*I–II.113.2 *corpus* & ad 2; 113.4; 114.1, 2 & 3.
55 *ST*I–II.85.3.
56 *ST*I–II.109.8.
57 *ST*I–II.85.1.
58 *ST*I–II.51.1.
59 *ST*I–II.109.2.ad 3.
60 Aristotle, *Nicomachean Ethics*, Book. II, ch. 1, 1103a 24–25, trans. W. D. Ross in *The Basic Works of Aristotle*, ed. R. McKeon (New York: Random House, 1941).
61 *In Ethica*, II.i.249.
62 *ST*I–II.49.2.ad 2.
63 *ST*I–II.51.1.

64 Ibid.
65 Ibid.; *ST*1–11.83.1.
66 *ST*1–11.85.1.
67 "The good of nature which is diminished through sin is the natural inclination to virtue" (*ST*1–11.85.2).
68 *ST*1–11.109.8.
69 Ibid.
70 *ST*1–11.109.2.
71 We are ignoring the distinction between operative and co-operative grace. Aquinas believes that both actual and habitual grace can be subdivided into operative grace, in which God acts "within us and without us," and co-operative grace, in which we in some way contribute to and co-operate with God's action (*ST*1–11.111.2). Though this distinction is important, it is not directly relevant to our concerns.
72 Like many terms in Aquinas's Latin, this very common one is very difficult to render in English. I will use the obvious English term *habit*, because it is best for the kinds of *habitus* with which we will be primarily concerned. The reader should be aware, though, that this English word does not adequately translate all uses of *habitus*, such as the *habitus* humors of the body have to health or beauty.
73 *ST*1–11.55.1.
74 *ST*1–11.111.2.
75 *ST*1–11.109.6.
76 *ST*1–11.113.3.
77 Luis de Molina (1535–1600), a Jesuit, held that God, by what he called middle knowledge (*scientia media*), knows what every free creature would do in every situation that God could bring about. The conditionally free future choice of the person is not determined by God. However, God can know and direct future free acts by bringing about a situation in which He knows by His middle knowledge that the person will freely act in a certain way.
     According to Molina, then, God can bring it about that two people, A and B, can receive the same grace, and in A's case it is efficacious and in B's case it is merely sufficient but not efficacious. This is because God knows by middle knowledge that, if grace is granted, A will freely respond in a salutary way and B will respond in a non-salutary way. When God grants the grace, then, A responds in one way and B in another.
     Domingo Báñez (1528–1604), a Dominican, argued against Molina and claimed that efficacious grace is *intrinsically* different from merely sufficient grace. In the case of A and B, if A receives efficacious grace and B receives merely sufficient grace, there must be some difference in what God gives each. But, Báñez held, God's giving efficacious grace to A and merely sufficient grace to B is compatible with the free choice of each. This is because, Báñez argued, *every* free act of a creature requires

a "premotion," a transitory created entity produced by God alone, which determines the act in its nature and actual existence. Hence the premotion God gives moves the person to a certain action, and yet the action is still free.

A vehement theological dispute broke out between Jesuits, who sided with Molina, and Dominicans, who sided with Báñez. Pope Clement VIII eventually intervened and both sides came together to discuss the matter in a series of meetings called *Congregationes de auxilliis*. The sessions were terminated when a formula was found to which both sides could agree. Further discussion was forbidden, but neither view triumphed over the other.

78 *ST*1–11.62.1.

79 *ST*1–11.62.1 & 85.2.

80 *ST*1–11.62.1.

81 *ST*1–11.68.2.

82 Ibid.

83 Ibid.

84 *ST*1–11.68.3.

85 Ibid.

86 On mortal sin leading to loss of sanctifying grace, see 1–11.85.2 & 4; on the loss of grace leading to loss of Gifts, see *ST*11–11.8.5.

87 *ST*11–11.4.4; 11–11.6.2. The faith of such a person would presumably be deficient in certainty, firmness, devotion and confidence (see *ST* 11–11.5.4).

88 *ST*1–11.103.2.

89 *ST*1–11.110.3.

90 *ST*1–11.112.4.ad 3; 62.1.ad 1.

91 *ST*1–11.50.2;110.4.

92 *ST*1–11.110.4.

93 *ST*1–11.62.1.ad 1.

94 "[Grace is] a certain condition which is presupposed by the infused virtues as their principle and root" (*ST*1–11.110.3.ad 3).

95 *ST*1–11.110.3.

96 *ST*1–11.64.1.

97 "For as the acquired virtues perfect the human person to walk in harmony with the natural light of reason, so the infused virtues perfect him to walk in harmony with the light of grace" (*ST*1–11.110.3).

98 11 Cor. 5:17 (RSV).

99 If his nature was corrupted by sin, he would be unable fully to acquire the virtue. The inability, however, would be due to the certain impediments; he would still possess the capacity (*ST*1–11.85.1 & 2).

6. THE LIGHT OF FAITH

1 *Intellect* is used here in its narrower sense to refer to the intellect in its first operation, the apprehension of quiddities. See chapter four.

2 *ST* II–II.1.1.

3 *ST* II–II.1.2.

4 *ST* II–II.1.2 & 8. W. C. Smith in *Faith and Belief* (Princeton University Press, 1979) offers an interpretation of Aquinas according to which faith does not essentially involve belief in a definite set of propositions at all. Smith takes Aquinas as suggesting that faith is fundamentally a relation to the First Truth (Prima Veritas) in which "the role of explicit belief (i.e. propositional belief) in his articulated view of faith is altogether subsidiary or minor and even at times negative" (83). In his article "*Fides* and *Credere*: W. C. Smith on Aquinas" (*The Journal of Religion*, 65 [1985], 339–412), Frederick J. Crossen argues, successfully I believe, that Smith's interpretation is based upon a faulty reading of Aquinas's distinction between the formal and material object of faith (404).

5 *ST* II–II.1.5; *De ver.* 14.1; *SSS* lib. III.ds. 23.q. 2. art. 1 & 2.

6 *ST* II–II.1.4 & 5; *SSS* III.d. 24.q. 1.art. 2. sol. 1.

7 *ST* II–II.1.5; II–II.2.4; 1.1.1. As I said in chapter one, the cognition one attains by a demonstration *quia* that God exists is not perfect *scientia*, for this requires a *propter quid* demonstration. It is an imperfect *scientia*, however, and distinct from faith.

8 *ST* I.2.2.ad 1.

9 *ST* II–II.1.1; II–II.2.2; *De ver.* 14.8.

10 *ST* II–II.2.1; *De ver.* 14.1; *SSS* III.ds. 23.q. 2.art. 1.

11 *ST* II–II.4.1; *De ver.* 14.1 & 2; *SSS* III. ds. 23.q. 2.art. 1 & 2.

12 *ST* II–II.2.9.

13 *ST* II–II.3.1 & 2.

14 This reading is embraced by John Hick in *Faith and Knowledge* (Ithaca: Cornell, 1966), 20–1; by Terence Penelhum in "The Analysis of Faith in St. Thomas Aquinas," in *Religious Studies* 3 (1977), 145; by Alvin Plantinga in "Reason and Belief in God," *Faith and Rationality: Reason and Belief in God*, eds. A. Plantinga & N. Wolterstorff (Notre Dame: University of Notre Dame Press, 1983), 40–7; and by Louis P. Pojman in *Religious Belief and the Will* (New York: Routledge & Kegan Paul, 1986), 32–40.

15 *ST* II–II.1.2.

16 Penelhum, 146.

17 Ibid.

18 Hick, 17.

19 Plantinga, 46.

20 *ST* II–II.6.1.

21 Penelhum, 146.

22 "The human intellect has a certain form – namely, the intelligible light

itself – which is of itself sufficient to apprehend certain intelligible realities; namely, the realities of which we can come to know through sense experience" (*ST*1–11.109.1).

23   *ST*11–11.8.1 & ad 2.
24   *ST*1–11.190.1.
25   *SSS* 111. ds. 23. q. 2.art. 1; *De ver.* 14.2.
26   *SSS* 1.*prologus*.q.1.art. 3. sol.3.
27   *De ver.* 14.1.ad 7.
28   *ST*11–11.2.4; see also *ST*1.1.1.
29   This argument is also put forward in A. Vos, *Aquinas, Calvin, and Contemporary Protestant Thought: A Critique of Protestant Views on the Thought of Thomas Aquinas* (Grand Rapids: Christian University Press, 1985). In this book Vos argues against an "evidentialist" interpretation of Aquinas, which seems quite similar to what I am referring to as the NI, and some of our arguments against the evidentialist-naturalist interpretation are similar. We differ, however, in many aspects of our positive account of Aquinas's views.
30   *ST*1.1.8.
31   Ibid. My italics. The reference to "Sacred Scripture" in this passage is somewhat confusing, but the article only makes sense if we take this as a reference to sacred doctrine, which is founded on and draws out the revelation in Sacred Scripture. We find the same use of "Sacred Scripture" in *ST*1.1.3.
32   Penelhum, 143.
33   Ibid., 145.
34   Ibid., 146.
35   Ibid.
36   Ibid., 143.
37   James 2:19 (New Revised Standard Version).
38   *ST*11–11.5.2.
39   *ST*11–11.5.2.ad 2.
40   *ST*1.64.1.ad 2.
41   *ST*1.64.1.ad 4.
42   *ST*1.64.1.ad 5.
43   *ST*11–11.5.2.ad 1.
44   *De ver.* 14.9.ad 4.
45   Penelhum raises other issues about Aquinas's account which we will take up below. Among these are: (1) Aquinas's claim that the assent to the propositions of faith is rational, even though these propositions "are not established conclusively [i.e. scientifically demonstrated]" (143); and (2) the role of the will in this assent.
46   Plantinga, 46.
47   *SCG* 1.6.41.
48   *SCG* 1.6.40.
49   SCG 111.101.2763.

50 *SCG* 1.6.36.
51 James Ross, "Aquinas on Belief and Knowledge," in *Essays Honoring Allan B. Wolter*, eds. W. A. Frank & G. J. Etzkorn (St. Bonaventure: The Franciscan Institute, 1985), 245–69; and "Believing for Profit," *The Ethics of Belief Debate*, ed. Gerald D. McCarthy, American Academy of Religion Series, eds. Charley Hardwick & James O. Duke, no. 41 (Atlanta: Scholars Press, 1986), 221–35. Eleonore Stump, "Aquinas on Faith and Goodness," in *Being and Goodness: The Concept of the Good in Metaphysics and Philosophical Theology*, ed. Scott MacDonald (Ithaca: Cornell, 1991), 179–207.
52 *De ver.* 14.1.
53 *De ver.* 14.2.
54 Ross, 249.
55 Ibid., 250.
56 Ibid., 261.
57 Ibid.
58 Ibid., 249.
59 Alvin Goldman, "What Is Justified Belief?" in *Justification and Knowledge: New Studies in Epistemology*, ed. George Pappas (Dordrecht: D. Reidel, 1979). Plantinga lucidly makes this point about Goldman's use of *justification* in *Warrant: The Current Debate*, 27–8.
60 Stump, 186.
61 Ross speaks explicitly of the will filling a "gap in the evidence" (261). Stump implies this when she presents, as an example of the will's influencing assent, the case of experimenters accepting a certain result "in consequence of their desire to have results turn out a particular way" (186) – though, presumably, the evidence did not support this conclusion.
62 *ST* II–II.2.1. Elsewhere Aquinas writes, "If the things apprehended were the sort to which the intellect naturally apprehends, *e.g. the first principles* [my italics], assent to or dissent from these are not within our power, but are according to the order of nature" (*ST* I–II.17.6).
63 Stump writes: "If a person believes that genes are the unit of inheritance because all reputable biologists say so, it does not seem as if will has a role to play in the formation of this belief" (190). However, she offers no textual evidence that this is Aquinas's view. And since this would certainly not be a case of *scientia*, it seems that Aquinas thinks the will does have a role to play here.
64 For a discussion of the distinction between a fully human act and its various components, as well as a brief and helpful summary of Aquinas's account of human action, see Alan Donagan's "Thomas Aquinas on Human Action," in *The Cambridge History of Later Medieval Philosophy*, eds. Kretzmann, Kenny & Pinborg, 642–54.
65 *ST* I–II.8.2; *De ver.* 22.13.
66 *ST* I–II.12.1; *De ver.* 22.13 & 14.

67 *ST* I–II.14.1, 2 & 3; "Reason proposes to the will a good as useful with respect to an end" (*De ver.* 22.15).

68 *ST* I–II.13.3; *De ver.* 22.15.

69 *ST* I–II.17; *De ver.* 22.12.ad 4.

70 Ibid., 252.

71 *ST* I–II 17.1.

72 "But to command is essentially an act of reason: for the one commanding orders the one he commands to do something by intimation or declaration, but to order in the manner of such an intimation belongs to reason. . . . Of the powers of the soul the first mover toward the performance of an act is the will. . . . Therefore, since a second mover does not move except in the power of the first mover, it follows that reason moves by a commanding is due to the power of the will" (ST I–II 17.1).

73 *SCG* I.6.

74 Stump writes that "although there are some superficial differences between my interpretation of Aquinas and that argued for by Ross, my account is in many respects similar to his" (191, n. 22).

75 Ibid., 188.

76 Ibid., 186.

77 Ibid., 195.

78 Ibid.,196–97.

79 Ibid., 198.

80 "Non enim fides de qua loquimur assentit alicui nisi quia est a Deo revelatum; unde ipsi veritati divinae innititur tanquam medio." A more literal translation of the last phrase would be:"[faith] relies on the Divine Truth as the middle [term in a syllogism]." Aquinas's point is that the one who has faith must reason thus: "p has been divinely revealed; that which is divinely revealed is true; hence, p." See also *ST* II–II.2.2, and *ST* II–II.5.3, especially the response to the second objection, where Aquinas says that although the heretic may accept nearly all the propositions of faith, he does not have faith, for he does not believe them "because of the first truth proposed to us in Scripture understood correctly according to the doctrine of the Church."

81 Ibid., 199.

82 Ibid., 197.

83 *De ver.* 23.4.

84 *ST* II–II.1.8.

85 See *ST* I–II.2.ad 1 and *ST* I.1.8.

86 I. T. Eschmann, OP, *A Catalogue of St. Thomas's Works*, in Gilson, *The Christian Philosophy of St. Thomas Aquinas*, 384–5.

87 Weisheipl, *Friar Thomas D'Aquino: His Life, Thought, and Work*, 385.

88 Weisheipl, 124–6.

89 Weisheipl, 361.

90 For a summary of and references to some of the scholarly literature, see

E. O'Conner, CSC, "The Evolution of St. Thomas's Thought on the Gifts," in *Summa Theologiae* (Blackfriars), vol. 24, *The Gifts of the Spirit* (London: Eyre & Spottiswoode, 1974), 118–19.

91 *SSS* III. ds. 34.q. 1.art. 1. It is clear he is not speaking only of merely human virtues here, for the example he uses to illustrate the point is that of faith and the Gift of Understanding.

92 "But holy fear, and initial fear insofar as it participates in holy fear, have the character (*ratio*) of a Gift. The reason for this is that it modulates its acts according to a higher measure than the human measure. For the measure of human works is the good of reason. Hence the virtuous abstain from evils, fleeing and fearing what is base insofar as it is unfitting to reason; and this belongs to any virtue. But the fear which is a Gift makes one abstain from evils because of a flight from the unfitting which is separation from God; and therefore it has God Himself for the measure of its works. And because the mode is caused by the measure, therefore it operates above the human mode and for this reason is a Gift" (*SSS* III. ds. 34 q. 2 art. 1 sol. 3). I was directed to this passage by O'Conner (120), and he has drawn attention to this contrast between the earlier and later works.

93 "As the intellectual virtues are placed before the moral virtues and rule them, so the theological virtues are placed before the Gifts of the Holy Spirit, and rule them" (*ST* I–II.68.8).

94 *ST* II–II.8.2.

95 *SSS* III. ds. 34 q. 1 art. 1. See also ibid., art. 2.

96 "But the fact that a human person with certainty recognizes what is to be done is beyond what is human. And this is the Gift of *Scientia*, which teaches living in the midst of a perverse and corrupt people" (*SSS* III. ds. 34 q. 1 art. 2).

97 Even if I am wrong in this and the Gifts are more closely related to the virtues in the early works, this will not undermine the central claim I am going to make about the justification and warrant of the assent of faith. For if I am wrong, I will have to add to what I say something about the role of the Gifts, but my claim that the assent of faith arises from some supernatural grace which heightens the individual's cognitive abilities will stand.

98 *SSS* III. ds. 24 q. 1 art. 3 sol. 3.

99 *De ver.* 14.2.

100 *SSS* III. ds. 23 q. 2 art. 1 ad 4.

101 *SSS* III. ds. 23 q. 2 art. 2 sol. 2.

102 We must account for Aquinas's explicit remarks in the *De veritate* that it is the good will's desiring eternal life which moves one to the assent of faith. This will be discussed in section 6.4.

103 *ST* II–II 8.6. See also *ST* II–II.6.1. In both these passages, Aquinas is speaking of the normal route to faith, and not that of those who saw the risen Christ, such as the Apostles.

104 *ST* II–II.2.3.ad 2.
105 E.g. *ST* II–II 8.1.
106 *ST* I.12.1.
107 *ST* II–II.8.7.
108 *ST* II–II.8.4.ad 2.
109 *ST* II–II.8.2.
110 *ST* II–II.9.1.
111 *ST* II–II.9.1.ad 1.
112 *ST* II–II.2.1.ad 1; II–II.2.9.ad 3; II–II.6.1.
113 *ST* II–II.6.1.obj. 1.
114 *ST* II–II.6.1.ad 1.
115 *ST* I.2.3 *corpus* & ad 3.
116 *ST* II–II.2.4. See also *De ver.* 14.9c and SSS III. ds. 24 q. 1 art. 2 quaestincula 3.
117 *De ver.* 14.9.obj. 9.
118 Ibid., ad 9.
119 One has an *opinio* when one "accepts one of two contradictory propositions with fear about the other" (*De ver.* 14.1). See also *ST* II–II.2.1.
120 *ST* II–II.9.1.ad 1.
121 G. E. M. Anscombe, "What Is It to Believe Someone?" in *Rationality and Religious Belief*, ed. C. F. Delaney (Notre Dame: University of Notre Dame Press, 1979), 145.
122 Penelhum, 139.
123 Ross, 259.
124 Stump, 188.
125 As Stump explains elsewhere, double-blind experimental design, for example, is meant to exclude the possibility that the experimenters' "wills may bring about assent largely in consequence of their desire to have the result turn out a particular way" (186). That is, it is mean to rule out assent which is not in accord with an objective consideration of the weight of the evidence.
126 *ST* I–II 13.6.
127 I say "*an* important basis", for it is not the only one. Even if this subjectivity in perception of goods did not occur, indeterminacy might still enter in because alternative prospective ends might in fact be equally good, or alternative prospective means might be equally eligible.
128 Aristotle, *Nicomachean Ethics*, 1114 a33–b2 (my translation).
129 This summary ignores the influence of passions on choice. The influence of passion is temporary, and makes one will not *simpliciter et secundum se*, but *prout nunc* (*In Ethica* III.xiii.520). This influence is not particularly relevant to the assent of faith and so I am leaving it aside.
130 *In Ethica* III.xii.512.
131 Ibid., xiii.520.

132 *ST*1–11.74.3.ad 2.
133 Ibid.; ST1–11 17.7; 109.8.
134 *In Ethica* 111.xii.512.
135 *ST*11–11 10.1.ad 3.
136 *ST*11–11.11.1.
137 Ibid., ad 2.
138 In accord with Aquinas's diachronic view of the will, there is no requirement that the person who assents to the articles entertain alternative possibilities before assenting. If the command is in accord with habits formed by past actions, it is free and voluntary, and can be meritorious or blameworthy.
139 "Responsible Action," in *The Philosophical Review* 92, no. 1 (January 1983), 36.
140 Ibid., 37.

7. THE *SCIENTIA* OF SACRED DOCTRINE

1 Thomas Aquinas, *Breve principium*, in *Thomae Aquinatis opera omnia*, ed. Robert Busa, SJ (1980), vol. 3, 648–49. A good translation of this work with helpful notes can be found in *Albert and Thomas: Selected Writings*, ed. Simon Tugwell, OP (New York: Paulist, 1988), 353–60.
2 *ST*11–11.2.1; 11–11.1.5.
3 *ST*1.1.2–8.
4 Scott MacDonald, "Theory of Knowledge," in *The Cambridge Companion to Aquinas*, eds. Kretzmann & Stump, 160–96.
5 MacDonald might respond that *scientia* has two senses in Aquinas. It can designate a "mental state or disposition"; but "it can also designate a set of propositions organized by subject matter and in accordance with the member propositions, logical and epistemic properties – what we might call an organized body of knowledge, a theory, or a science" (189, n. 13). When Aquinas claims that sacred doctrine is a *scientia*, MacDonald might argue, he is not claiming that our assent to the truths of sacred doctrine meet the conditions for *scientia* as a positive epistemic state. He is claiming simply that sacred doctrine is a set of propositions organized in a certain way.

This response seems unsatisfactory for two reasons. First, this second sense of *scientia* does not seem to be in Aquinas. The *PA* clearly introduces the term to designate a cognitive perfection, and when MacDonald distinguishes the two senses of *scientia*, he cites no passage in which the term clearly has another sense. In the absence of evidence that the term has a second sense, we should take it in the sense it was explicitly said to have. Moreover, among the conditions for a proposition being in some way part of a *scientia* is that it *is known in a certain way* (i.e. the premises must be better known that the conclusion). But a proposition or set of propositions cannot be known in any way apart from reference to an actual or possible knower.

Secondly, it does not seem that *Summa theologiae* 1.1.2 can be read as asking whether sacred doctrine is a body of propositions bearing certain relationships to one another, for the body of the article is concerned with the way we humans *know* the truths of sacred doctrine – we know them not by the light of our own intellect but by the light of God's *scientia*.

6 *ST* II–II.2.6.
7 *ST* II–II.4.1.
8 *In Post. anal.* I.ii.15.
9 *ST* I.1.4.
10 Ibid.
11 *ST* II–II.1.2.
12 *ST* II–II.4.4.
13 *ST* I–II.5.7.
14 *ST* II–II.*prologus*.
15 *ST* I–II.6.*prologus*.
16 *Nicomachean Ethics* VII.9, 1151a 16–17.
17 *ST* I.82.1; I–II.8.2.
18 *ST* III.*prologus*.
19 *Posterior Analytics* I.33, 89a 37.
20 *In Post. anal.* I.xliv.404.
21 I owe this point, as well as a clear statement of the objection being considered here, to a comment on an earlier draft of this chapter by Alasdair MacIntyre.
22 The versions of the five ways in the *Summa theologiae* are briefer and simpler than those in other works of Aquinas. This suggests that he was recapitulating arguments pursued at greater length elsewhere, and not attempting a rigorous demonstration of a conclusion.
23 For a good exposition of this reading of the "five ways" and succeeding questions on God in the *Summa theologiae*, see David Burrell, CSC, *Exercises in Religious Understanding* (Notre Dame: University of Notre Dame Press, 1974), 82ff.; and his *Aquinas: God and Action* (Notre Dame: University of Notre Dame Press, 1979), Part I.
24 Burnyeat, "Aristotle on Understanding Knowledge," 139.

Bibliography

LATIN EDITIONS OF AQUINAS'S WORKS

Summa theologiae, ed. P. Caramello (Rome: Marietti, 1948).

Liber de veritate Catholicae fidei contra errores infidelium, qui dicitur Summa contra gentiles II–III, eds. Petrus Marc, Ceslao Pera & Petrus Caramello (Rome: Marietti, 1961).

In quattuor libros Sententiarum, in *S. Thomae Aquinatis Opera Omnia* 1, ed. Robert Busa, SJ (Stuttgart: Frommann-Holzboog, 1980).

Quaestiones disputatae II, eds. P. Bazzi, M. Calcatera, T. S. Centi, E. Odetto & P. M. Pession (Rome: Marietti, 1965).

Quaestiones disputatae de veritate, in *Opera omnia* (Leonine) XXII, i & ii (Rome: Editori Di San Tomasso, 1982–).

Sententia libri De anima, in *Opera omnia* (Leonine) XLV, i & ii (Rome: Editori Di San Tomasso, 1982–).

Sententia libri ethicorum, in *Opera omnia* (Leonine), XLVII, i & ii. (Rome: Editori Di San Tomasso, 1982–).

In duodecim libros Metaphysicorum Aristotelis expositio, eds. M.-R. Cathala & R. M. Spiazzi (Rome: Marietti, 1964).

Expositio libri Peryermenias in *Opera omnia* (Leonine) I*1 (Rome: Comissio Leonina, 1982–).

In octo libros Physicorum Aristotelis expositio, ed. P. M. Maggiolo (Rome: Marietti, 1965).

Expositio libri posteriorum in *Opera omnia* (Leonine) I*2 (Rome: Comissio Leonina, 1982–).

Super Boethium de Trinitate & *Expositio Libri Boethii de Ebdomadibus* (Leonine) L (Rome: Comissio Leonina, 1982–).

ENGLISH TRANSLATIONS OF AQUINAS'S WORKS

Summa Theologiae, trans. by English Dominicans (London: Burns, Oates, and Washbourne 1912–36; repr. New York: Benziger 1947–8; repr. New York: Christian Classics, 1981).

Summa Contra Gentiles, trans. by English Dominicans (London: Burns, Oates, and Washbourne, 1934).

The Disputed Questions on Truth, vol. 1 trans. by Robert William Mulligan, SJ (Chicago: Henry Regnery Co., 1952; vol. 2 trans. by James V. McGlynn, SJ (Chicago: Henry Regnery Co., 1953); vol. 3 trans. by Robert W. Schmidt, SJ (Chicago: Henry Regnery Co., 1954).

Aristotle's De Anima with the Commentary of St. Thomas Aquinas, trans. by K. Foster and S. Humphries (New Haven: Yale University Press, 1951).

Commentary on the Nichomachean Ethics, trans. by C. I. Litzinger (Chicago: Regnery, 1964).

Commentary on the Metaphysics of Aristotle, trans. by J. P. Rowan (Chicago: Regnery, 1964).

Aristotle on Interpretation: Commentary by St. Thomas and Cajetan, trans. by J. T. Oesterle (Milwaukee: Marquette University Press, 1962).

Commentary on Aristotle's Physics, trans. by R. J. Blackwell *et. al.* (New Haven: Yale, 1963).

Commentary on the Posterior Analytics of Aristotle, trans. by F. R. Larcher (Albany, NY: Magi Books, 1970).

The Division and Methods of the Sciences, Questions V–VI of the Commentary on Boethius' De Trinitate, trans. by Armand Maurer (Toronto: Pontifical Institute of Mediaeval Studies, 1953).

Faith, Reason, and Theology, Questions I-IV of the Commentary on Boethius' De Trinitate, trans. by Armand Maurer (Toronto: Pontifical Institute of Mediaeval Studies, 1986).

On the Virtues in General, trans. by J. P. Reid (Providence, RI: The Providence College Press, 1951).

Questions on the Soul, trans. by James H. Robb (Milwaukee: Marquette University Press, 1984).

OTHER WORKS CITED

Aristotle. *Posterior Analytics. Translated with a commentary by Jonathan Barnes*, 2nd edn. New York: Oxford University Press, 1992.

Anscombe, G. E. M. "What Is It to Believe Someone?" in *Rationality and Religious Belief*, ed. C. F. Delaney Notre Dame: University of Notre Dame, 1979.

Asztalos, Monika. "The Faculty of Theology". In *Universities in the Middle Ages*, ed. Hilde de Ridder-Simoens (Cambridge University Press, 1992), vol. 1 of *A History of the University in Europe*, ed. Walter Rüegg.

Barnes, Jonathan. "Aristotle's Theory of Demonstration," in *Articles on Aristotle: 1. Science*, eds. Jonathan Barnes, Malcolm Schofield & Richard Sorabji. London: Duckworth, 1975.

Boyle, Leonard E. *The Setting of the Summa theologiae of Saint Thomas*. The Etienne Gilson Series 5. Toronto: Pontifical Institute of Mediaeval Studies, 1982.

Burnyeat, M. F. "Aristotle on Understanding Knowledge," in E. Berti , ed.,

Aristotle on Science: The Posterior Analytics. Proceedings of the Eighth Symposium Aristotelicum. New York: Editrice Antenore, 1981.

Burrell, David. *Analogy and Philosophical Language.* New Haven: Yale University Press, 1973.

Exercises in Religious Understanding. Notre Dame: University of Notre Dame Press, 1974.

Aquinas: God and Action. Notre Dame: University of Notre Dame Press, 1979.

Chenu, Marie-Dominique. *La Théologie comme science au XIIIe siècle.* 2nd edn. 1943.

Towards Understanding Saint Thomas, trans. A. M. Landry & D. Hughes. Chicago: Regnery, 1964.

Chisholm, R. *Theory of Knowledge.* eds. by Elizabeth & Monroe Beardsly. Englewood Cliffs: Prentice-Hall, 1966.

Crossen, Frederick J. *"Fides and Credere:* W.C. Smith on Aquinas," in *The Journal of Religion* 65 (1985) 339–412.

Dancy, Jonathan & Ernest Sosa, eds. *A Companion to Epistemology.* Oxford: Blackwell, 1993.

Davies, Brian. *The Thought of Thomas Aquinas.* Oxford University Press, 1992.

Dretske, F. I. *Knowledge and the Flow of Information.* Oxford: Basil Blackwell, 1981.

Ferejohn, Michael. *The Origins of Aristotelian Science.* New Haven: Yale University Press, 1991.

Finnis, J. *Natural Law and Natural Rights.* Oxford University Press, 1980.

Frankfurt, Henry. "Presidential Address of the Eastern Division of the American Philosophical Association," in *Proceedings and Addresses of the American Philosophical Association* (November, 1992), vol. 66, no. 3.

Gettier, Edmund. "Is Justified True Belief Knowledge?" in *Analysis* 23 (1963), 121–3.

Gilson, Etienne. *Thomist Realism and the Critique of Knowledge,* trans. by Mark A. Wauck. San Francisco: Ignatius Press, 1986.

The Christian Philosophy of St. Thomas Aquinas, trans. L. K. Shook. New York: Random House, 1956.

History of Christian Philosophy in the Middle Ages. London: Sheed & Ward, 1955.

Goldman, Alvin. "What Is Justified Belief?" in *Justification and Knowledge: New Studies in Epistemology,* ed. George Pappas. Dordrecht: D. Reidel, 1979.

Grisez, G. "The First Principle of Practical Reason: A Commentary on the *Summa Theologiae,* 1–2, Question 94, Article 2," in *Natural Law Forum* 10 (1965), 168–201.

Grisez, G. & J. Finnis. "The Basic Principles of Natural Law: A Reply to Ralph McInerny," in *The American Journal of Jurisprudence* 26, (1981), 21–31.

Hankinson, R. J. "Philosophy of Science," in *The Cambridge Companion to Aristotle*, ed. Jonathan Barnes. Cambridge University Press, 1995.

Hick, John. *Faith and Knowledge*. Ithaca: Cornell, 1966.

Hinnebusch, William A. *The History of the Dominican Order*, vol. 2, *The History of the Dominican Order: Intellectual and Cultural Life*. New York: Alba, 1973.

Hoenen, Peter. *Reality and Judgement According to St. Thomas*, trans. by Henry F. Tiblier. Chicago: Regnery, 1952.

Hutchison, Keith. "What Happened to Occult Qualities in the Scientific Revolution?" in *Isis* 73 (1982), 233–53.

Irwin, T. H. *Aristotle's First Principles*. Oxford University Press, 1988.

Jenkins, John. "Expositions of the Text: Aquinas's Aristotelian Commentaries," *Medieval Philosophy and Theology* 5 (1996), 39–62.

"Aquinas on the Veracity of the Intellect," in *The Journal of Philosophy* 88 (Nov. 1991), 623–32.

"Good and the Object of Natural Inclination in St. Thomas Aquinas," in *The Journal of Medieval Philosophy and Theology* 3 (1993), 62–96.

Kenny, Anthony, *Action, Emotion and Will*. London: Routledge & Kegan Paul, 1963.

Kenny, Anthony, ed. *Aquinas: A Collection of Critical Essays*. Notre Dame: University of Notre Dame Press, 1969.

Kornblith, Hilary. "Responsible Action," in *The Philosophical Review* 92, no. 1 (January 1983).

Kretzmann, Norman. "Infallibility, Error, and Ignorance," in *Aristotle and His Medieval Interpreters*, eds. Richard Bosley & Martin Tweedale, *Canadian Journal of Philosophy*, Supplementary Volume 17 (1991), 159–94.

Kretzmann, Norman, Anthony Kenny & Jan Pinborg, eds. *The Cambridge History of Later Medieval Philosophy*. Cambridge University Press, 1982.

Kretzmann, Norman & Eleonore Stump, eds. *The Cambridge Companion to Aquinas*. Cambridge University Press, 1993.

Leff, Gordon. *Paris and Oxford Universities in the Thirteenth and Fourteenth Centuries*. New York: John Wiley & Sons, 1968.

"The *Trivium* and the Three Philosophies," in *A History of the University in Europe*, ed. Walter Rüegg, vol. 1, *Universities in the Middle Ages*, ed. Hilde de Ridder-Symoens. Cambridge University Press, 1992, 307–36.

Lonergan, Bernard. *Verbum: Word and Idea in Aquinas*. Edited by David Burrell. Notre Dame: Notre Dame Press, 1967.

McGinn, C. "The Structure of Content". In *Thought and Object*. Edited by Andrew Woodfield Oxford: Clarendon Press, 1982.

McInerny, Ralph. *Studies in Analogy*. The Hague: Marinus Nijhoff, 1968.

Ethica Thomistica. Washington: Catholic University of America Press, 1982.

McKirahan, Richard. *Posterior Analytics, Principles and Proofs: Aristotle's Theory of Demonstrative Science*. Princeton University Press, 1992.

MacIntyre, Alasdair. *Whose Justice? Which Rationality?* Notre Dame: University of Notre Dame Press, 1988.

Three Rival Versions of Moral Enquiry: Encyclopaedia, Genealogy, and Tradition.
Notre Dame: University of Notre Dame Press, 1990.

First Principles, Final Ends and Contemporary Philosophical Issues. Milwaukee:
Marquette University Press, 1990.

Maréchal, Joseph. *The Starting Point of Metaphysics: Lessons on the Historical and
Theoretical Development of the Problem of Knowledge, Cahier One: From Antiquity
to the End of the Middle Ages: The Critique of Knowledge,* trans. by Joseph
Donceel. In *A Maréchal Reader.* New York: Herder and Herder, 1970.

Maritain, Jacques. *Distinguish to Unite, or The Degrees of Knowledge* trans. by
Gerald B. Phelan. New York: Charles Scribner's Sons, 1959.

Essence and the Existent, trans. by Lewis Galantiere and Gerald B. Phelan.
New York: Pantheon, 1948.

Noël, L. *Le Réalisme immédiat.* Louvain, 1938.

Nozik, R. *Philosophical Explanations.* Oxford: Clarendon Press, 1981.

O'Conner, E. "The Evolution of St. Thomas's Thought on the Gifts," in
Summa Theologiae (Blackfriars), vol. 24, *The Gifts of the Spirit.* London:
Eyre & Spottiswoode, 1974.

Pappas, G. S., ed. *Knowledge.* Dordrecht: D. Reidel, 1979.

Penelhum, Terence. "The Analysis of Faith in St. Thomas Aquinas," in
Religious Studies 3 (1977), 145.

Pieper, Josef. *Guide to Thomas Aquinas,* trans. by Richard & Clara Winston.
Notre Dame: University of Notre Dame Press, 1962.

Plantinga, Alvin. *Warrant: The Current Debate.* New York: Oxford University
Press, 1993.

Warrant and Proper Function. New York: Oxford University Press, 1993.

"Reason and Belief in God," in *Faith and Rationality: Reason and Belief in
God,* eds. Alvin Plantinga & Nicholas Wolterstorff. Notre Dame:
University of Notre Dame Press, 1983.

Pojman, Louis P. *Religious Belief and the Will.* New York: Routledge & Kegan
Paul, 1986.

Porter, Jean. *The Recovery of Virtue: The Relevance of Aquinas for Christian Ethics.*
Louisville: Westminister/John Knox Press, 1990.

Rahner, Karl. *Spirit in the World,* trans. Translated by William Dych. New
York: Herder and Herder, 1968.

Ross, James. *Portraying Analogy.* Cambridge University Press, 1981.

"Aquinas on Belief and Knowledge," in *Essays Honoring Allan B. Wolter,*
eds. W. A. Frank & G. J. Etzkorn, St. Bonaventure: The Franciscan
Institute, 1985.

"Believing for Profit," in *The Ethics of Belief Debate,* ed. Gerald D.
McCarthy. American Academy of Religion Series, eds. Charley Hardwick & James O. Duke, no. 41. Atlanta: Scholars Press, 1986.

Smith, W. C. *Faith and Belief.* Princeton University Press, 1979.

Stump, Eleonore. "Aquinas on the Foundations of Knowledge, in *Aristotle
and His Medieval Interpreters,* eds. Richard Bosley & Martin Tweedale.
Canadian Journal of Philosophy, Supplementary volume 17, 125–58.

"Aquinas on Faith and Goodness," in *Being and Goodness: The Concept of the Good in Metaphysics and Philosophical Theology*, ed. Scott MacDonald, Ithaca: Cornell, 1991.

Taylor, C. C. W. "Aristotle's Epistemology," in *Epistemology*, ed. by S. Everson. Cambridge University Press, 1990.

Vos, A. *Aquinas, Calvin, and Contemporary Protestant Thought: A Critique of Protestant Views on the Thought of Thomas Aquinas*. Grand Rapids: Christian University Press, 1985.

Weisheipl, James A. *Friar Thomas D'Aquino: His Life, Thought, and Work*. New York: Doubleday, 1974.

Index

.